# THE ENGLISH UTILITARIANS

# MILL'S UTILITARIANISM

REPRINTED WITH A STUDY OF

# THE ENGLISH UTILITARIANS

By JOHN PLAMENATZ

Fellow of All Souls College, Oxford

BASIL BLACKWELL
OXFORD
1949

Printed in Great Britain for Basil Blackwell & Mott Limited
by A. R. Mowbray & Co. Limited, London and Oxford

# CONTENTS

## THE ENGLISH UTILITARIANS

## MILL'S UTILITARIANISM

# THE
# ENGLISH UTILITARIANS

## CHAPTER I

## THE THEORY AND ITS ORIGINS

### 1. THE THEORY DEFINED

THERE is scarcely a writer on moral and political theory who is free
from every taint of utilitarianism. Since all men often seek pleasure
and avoid pain, no one anxious to have an audience will preach
complete indifference to either. That is why the more enthusiastic
utilitarians have sometimes been tempted to assert that all men are
with them even when they think otherwise. Bentham never
doubted that when the nonsense is eliminated from rival theories,
what remains behind is always his own. James Mill was inclined
to believe that when others thought they disagreed with him they
were, without knowing it, caught up in the intricacies of language.
He believed that all men are utilitarians in practice, though many
of them, having illusions of which they cannot get rid, are unwilling
to admit it. Whether the utilitarian theory is true or false, it is at
least plausible. In one form or another, it occurs readily enough to
anyone who reflects on the moral or political behaviour of mankind. There can be little purpose, then, in noticing the many
traces of the doctrine to be found in a great variety of European
philosophies. What is profitable is not to discover the sense in which
all men are utilitarians, but to define the doctrine so narrowly
that only those thinkers who are usually called utilitarians deserve
the name.

The utilitarians, properly so called, flourished in this country for
a period of over a hundred years, from the middle of the eighteenth
to the middle of the nineteenth century. There were also utilitarians
in France and in other parts of Europe, but the doctrine is essentially

English. Indeed, in its many varieties, it constitutes the larges
contribution made by the English to moral and political theory
It is intimately connected with English empiricism, although there
is no logical necessity in the connexion. And if the greatest o
English political philosophers was not a utilitarian, he exercised th
most powerful influence on those who were. Bentham and Jame
Mill lived in the shadow of Hobbes all their intellectual lives an
Hume learnt more from him than he ever acknowledge
M. Halévy, in his book on *Philosophic Radicalism*, found much t
say about continental utilitarians. But in spite of M. Halévy, it i
I think, possible to confine one's attention to English writers and to
miss very little that is important. And that little is to be found in
Helvetius and Beccaria.

The four most important utilitarians are Hume, Bentham, James
Mill and his son, John Stuart Mill. What is it that is common to
all their theories? Part of the answer to this question is the definition
of utilitarianism. But I hope, in this essay, to do more than just
define the doctrine; I hope, also, to give the reader an idea of the
great variety and richness of the systems of which it forms a part.

I had better begin with a short definition of the utilitarian
doctrine. It seems to me that all its adherents assert or assume
(more often the latter) the truth of the following propositions:

(i) Pleasure is alone good or desirable for its own sake; or else
men call only those things good that are pleasant or a means to
what is pleasant.

(ii) The equal pleasures of any two or more men are equally
good.

(iii) No action is right unless it appears to the agent to be the
action most likely, under the circumstances, to produce the greatest
happiness; or else men do not call any action right unless it is one of
a type that usually produces the greatest happiness possible under
the circumstances.

(iv) Men's obligations to the government of the country in which
they live, and that government's duties to them, have nothing to
do with the way in which the government first acquired power or
now maintains it, except to the extent to which these origins and
methods affect its ability to carry out these duties.

I must first insist that this definition is not a precise statement of
the opinions common to all the utilitarians. To offer precision

where there is no place for it is only to mislead. Every one of the four propositions set out above can be interpreted in several different ways. Indeed, had this not been so, they would have been useless for my purpose.

In case I should be accused of paradox, I must explain my meaning. In the sphere of morals and politics, a definition, to be precise, would have to be indefinitely long; and to be useful as well as precise, it would have to be, not one definition, but many, of which each gave one of the meanings of the term in question. Now, my business is not to define terms precisely but to set a limit to their possible definitions. Though the utilitarians aimed at clarity and consistency, and came nearer to achieving both than most philosophers have done, they used, when they discussed morals and politics, the old vocabulary that had served so many purposes in its time. No one can know what exactly they meant when they used this vocabulary. The reader is therefore to understand no more than this: that, in my opinion, anyone may properly be called a utilitarian if he believes that these four propositions are true, provided only that his interpretation of them does no violence to the usual meanings of the words they contain. There are many questions that most of the utilitarians never bothered to ask. What are pleasure and pain? Are they capable of measurement? If they are not, is there still some sense in which one pleasure or pain may be said to be greater, equal to or less than another? What is implied by the statement that pleasure is good and pain evil? A man may, if he has the necessary training in logic, make a long list of the senses in which the utilitarians may have used any one of their favourite words or phrases. But whatever the answers to these questions, and the lists prepared by our imaginary logician, there are limits to what the utilitarians could have meant. And these limits are set, not merely or even primarily by the definitions they themselves offer, but by the uses to which they put some of the commonest words in the vocabulary of the moralist and the politician.

I hope my definition is adequate, but I know it cannot be and believe it ought not to be precise. Even if, since their time, ethics and politics had acquired a precise vocabulary, it would be difficult to use it to describe the doctrines of the utilitarians; for their doctrines would not lend themselves to such treatment. To use a scientific vocabulary to define unscientific notions is like trying to chop wood with a razor; there is no end to the work, and the instrument, improperly used, is soon blunted. But there, in fact, exists no scientific vocabulary for the use of the political and moral philosopher. He must make do with words that are among the most frequently used in every language. When he is trying to describe the phenomena that constitute the moral and political behaviour of mankind, his disadvantage, if he understands its nature, is almost intolerable. But when his task is to describe doctrines, put together in their time by men no better provided than himself, he need not feel unequal to it. The same rough methods that suited them must also be good enough for him. And there is this much to be said for the utilitarians, that, though they did not speak like scientists, they always spoke sensibly. They were content with as much elasticity in the language as it naturally possessed. They did not distort or inflate it. They used it like Englishmen and not like philosophers, and so they never did to it the almost irreparable damage which, if we are to believe some Germans, was done to their language by philosophers. Even Bentham had a proper instinct in this matter; he wanted to create a technical vocabulary separate from the one in ordinary use.

But though these four propositions give us, as I believe, the essence of utilitarianism, this does not mean that the utilitarians do not often make statements inconsistent with them; that is to say, inconsistent with any reasonable interpretation of them. They do so either because they are not aware of the inconsistencies involved or else because they think they are making qualifications of only minor importance. These four propositions, in the sum of their usual meanings, embrace most of the beliefs to which the utilitarians attach the greatest importance and which they most often assert or assume. This is, I think, as much as can be expected of a set of propositions, not too complicated to be useful, and intended to cover the essential doctrines of a numerous school of philosophers. A definition of this kind is like the great bed at Ware, that will hold all the members of a large family, though the limbs of one or two of them hang over its sides.

There are two further points about this definition that call for comment. In the first place, so far as this definition goes, a utilitarian theory of morals may or may not be what Professor G. E.

Moore has called naturalistic. By a 'naturalistic' theory of morals Professor Moore means any theory that asserts or assumes that goodness denotes some property, simple or complex, of a natural object. And by a natural object he means anything that is the subject matter of the natural sciences.[1] I do not think that Professor Moore has made his meaning clear. Goodness, whatever it is and even if his account of it is correct, must be a property of what exists, and nothing does exist, if we are to believe Professor Moore, except natural objects. What Professor Moore probably means is that a theory of morals is naturalistic if it asserts or assumes that goodness is a property of which any natural science takes account. Or in other words, a theory of morals is naturalistic if it reduces ethics to a branch of psychology, sociology or any of the other natural sciences. Professor Moore himself believes that ethics is not a natural science, and that goodness is a simple, indefinable, unanalysable quality that is neither a constituent nor a relational, but a resultant, property of the things called good. A resultant property is, he thinks, neither spatial nor temporal, though what it belongs to may be the latter or both. Professor Moore believes that anyone who disagrees with him, who asserts, for instance, that good means pleasant or approved of or desired (however many qualifications are introduced for the sake of plausibility), is guilty of what he calls the naturalistic fallacy. He is guilty of assuming that goodness is the same thing as some one or other of the properties always or often possessed by the things called good, these properties being constituent or relational. Professor Moore himself thinks that goodness, alone of moral notions, is simple and indefinable, rightness being no more than conduciveness to what is good. But it is possible to be as absolute about the one notion as the other, and to insist, as some moralists have done, that they are both simple and indefinable.

Now, I will not say that the utilitarians are guilty of the naturalistic fallacy, for, unless Professor Moore is right, there can be no such fallacy. But it is very probable that most of their theories are, in his sense of that word, naturalistic. They would, most of them, had they considered the matter, probably have denied that there are such simple unanalysable qualities, different in kind from all others, as Professor Moore would have *goodness* to be, and other

[1] *Principia Ethica*, pp. 40-1 (1903 edition).

philosophers *rightness* as well. But though it is very probable that they would, most of them, have denied this, it would still have been a mistake to define their doctrine in such a way as to entail this denial. Professor Moore's distinction was never present to the minds of the utilitarians. It would therefore be misleading to define the doctrine in such a way as would suggest that they all made the same answer to a question never put by any of them. Of the major utilitarians, Hume and James Mill alone express themselves so clearly and consistently that it is never possible, for one moment, to doubt that their theories are naturalistic. But Bentham, with his usual lack of interest in a distinction from which no important practical consequences are to be drawn, speaks with many voices. There are times when he talks as if good and pleasant meant the same thing; at other times his words suggest that good means desired or approved of; and at still other times, what he says would be nonsense unless he were understood to mean that good and desirable are synonymous. Bentham is more concerned with the notion of rightness than goodness, and his usual account of it is that it is the same thing as utility. But he also often implies that it is not, that rightness and utility, though inseparably connected, are different. For he calls utility the criterion of morality, which is to suggest that they are two and not one. Yet the most cautious man, though he might say that doubts about Bentham are permissible, would hazard the guess that, on this question, he shares the opinion of Hume and James Mill. The most difficult case is that of John Stuart Mill. His general philosophy requires that his moral theory should be naturalistic, and the principles on which he rests that theory are in fact naturalistic, but some of the modifications he introduces at later stages in his argument are hardly to be reconciled with these principles. This does not mean that they cannot be reconciled with other principles which, though they are not utilitarian, are naturalistic; and in fact I believe that they can. There is, indeed, better reason for believing that the younger Mill's theory is consistently naturalistic than that it is consistently utilitarian. And in any case his fundamental principles are clearly both. For he tells us that rightness is conduciveness to pleasure, and also that to think of a thing as desirable is to think of it as pleasant. But though it is highly probable that the moral theories of the four greatest utilitarians are naturalistic, it is impossible to hold that none of the others differs from them in this respect. Godwin, for instance, asserts that justice is eternal, and by this assertion he seems to mean that it follows from the very fact that sentient and intelligent beings are living together that it is the duty of each, whatever his desires and emotiòns, to promote to the best of his ability the happiness of the others. This being so, it follows that the greatest happiness of the greatest number is an end desirable for its own sake, and that morals can never be reduced to a branch of psychology or of any other of the natural sciences. That sentient and intelligent beings ought to act in this way is, apparently, a proposition whose truth is borne in upon us as soon as we have understood it. The notion of obligation expressed in this proposition is not to be explained in terms of human desires or feelings. It is simple and unanalysable, just as Professor Moore supposes goodness to be. Godwin does not tell us this, but it is what his theory implies. For though he, like every other utilitarian, knows nothing of a distinction first made by Professor Moore, and is not even aware that the ultimate principle from which he starts is different from any advocated by Hume, whose general philosophy he accepts, it is clear that his moral theory is not naturalistic. And what is clearly true of Godwin may also be true of several other utilitarians, who are even less anxious than he to discuss the logical status of their fundamental principles. No more need, I think, be said to show that it would be a mistake so to define utilitarianism as to suggest that every utilitarian theory must be naturalistic.

More important, when we discuss the utilitarians, is the distinction between those who say that the criterion of morality is objective and those who believe that actions are right or wrong only because they are approved or disapproved by all or most of the persons who contemplate them. Hume belongs clearly to the latter class; Bentham, and those in the intellectual descent from him, to the former. But even this distinction does not enable us to place every utilitarian in one of two classes, for it is a distinction without interest to many of them.

In the second place, this definition of the utilitarian doctrine excludes the theory of morals called egoistic hedonism, whose most famous English exponent is Hobbes. It cannot be said that Hobbes, in the same sense as Hume, Bentham and the Mills, regards one man's

pleasure as equally valuable with any other's. Hobbes says no more
than that a man desires only his own pleasure, and that whatever
he desires he calls good. Since every man desires his own pleasure,
it follows that every human pleasure is called good by some man.
Hobbes might therefore say that any man's pleasure is just as good
as any other man's. But this is not the sense in which, according
to the utilitarians, one man's pleasure is as good as another's. For
the utilitarian regards the greatest happiness of the greatest number
as in itself desirable. If this means anything, it implies that it is as
much a man's duty to give pleasure to other people as to secure it
for himself. But Hobbes's system implies no such thing. The
greatest happiness of the greatest number as the supreme end of
human action can mean nothing to Hobbes. A man will seek other
men's pleasures only as a means to his own, and he will call no
pleasures good except his own. If, in the order of possible worlds,
his own happiness varied inversely with that of other men, he would
call that world best in which the sum of human misery was the
greatest.

It is true that several utilitarians, including Bentham and James
Mill, adopt, either occasionally or invariably, the egoistic hedonism
of Hobbes. And many others, though they say nothing definite, use
language that suggests that it is somehow more obviously right
that a man should seek his own pleasure than other people's.
Egoism, they appear to assume, stands in no need of either explanation or justification, but altruism does. And in their attempt to
justify it, they suggest that altruism arises out of egoism, or else
that it is a subtle and refined form of it. But for all this, they do not
cease to be utilitarians. They either make an attempt to reconcile
their egoistic hedonism with their belief that the end of all human
action ought to be the greatest possible happiness, no matter whose,
or else they believe that the two doctrines are so obviously
compatible that no reconciliation is necessary. In any case, what
they are primarily interested in advocating and defending is some
form or other of utilitarianism. It can be said of them all, even of
James Mill, that at heart they are utilitarians, though their minds
are full of the prejudices to which Hobbes gave such striking expression. Only Hume and the utilitarians who, like Adam Smith,
follow closely in his footsteps, succeed in avoiding the traps laid for
future generations in the *Leviathan*. And even Hume, who finds it

easy to accord to altruism a separate existence in its own right, continually insists on the predominant selfishness of man.

Utilitarianism and egoism are, of course, incompatible doctrines. If men desire only their own pleasure, or if their own pleasure is all they ought to desire, there can be no sense in saying that the greatest happiness of the greatest number is desirable. Even if it were true that no man could attain his own greatest happiness unless all other men did the same, it would still be impossible to reconcile egoism and utilitarianism. For it must still follow, if egoism is true, that nothing can be desired or desirable, except each man's happiness by himself, so that the greatest happiness of the greatest number neither can nor ought to be desired by any man for all men's sake but only for his own. No harmony of interests, natural or contrived, can affect a reconciliation between the two doctrines, though, should such a harmony exist, it cannot be important which of the two doctrines is true. For in that case, what the enlightened egoist desires as a means is desired as an end by the enlightened utilitarian; and whichever of the two realizes his desire, mankind are equally happy. But though it may well be that, under certain ideal circumstances, it is practically indifferent which of the two doctrines is true, this does not alter the fact that they cannot, under any conceivable circumstances, both be true.

Now, it cannot be denied that Bentham and James Mill asserted that both are true, and James Mill at least attempted to reconcile each with the other. The attempt was, of course, unsuccessful, but this lack of success is no reason for denying that the elder Mill was a utilitarian. Had he not believed that utilitarianism is true, he could not have wished to reconcile egoistic hedonism with it. Nor, I think, should we deny the name utilitarian to Bentham, who never felt the need to effect such a reconciliation. It never even occurred to him that the two doctrines might appear incompatible, since he was the happy possessor of both. It was his mission in life to teach men how they might contrive a harmony of selfish interests, so that it might at last be possible for them to desire as a means what they ought to promote for its own sake. The suspicion that an end so defined is a contradiction in terms never entered the head of this practical man. He may not have known how to define it but he knew what he wanted; and had he achieved it, it would not have mattered how he defined it. Bentham and James

B

Mill were egoistic hedonists. But this is a fact about them much less important than that they were also utilitarians. It is the utilitarian doctrine that is the major premise of all their favourite practical arguments. And that it is so is not a matter of indifference, for until a harmony of selfish interests is established, egoism and utilitarianism cannot justify the same rules of conduct. But it was the rules justified by utilitarianism that they both wished to establish. Hobbes tried to prove that one of the necessary means to each man's happiness, the existence of a sovereign able to enforce obedience to his commands, is also the means to other men's happiness. Neither Bentham nor Mill would have denied this. But Hobbes never justified the institution of the sovereign on the ground that the harmony of interests created by it must increase the sum of human happiness. Bentham and Mill, on the other hand, wished to establish a more perfect harmony than any conceived by Hobbes for precisely this reason. They did not say: let everyone strive to create a harmony of selfish interests, for until it is created he cannot hope to be happy. They said: the best society is the one in which there is the greatest happiness of the greatest number, and we must therefore strive to create a harmony of selfish interests, for unless we do so, this desirable end cannot be achieved. This is the great difference between Hobbes and the two utilitarians who came closest to an uncritical acceptance of his doctrines; and in virtue of it, it is but just that they should be called utilitarians and he always an egoist.

## 2. HOBBES AND THE UTILITARIANS

Hobbes had a bad reputation and later philosophers were not anxious to acknowledge their debt to him. But in the *Leviathan* there is such an abundance of riches that several generations could borrow freely from it and be satisfied. It is not difficult, in spite of their discreet silence, to see how much the utilitarians owe to Hobbes.

Hobbes did not invent all the theories that are to-day so strongly associated with his name. No man can be an innovator on such a scale. But Hobbes did step aside from the European tradition of his day. He put his questions differently and gave different answers. The extent of the difference is disguised by his political vocabulary, which is less unlike that of other men than his ideas.

From the time of Plato until that of Hobbes, two sorts of moral theory had prevailed among European philosophers. The one makes the supreme object of human endeavour the full and harmonious development of all the powers of the individual; while the other declares that virtue consists in behaviour according to rules that man can discover by the use of his reason. These two kinds of theories can be combined in many ways and they can also be related to many different conceptions of the universe. It can, for instance, be said that a man will 'realize' himself, will become the best that he has it in him to be, if he behaves according to the laws of nature revealed to him by his reason. Or it can be said, as it was by Plato and Aristotle, that man will attain his full development only in the perfectly constituted state. Nor is there anything to prevent a man from saying that the laws of reason are the laws of God. Some philosophers have been loath to reject any part of what they considered to be the inherited and divinely inspired wisdom of mankind. Such a philosopher was St. Thomas Aquinas, in whose house there are many mansions in which all the great thinkers of the past are honourably received.

But respect for the past and hospitality to its traditions are not among the virtues of Hobbes. He finds no room for any essential part of either of the two most important European moral philosophies. According to his system, no man can be better or worse than he was before; he can only be more or less successful in acquiring pleasure. Nor are there any rules which all men, who have the use of their reason, discover to be binding upon themselves merely because they are rational and sentient beings and live in society with others like themselves. The laws of morality, in the opinion of Hobbes, have no such validity; they are merely rules that men, since they wish to be happy, would do well to obey, provided that other men do likewise. The state is no more than a contrivance to ensure that all men do obey these rules, so that it may be the interest of each of them to do so. For a man who obeys them, while others do not, is no better than a fool.

The utilitarians share with Hobbes a complete indifference to the notion of self-improvement as a thing desirable for its own sake. The single exception is John Stuart Mill, but this is merely one of several ways in which he is untrue to the doctrine inherited from his father. The later utilitarians are as great enthusiasts as Plato for education, but its only purpose, in their opinion, is to make men more efficient producers of happiness. And like Hobbes, all the utilitarians, with the exception, once again, of John Stuart Mill, that unhappy and unconscious traitor to their creed, deny that virtue, which is obedience to the moral law, has a value for men independent of its power to promote their happiness.

The influence of Hobbes on some utilitarians is much greater than on others. The man of virtue, for both Hobbes and Bentham, is the excellent calculator. Nor are the calculations they advocate very different from one another. Though Bentham's supreme end can mean nothing to Hobbes, yet the actions that promote it are those most likely to make the agents themselves happy. Bentham's legislator makes the laws that ensure that each man from selfish motives will promote the greatest happiness of the greatest number; while Hobbes's sovereign ensures that each man will pursue his own happiness unmolested by the others. The two philosophers define their terms differently, but the sort of considerations that they think ought to weigh with men when they act are pretty much alike.

But it is in the sphere of political philosophy that Hobbes has the most direct and obvious influence on the utilitarians, even on Hume, whose theory of morals, except in its rejection of the two great European traditions, is so unlike that of the *Leviathan*. The utilitarians, like Hobbes, regard the state as a means of reconciling men's selfish interests. It exists, not to protect their rights, but to give men more abundantly the happiness they always seek. Hobbes, it is true, speaks of 'natural rights' that men possess before they enter political society, but he does not mean by this phrase what others have meant who used it. When Hobbes says that, in the state of nature, men have an unlimited right to acquire whatever takes their fancy provided they have the strength to do so, he can only mean that, outside society, there is no sense in saying that it would be wrong for them to take it. Right for Hobbes is therefore mere absence of wrong. But when we say that a man has a right to do something, we imply that it would be wrong for other men to try to prevent him. This is also implied by what most philosophers, who use the term, say of natural rights. But the case with Hobbes is different. He uses the phrase in a meaning all his own. The natural rights of Hobbes are not rights at all, and no state can exist for their protection.

Hobbes misleads his reader, and perhaps also himself by his account of the sovereign's institution, of which he says that it involves the transfer of their natural rights by the persons who form a political society to the man who is to be their sovereign. Now, a natural right of the sort described by Hobbes cannot be transferred. Though the men who agree to form a political society so act that one man among them can exercise effectively over the others the power that they, all of them, in the state of nature vainly tried to exercise, there is no transference of power, let alone of right. For the power that belongs to the sovereign in political society belonged to no one in the state of nature. What Hobbes has done is to call powers rights and then treat them as if they were what other people call by that name. Natural rights, in the traditional sense, are as unnecessary to Hobbes's political philosophy as to that of any of the utilitarians.

Though Hobbes describes the transfer of rights and speaks of the sovereign as bearing the 'persons' of his subjects, the whole of his long account of the matter is foreign to the main body of his doctrines. It is a piece of mysticism that can mean nothing to whoever has accepted the other parts of his theory. There is no sense compatible with Hobbes's premises in which the sovereign can do no wrong and his subjects can do it. If a subject finds it his interest to obey the laws, while the sovereign can often afford, when it suits his purpose, to ignore them, this is only because the subject has little power and the sovereign a great deal. Hobbes's principles once accepted, no covenant can create obligations or rights, either in the parties to it or in any person who receives power in consequence of it. All that a covenant can do, if those that make it keep it, is to alter the circumstances in which men act, so that it becomes their interest to act otherwise than they would have done without it. The political theory of Hobbes differs from that of most of the utilitarians, not because he admits the existence of natural rights and they do not, but because his theory, unlike theirs, allows of no rights at all other than legal powers. Though no one made a more frequent use of the words, 'laws of nature' and 'natural rights', it is clear that the things themselves have no place in his philosophy.

The purpose of Hobbes's sovereign is to create a harmony where none existed. The sovereign, however often he may himself disregard them or allow his favourites to do so, has the strongest interest in obliging the great majority of his subjects to obey his laws. And he has the power so to oblige them, because, though no man desires to be restrained, every other man has an interest that he should be. Thus it is that, when the sovereign forces any man to obey his laws, all other men, if they know their own interests, are his allies. The state is a society in which it is made one man's (or several men's) selfish interest to oblige every other man to behave in ways that suit his neighbours. But no man has an interest in himself obeying the laws except that his disobedience, by weakening the sovereign, makes it less likely that others will obey them. It is this, and not the flow of words about natural rights and sovereign impersonations, that is the hard core of Hobbes's political theory. It is also the doctrine that Hume, Bentham and James Mill borrow from him.

The utilitarians take little interest in the origin of the state, while Hobbes devotes many pages to its description. Hobbes is regarded as one of the great exponents of the theory of the social contract. But Hobbes's contract is unlike anyone else's. It is not a true covenant imposing real obligations on the parties to it. Hobbes, like many of the other contract theorists, does not suppose that he is describing an historical fact. The theory, for him as for them, is a convenient fiction. But its convenience lies elsewhere. His purpose is not to explain why and to what extent subjects are obliged to obey their rulers, but only to prove that it is, on all but the most rare occasions, their interest to do so. He therefore imagines a state of nature and contrasts its miseries with the comparative ease of political society. Having imagined men without government, he finds it necessary to describe the motives that could induce them to create it. But having described these motives, and introduced into his account of the institution of the sovereign a superfluous mystical element, he quietly tells us that the conqueror has the same right to rule as the sovereign established by covenant. What more could he say to prove that, in his opinion, whatever the origin of the sovereign's power, his subjects' motives for obeying him remain the same? But this is also the opinion of the utilitarians.

Hobbes, like the utilitarians after him, thought it the great function of government to reconcile selfish interests, to make it worth every man's while to obey laws giving security to all men. It is this, more than any other part of his theory, that is the essence of it, in the sense that it gives it a unity it would not otherwise possess. The state, according to him, is neither the promoter of the good life nor the protector of rights; it is the conciliator of interests. Unlike the utilitarians, Hobbes calls interests 'natural rights', and so makes it appear that, like the contract theorists before him, he regards the state as the protector of rights. Yet it is, I think, easy to see that he means no such thing, though his special use of the words 'natural rights' misleads not only his readers but sometimes also himself. For he not only calls interests rights, but applies arguments to them that could only hold if they were rights, in some sense of that word precluded by his assumptions. This is the price that anyone is liable to pay who uses words in unusual meanings.

The most important difference, in the political sphere, between Hobbes and the utilitarians, is not that he regards the state as the protector of natural rights and they do not. It is rather that his fear of anarchy leads him, against all the evidence of history, to exaggerate the need for an absolute sovereign of unquestioned authority. That he magnifies man's egoism, his vanity and his love of power matters much less, for it is by no means obvious that what he wishes us to conclude from these qualities is really made necessary by them. There can be no valid argument from human selfishness, jealousy and pugnacity to the need for unbridled government. For these qualities, though less universal than Hobbes supposes, are evenly distributed among the peoples of the world, who have known not one but many forms of stable government. From men's selfishness, vanity and need for security it is no more possible to deduce the form of government that would suit them best, than the clothes they should wear from their susceptibility to heat and cold and their love of finery. Several of the utilitarians, though they use milder language, think hardly better of mankind than does Hobbes, but not one of them is an apologist for absolute government. It is his greater fear of anarchy and not his worse opinion of his species that makes Hobbes so anxious to prove that subjects owe an almost unlimited obedience to their sovereign. Be so foolish as to challenge his authority, Hobbes tells us, and you will be plunged at once into the war of all against all.

History teaches us that Hobbes's threat is an idle one. The sovereign is strong, and the subject who dares defy him, unless he can persuade others to join him, must be a mere fugitive from justice. It is only the united strengths of many subjects that can suffice to destroy the sovereign's power. But there cannot be a union without discipline. Rebels cannot succeed unless they maintain order in their own ranks; and they cannot have security until they have made their power effective throughout the state. Those who destroy governments nearly always replace them, maintaining their power by the same means that they gained it. This is not always so. The rebels may quarrel among themselves, or there may from the first have been several claimants to the authority of the dispossessed sovereign. But the period of civil war need not last long and it may involve very little suffering for most people. Hobbes's argument is only plausible if we accept his description of the alternatives (continued obedience to the existing sovereign, and the most hideous anarchy) between which we have to choose. But if we prefer to take history for our guide, we find the alternatives more difficult to assess, and it is far from obvious that submission is the wisest policy.

The utilitarians seldom look to history for political lessons. If they do not share Hobbes's preference for absolute government, it is only because they have different prejudices. Bentham and the elder Mill, for instance, were as certain as Hobbes that men ought not to trust one another. But they happened to be more afraid of misgovernment than anarchy. They therefore argued that, because men are selfish, vain, and naturally abusive of power, only a democratic government could secure them against each other's ill-usage. They accepted the opinion of Hobbes that the great function of government is to conciliate interests, and they did not quarrel with his estimate of mankind. But they did not share his fear of anarchy.

Hobbes used a traditional vocabulary unsuited to his political theory, and it was precisely this vocabulary that the utilitarians abandoned. That is why the difference between them appears so much greater than it is. But eliminate from Hobbes's statement of that theory the phrases that only serve to obscure his meaning, and what remains, except for his extravagant fear of anarchy, is strikingly similar to the fundamental political doctrines of the utilitarians.

### 3. LOCKE AND THE UTILITARIANS

There are some respects in which Locke, the moralist, stands closer to the utilitarians than does Hobbes. But their debt to him is much smaller. It was from the richer man that the greater sum was borrowed. And yet what was borrowed from Locke, though smaller in amount, was more easily convertible into the utilitarian currency.

Most of Locke's theory of morals, such as it is, is to be found in three chapters of his *Essay Concerning Human Understanding*.[1] By the time he has got to the last of these chapters,[2] Locke has apparently forgotten what he said in the other two. There is little that is consistent in his theory of morals; but the greater part of it resembles either the egoistic hedonism of Hobbes or the utilitarianism of a later age. His one consistent belief is that nothing is good or evil except pleasure and pain or the means to them.

Like Hobbes and the utilitarians, Locke asserts that there are no moral laws, whose validity is immediately recognized without regard to their consequences. He believes that the great variety of opinions about morals held in different societies, or in the same society at different times, are sufficient evidence that this assertion is true. 'The saints who are canonized among the Turks', he says, 'lead lives which one cannot with modesty relate.'[3] He also says that 'God, having, by an inseparable connexion, joined virtue and public happiness together, and made the practice thereof necessary to the preservation of society, and visibly beneficial to all with whom the virtuous man has to do; it is no wonder that every one should not only allow but recommend and magnify these rules to others, from whose observance of them he is sure to reap advantage to himself.'[4] That is to say, God has made it worth every man's while to behave in ways that promote the public happiness, and it is this behaviour that constitutes virtue. This is as close to the utilitarian theory of morals as Locke ever comes, and it is the doctrine that Paley borrows from him. But Locke does not, in so many words, say

---

[1] These are, chapter 3, of Book I; chapter 21 of Book II; and chapter 3 of Book IV.

[2] In it he says that morals is a demonstrable science, like mathematics, although he has said, in the third chapter of Book I, that there are no universally valid moral laws.

[3] *Essay Concerning Human Understanding*, Book I, chap. 3, 9.

[4] *Ibid.*, I, 3, 9.

that the public happiness is the measure of right and wrong. He suggests that it is God who must supply men with motives for pursuing it; their object, in obeying his laws, being always their own advantage and not the public interest. There is more of egoistic hedonism than of utilitarianism in this, and yet it is a step towards the doctrine of Bentham and James Mill that Hobbes never took. Though Bentham often, and James Mill always, asserts that no man can desire any pleasure except his own, they both insist that the greatest happiness, no matter whose, is the only criterion of morality. It is this, whether or not it is consistent with their egoistic premises, that makes utilitarians of them. But Locke, like Hobbes, will have it that 'what has an aptness to produce pleasure in us is what we call good, and what is apt to produce pain in us we call evil'.[1]

There is more of the utilitarian doctrine in Locke's moral than in his political philosophy. The social contract is his central theme, and what he describes is a true covenant imposing real obligations on the parties to it. The rights that men possess in the state of nature are not, for him, mere powers, of which it would be meaningless to say that they ought or ought not to be exercised; they are powers in the exercise of which they ought to be protected by their neighbours. And it is because men have these rights and obligations in the state of nature that they can establish a ruler over them to whom they owe a duty of obedience. Their object in establishing him may be the more efficient protection of the rights on which public happiness depends, but his right to rule rests, not only on his efficient government, but much more on his subjects' consent. The conquest of power, however excellent the conqueror's government, is no sufficient title to the obedience of his subjects.

It is true that, having made consent a necessary ground of political obligation, Locke finds himself in great difficulties, and that his only way out of them is to call by that name many things that obviously are not consent. Whenever he thinks it in the public interest that men should obey their governors, he undertakes to prove that they have consented to do so. This may be, as Bentham would have suggested, an unconscious tribute to the utilitarian doctrine, but it is also evidence that it could not satisfy Locke. In chapter fourteen of the *Second Treatise of Civil Government*, Locke has an argument

---

[1] Ibid., II, 21.

designed to pr......t when a government harms its subjects, it is acting without.....r consent. He thinks it obvious that people will never consent 'that anybody should rule over them for their harm.' Even at this point, when a man with not half his reputation for sagacity might have been satisfied with the utilitarian argument —that subjects have the right to revolt against rulers who harm them—Locke must bring in the notion of consent.

Locke's theories of property and of punishment, two of the greatest subjects in the domain of political philosophy, have little that is utilitarian about them. Every man is to keep the fruits of his labour because he has a natural right to them. Locke does not deny that his keeping them is in the public interest, but his title is grounded in a natural right and not in utility. Locke is a utilitarian only when he comes to explain why it is that a man may not retain more of the perishable fruits of his labour than he can consume before they spoil. Of punishment Locke tells us that by the Law of Nature every man in the State of Nature has the right to punish anyone who transgresses that Law. It is only because every man has this right in the State of Nature that a government can have it in Civil Society. We are to understand that, though punishment is useful, no government has the right to inflict it because, by so doing, it can promote the public happiness. In the political philosophy of Locke, the question of origins is always the most important. But with Hobbes its importance is more apparent than real, and all the utilitarians neglect it.

I have made a number of distinctions that some of my readers may think arbitrary. To the social contract Hobbes assigns as large a place in his political philosophy as does Locke, and yet I have said it is not as essential to it. I have also said that the utilitarians have more in common with Hobbes than with Locke, and yet the public happiness is as important to Locke as it is insignificant to Hobbes. But the public happiness as the end of government is the favourite notion of the utilitarians. Would it not have been as easy to prove that the spiritual ancestor of Bentham was Locke rather than Hobbes?

There is one concession that every writer on politics must make to the less easily satisfied of his readers. This is a subject, as Burke saw, in which there is little enough room for novelty. Or rather, novelty, if it is to be had at all, must be the fruit of patience observation and extensive knowledge. The study of society is of all studies the least rewarding; it brings a small return on a large intellectual effort. Political thinkers have, therefore, been manipulators of ideas rather than extenders of knowledge. They had, by the seventeenth century, inherited a considerable stock of these ideas, and their originality, when it existed, consisted, as often as not, in the special uses to which they put them. This stock of ideas was not so great that an ingenious and imaginative writer could not find some place for most of them in his own system. We need not wonder, then, if we find in the political writings of Locke most of the ideas of Hobbes, except those explicitly rejected by the younger philosopher.

But this does not mean that the systems of Hobbes and Locke are not profoundly different. They are not just two varieties of the social contract theory. Locke accepts a traditional doctrine and elaborates it, so that it can serve as the theoretical justification of limited monarchy and parliamentary supremacy. The idea round which his entire political philosophy turns is that every legitimate government is the protector of rights uncreated by it and that subjects are bound to obedience only so long as their rights are protected. But the essence of Hobbes's theory is that government is the conciliator of selfish interests. If he was not the inventor of this idea, he was certainly the first modern thinker to place it at the foundation of his political philosophy. Anything unnecessary to a philosophy so grounded, though Hobbes may expatiate upon it in one place, is quietly sacrificed, should the occasion require it, in another. Thus it is that, after a long description of the institution of sovereignty, and after telling us that the subjects are the true authors of all their ruler's actions (a description not altogether unlike Rousseau's account of the General Will, and with the same air of mystery about it), Hobbes announces that conquest is as good a title as any other to government. In the last resort, all that matters with him is security or, in other words, the discipline of law under which every man finds his selfish account. To Hobbes, this discipline of law creates a harmony of interests, that is not desirable in itself though desired by every prudent man as the surest means to his own happiness. To the utilitarians, this harmony of interests is the public happiness, which is either the objective criterion of morality or else the end to which our moral sentiments are in fact directed. But this idea of government as the conciliator of interests, though Locke neither ignores nor rejects it, is not central to his philosophy. This is surely reason enough for saying that it is to Hobbes rather than Locke that the utilitarians are indebted.

# CHAPTER II

# HUME

## 1. His Theory of Morals

DAVID HUME is rightly regarded as the founder of utilitarianism, though, like many founders, he is less uncompromising than most of his successors. He is also the inventor of the subjectivist system of ethics, which many later utilitarians adopted, either in part or as a whole, although it does not form an essential part of the doctrine. I do not mean by this that it is not an essential part of Hume's moral theory, for that it certainly is, but only that a man can be a utilitarian, in the usual meaning of the word, without adopting Hume's subjectivist system or any variety of it.

Hume does not use the word 'utilitarianism', which John Stuart Mill claims to have invented. If Mill's claim is true, the word was introduced into the English political vocabulary at about the same time as two others, both of them destined to be even more widely used and misused, namely, 'liberalism' and 'socialism'. Nor does Hume ever use the expression 'the greatest happiness of the greatest number', which is, according to F. C. Montague, to be found in the fifth edition of Hutcheson's *Enquiry into our Ideas of Beauty and Virtue*. This edition was published in 1753, six years after Hutcheson's death. But if Hume does not name the doctrine, nor invent the sacred formula, he does provide his successors with the word 'utility' of which they stand more in need than any other if they are to express their theory concisely and without ambiguity.

Leslie Stephen once said of Hume that 'the essential doctrines of Utilitarianism are stated (by him) with a clearness and consistency not to be found in any other writer of the century', and that 'from Hume to J. S. Mill, the doctrine received no substantial alteration'.[1]

It is not possible, I think, to quarrel with this verdict, provided it is understood that the 'essential doctrines' correspond, more or less, to the four criteria given at the beginning of this essay. There are many varieties of utilitarianism besides the one advocated by

[1] *History of English Thought in the Eighteenth Century*, Vol. II, p. 87.

Hume, and from the essential doctrines it is possible, if certain further assumptions are made, to draw conclusions very different from any with which Hume would have been inclined to agree.

The virtues of clarity and consistency have often been ascribed to Hume. He deserves the praise at least as much as any other important philosopher of the eighteenth century. But Hume is a careless writer; he is certainly not always consistent in his use of words, and so he sometimes gives an appearance of logical inconsistency when he is in reality perfectly aware of the implications of what he is saying. He deliberately uses the same words in different meanings, or different words in the same meaning, because he finds it convenient to do so and does not wish to appear clumsy or pedantic. Unwary readers, especially of the academic type, sometimes imagine they have caught him out when they have done nothing of the kind. Hume, like everyone who discusses difficult philosophical problems, is sometimes guilty of genuine inconsistencies, but his great defect, as a moral and political thinker, is much more often inadequacy than inconsistency. He does not take all the relevant facts into account. But even in this respect, he is greatly the superior of most of his contemporaries, and is much less inclined than they are to over-simplify.

Utilitarianism is above all a theory of morals. The political doctrines put forward by any utilitarian philosopher are no more than the conclusions he draws from his moral premises and from certain other propositions which, rightly or wrongly, he believes to be generalizations from experience. We must, therefore, first deal with Hume's theory of morals. It is to be found in the third book of his *Treatise of Human Nature*, and also in the *Enquiry Concerning the Principles of Morals*. Of these two, the latter is the more readable; but it only repeats in more elegant and less precise language what Hume had already said in the former. It will be best, therefore, to attend mostly to what he says in the *Treatise*, making only occasional references to the *Enquiry*, although Hume considered it 'incomparably the best thing' he had ever written.

Hume's ambition, as a moral philosopher, was the exact opposite of Locke's. Whereas Locke had hoped that it might one day be given to him to show that Morals is a demonstrable science, Hume's purpose, which he believed he had achieved, was to introduce the experimental method into it.

He explains to us what he thinks Ethics is in an often-quoted passage. 'The only object of reasoning' (and he means reasoning about morals) 'is to discover the circumstances on both sides which are common to these qualities' (he means the qualities that men call estimable or blameable), 'to observe that particular in which the estimable qualities agree on the one hand, and the blameable on the other; and thence to reach the foundation of ethics, and find those universal principles from which all censure or approbation is ultimately derived. As this is a question of fact, not of abstract science, we can only expect success by following the experimental method, and deducing general maxims from a comparison of particular instances.'[1]

Hume does not treat his reader to the examination of many particular instances, but passes almost immediately to his conclusions. 'Morals', he says, 'excite passions, and produce or prevent actions. Reason of itself is impotent in this particular. The rules of morality, therefore, are not conclusions of our reason.' '. . . Reason . . . can have an influence on our conduct only after two ways: Either when it excites a passion by informing us of the existence of something which is a proper object of it; or when it discovers the connexion of causes and effects, so as to afford us the means of exciting any passion.'[3] Hume means that it is not reason but our emotions that prescribe the ends we are to pursue. We can, according to him, no more expect reason to prescribe to us what we ought to desire for its own sake than to determine what we do desire. We must, of course, use our reason in order to understand what sort of creatures we are and how our behaviour is in fact determined; but there are no things, good or evil in themselves, or actions, right or wrong in themselves, whose moral qualities are independent of our own attitude to them and which we can but recognize. Hume invites the reader to examine any action usually called vicious. 'Wilful murder, for instance; examine it in all lights, and see if you can find that matter of fact or real existence which you call vice. In whichever way you take it, you find only passions, motives, volitions and thoughts. . . . The vice entirely escapes you, as long as you consider the object. You never can find it, till you

---

[1] *Enquiry Concerning the Principles of Morals*, Sec. 1, § 5.
[2] *Tr. H. Nat.*, Bk. III, Pt. 1, Sec. 1, p. 457 (Selby-Bigge edition, Oxford, 1896).
[3] Ibid., III, 1, 1, p. 459.

turn your reflection into your own breast, and find a sentiment of disapprobation, which arises in you, towards this action.'[1] His conclusion is that 'an action or sentiment, or character is virtuous or vicious . . . because its view causes a pleasure or uneasiness of a particular kind'. Things are good and bad, therefore, because the contemplation of them causes pleasure or displeasure to the persons who observe them or who think about them; and this pleasure or displeasure is always of a particular kind, which Hume does not define (though he does not say it is indefinable) but which he considers to be the same thing as approval and disapproval.

Hume altogether rejects egoistic hedonism. He says that we do not approve or disapprove of characters and actions because they are or are not beneficial to ourselves. He says: 'The good qualities of an enemy are hurtful to us; but may still command our esteem or respect. 'Tis only when a character is considered in general, without reference to our particular interest, that it causes such a feeling or sentiment, as denominates it morally good or evil'.[2] The dismay that we feel when someone does what will injure us, or our violent delight when we receive a great benefit, must not, according to Hume, be confused with disapproval and approval. These two latter sentiments are, as he is never tired of telling us, always disinterested. Even when someone is good to us, we can distinguish between our approval of his benevolence and our pleasure at the good done to us. Both these sentiments are pleasant, but they are quite different from each other. Had our benefactor been equally good to someone else, we would, presumably, have felt the former sentiment but not the latter.

Hume is a careless writer. His words sometimes imply that we approve or disapprove of an action or a character whenever the contemplation of it causes us pleasure or pain. At other times, he speaks of pleasure or pain of a certain kind; and it is then clear that he has come nearer to his real meaning. But the phrase 'pleasure or pain of a certain kind' is ambiguous. When we say that we distinguish between kinds of pleasure, we may mean only between kinds of pleasant things or between pleasures having different causes, without suggesting that they are pleasant in different ways; or we may mean that we distinguish (if that is possible) between kinds of pleasure in the same way as we distinguish between colours.

[1] Ibid., pp. 468–9.      [2] Ibid. p. 472.

C

Hume's meaning is not clear. He often speaks as if approval and disapproval were particular kinds of pleasure and pain, but his words also suggest that there are only differences of degree between different pleasures and different pains, the peculiarity of approval and disapproval consisting only in this, that they are pleasure and pain caused by the disinterested contemplation of a character or an action. By 'disinterested contemplation' no more is meant than contemplation unaffected by any hope of benefit or fear of injury likely to accrue to the contemplator or to any person to whom he is not indifferent. Hume is right in believing that we can contemplate in this way actions that benefit or injure ourselves. We can, as it were, consider our own predicament as if it were anyone else's.

It is probable that Hume means by approval and disapproval, not a special kind of pleasure or pain, but a pleasure or pain caused in a particular way. Yet this is an interpretation on which it would be a mistake to insist, not only because no one can be certain what Hume does mean, but also because it is likely that, whatever he means, he is wrong. Approval and disapproval are emotions, while pleasure and pain are not, but are merely qualities that emotions or feelings sometimes possess. Moreover, approval can be unpleasant and disapproval pleasant. Indeed, in the countries of Northern Europe and North America, disapproval is a favourite form of self-indulgence.

The reader may have noticed, from the passages so far quoted, that Hume does not distinguish between good and right, or between evil and wrong. A state of mind, a motive or a disposition of the character is good or evil because we approve or disapprove of it; and an action is right or wrong for exactly the same reasons. As for the obligatoriness of an action, it consists, in Hume's opinion, in nothing more than the fact that the thought of not performing it, when we are able to do so, causes us displeasure of the kind which is disapproval. Thus obligatoriness and rightness are not, for Hume, the same thing. When I approve the performance of an action, I call it right; when I disapprove the non-performance of it I say that the prospective agent, whether myself or somebody else, is under an obligation to perform it. And when the action is one that I could myself perform, then my disapproval of the non-perform-ance of it is a motive for performing it. That is to say, it is an emotion which might cause me to perform it, and in fact always would cause me to do so if there were not other motives operating in the contrary direction.

So much, then, for Hume's views about good and evil and right and wrong. The reader will observe that nothing yet said about him is a reason for considering Hume a utilitarian. Though most utilitarians have shared many or at least some of the opinions of Hume so far discussed, they are none of them essential parts of the utilitarian doctrine. We cannot say that because Hume has these opinions he is a hedonist; all that we can say is that, if he is a hedonist, he cannot be an egoistic one after the manner of Hobbes. We can also say that, if he is a hedonist, he is a utilitarian; but we must first establish that he is a hedonist.

Now it is clear that Hume is not a simple hedonist, such as Hobbes and Bentham always were, and Locke sometimes. He nowhere asserts that nothing is good except pleasure and nothing evil except pain. All that he does say is that men usually approve or disapprove whatever, in the society in which they live, is either pleasant or a means to pleasure, or else is painful or a means to pain. This, he would have us believe, is a fact about human nature that we can do nothing but accept. It is by observation of human behaviour, and in no other way, that we come to know it. Hume does not equate pleasure and goodness, nor does he claim to apprehend any necessary connexion between them. That the two are connected is, he thinks, vouched for by our experience. It is one of those generalizations that their author says are empirical though he produces no evidence to support the assertion.

It is easy to see that Hume does not equate pleasure and goodness. He says that men usually approve, not only what is pleasant, but what is a means to pleasure. But it is clear that the means to pleasure (for instance, a virtuous action requiring great courage) may be very painful. Hume, therefore, must believe that we can approve of what is very painful; from which it follows that what is very painful may be good. And observe that Hume does not assert, what Bentham did assert, that what is painful may be a means to the good but must itself be evil. On Hume's theory, what is a means to pleasure can be just as good as what is pleasant; for all that is required for a thing to be good is that the disinterested contemplation of it should normally arouse pleasure. Hume is explicitly committed to the view that we approve the means to pleasure as much as pleasure itself; and therefore that many other things besides pleasure are good. If a hedonist is defined as a person who maintains that only pleasure is good, and if utilitarianism is treated as a variety of hedonism, then it is clear that Hume is not a utilitarian. Whoever does not wish to come to the absurd conclusion, that the founder of utilitarianism is not a utilitarian, will take good care to define the doctrine in such a way as not to be obliged to do so.

Hume's utilitarianism consists, therefore, in this: that he maintains that men normally approve of those states of mind or actions that are pleasant or a means to pleasure, and disapprove of those that are painful or a means to pain, no matter whose the pleasure or pain. It is the primary importance he attaches to pleasure and pain, his opinion that a pleasure or pain, no matter whose, is as good or evil as any other equal to it, that make him a utilitarian. He says: 'Every quality of the mind is denominated virtuous, which gives pleasure by the mere survey; as every quality, which produces pain, is call'd vicious. This pleasure and this pain may arise from four different sources. For we reap a pleasure from the view of a character, which is naturally fitted to be useful to others, or to the person himself, or which is agreeable to others, or to the person himself. One may, perhaps,' Hume goes on, 'be surpriz'd, that amidst all these interests and pleasures, we should forget our own, which touch us so nearly on every other occasion. But we shall easily satisfy ourselves on this head, when we consider, that every particular person's pleasure and interest being different, 'tis impossible men cou'd ever agree in their sentiments and judgments, unless they chose some common point of view. . . . Now, in judging of characters, the only interest or pleasure, which appears the same to every spectator, is that of the person himself, whose character is being examined; or that of persons who have a connexion with him.'[1] This, if it means anything, means that the moral sentiments are disinterested; and it also means that they are shared, though felt more intensely by some than by others, by all or nearly all men.

Hume, then, is a utilitarian but he is not a complete one. He thinks that the characters and actions approved or disapproved by nearly all men are for the most part those that usually promote pleasure or pain. But he is not sure that this is so always. He says

[1] *Treatise*, p. 591.

'. . . these sentiments' (he means approval and disapproval) 'may arise either from the mere . . . appearance of characters and passions, or from reflexion on their tendency to the happiness of mankind . . . My opinion is that both these causes are intermix'd in our judgments of morals. . . . Tho' I am also of opinion, that reflexions on the tendencies of actions have by far the greatest influence, and determine all the great lines of duty.'[1]

This passage is interesting, not only because it shows us that Hume is not a complete utilitarian, but also because of the great importance it ascribes to reason. Hume goes so far as to say that reflexions on the tendencies of actions determine all the great lines of duty. But he does not usually ascribe as much importance to reason as he does in this passage. It it experience that teaches us which actions usually have pleasant consequences and which have painful ones; and learning from experience involves the use of reason. But Hume does not mean that we must each of us come to the conclusion that a certain type of action is usually productive of pleasure before we come to approve it. His view is rather that we imitate, in this respect, the fashions prevalent in the society in which we live. All of us most of the time, and many of us all the time, approve and disapprove from mere habit, without worrying our heads about the probable consequences of the actions approved or disapproved. But these habits are themselves, over long periods of time, directed by the 'collective' experience of mankind or of the society in which we live. It is, so Hume believes, a law of human nature that men will never long approve what injures them or disapprove what causes them to be happy.

Hume lived in a society more stable, in many respects, than our own. I do not mean that it was less liable to disorder, but merely that it changed more slowly. Scotland, Hume's native land, did, of course, change rapidly during the eighteenth century, but only to become more like England than she had been before. The standards of behaviour prevalent in his own day among the educated classes of Western Europe seemed to Hume to be fairly stable; and he quite simply assumed that conformity to them would lead, on the whole, to as much happiness and as little unhappiness as men could reasonably expect. He did not consider the case of a rapidly changing society, in which men's habits, formed in an earlier

[1] Ibid., pp. 589–90.

age, no longer suit the one in which they live. In such a society, men might approve of many things, formerly beneficial but now injurious, and disapprove of others, formerly injurious but now beneficial. Since, according to Hume, it takes time to form the habits that direct the moral sentiments, it must always be true that, in a rapidly changing society, the prevailing moral standards will never promote the greatest happiness possible.

No theory of morals assigns a larger role to sympathy than does Hume's. Hume explicitly rejects the notion that egoism is in any sense fundamental, and altruism either a disguised form of it or else its derivative. In rejecting Hobbes's psychological hedonism, he borrows the simple argument of Bishop Butler, that a man must be able to desire other things besides his own pleasure, because, before anything can please him, he must first desire it. A man must, before he can get pleasure from quenching his thirst, feel thirsty. And if he can desire other things besides his own pleasure, there is no reason why other people's pleasures should not be among those things. Egoistic hedonism is usually of the psychological kind. It is not absurd to hold that, though men can desire pleasures not their own, it is their own pleasures that they should strive to obtain. But few people have ever been tempted to accept this theory, which, though it is logically impregnable, is far less plausible than the one adopted by Hobbes. What Butler and Hume, therefore, most desire to do is to refute Hobbes. For the egoistic hedonism of Hobbes is not properly a theory of morals. It does not explain the facts of our moral experience but obliges us to reject them as illusions. Hume is as well aware as anyone, and much better aware than either Bentham or James Mill, that no true moral philosophy can make an accommodation with Hobbes.

Hume defines sympathy as the pleasure or pain we feel whenever we contemplate the pleasures or pains of other people. And from sympathy springs benevolence; because the pleasure of other people gives us pleasure, we wish to give pleasure to them, and because the pain of other people gives us pain, we wish to relieve them. This, of course, is not to reduce benevolence to egoism. We do not desire to give pleasure to other people in order that their pleasure should give us pleasure; on the contrary, our own pleasure, so far from being the object of our desire, is merely the cause of it. There is no trace of Hobbesian egoism in what Hume has to say about sympathy and benevolence.

Having established its right to an existence independent of egoism, Hume is anxious not to make too much of sympathy, for all that it must play so important a part in his system. Our sympathy, he says, is seldom intense, except when the pleasures and pains of those to whom we are most closely bound by blood or friendship are concerned. Sympathy is a weak emotion on most occasions when we feel it and the benevolent impulses aroused by it are usually much weaker than our selfish passions.

But though sympathy is a weak emotion, it is one to which we are all liable. Human souls are so much alike that no sooner does one man approach another than the bonds of sympathy are established between them. Though they may not like one another, they will not, unless they are mere passers-by, be indifferent. This does not mean that Hume would deny that we are indifferent to many people whom we see or hear during the course of the day, for we may know nothing of them. But if we converse with any of them, however small our interest, we cannot listen to what they say about themselves without some faint sympathy or antipathy. If this much is admitted, Hume thinks it enough for his purpose, which is to prove that the moral sentiments, though strong enough to control the behaviour of all mankind, are yet derived from sympathy.

Hume puts the gist of his argument into a short passage in which he says: '. . . tho' sympathy be much fainter than our concern for ourselves, and a sympathy with persons remote from us much fainter than that with persons near and contiguous; yet we neglect all these differences in our calm judgments. . . . Besides, that we ourselves often change our situation . . ., we every day meet with persons, who are in a different situation from ourselves and who cou'd never converse with us on any reasonable terms, were we to remain constantly in that situation and point of view, which is peculiar to us. The intercourse of sentiments . . . makes us form some general unalterable standard, by which we may approve or disapprove of characters and manners. And tho' the heart does not always take part in those general notions . . . yet they are sufficient for discourse, and serve all our purposes in company, in the pulpit, on the theatre, and in the schools.'[1]

It is easy to see how Hume distinguishes between sympathy and the moral sentiments. Sympathy is the pleasure or pain we feel when we contemplate the pleasures or pains of other people. The moral sentiments are the pleasures and pains we feel when we contemplate actions or characters without regard to any benefit or injury that may result from them to ourselves or to persons in whom we take a special interest. Sympathy and the moral sentiments have different objects; they are aroused in us by the contemplation of different things. Moreover, the moral sentiments are disinterested, while sympathy is not. But though the distinction between them is clear enough, it is difficult to see how Hume derives the moral sentiments from sympathy. How does an emotion that is strong only when persons close to us are involved give rise to sentiments that are completely disinterested? Hume sees the difficulty and often refers to it, but not every one will agree that he has solved it. What are the calm judgments in which we neglect all the differences in sympathy so natural to us? They are presumably judgments about the consequences of human actions and characters. We may, for instance, reasonably conclude that a crime committed in China two thousand years ago caused as much unhappiness as one committed yesterday in our neighbourhood and involving our closest friends in hopeless misery. In the one case we feel only the faintest sympathy, and in the other our hearts go out to our friends. If our feelings of disapproval in the two cases are equal, or at least much nearer equal than our feelings of sympathy, how is it that the former are derived from the latter? Our calm judgments can, perhaps, explain how it is that we disapprove the two crimes equally, but they cannot make more intelligible the derivation of the moral sentiments from sympathy. It is not enough to say with Hume that the one class of feelings derives from the other, to admit the greatest differences in the operations of the two and to say that these differences are accounted for by the influence of our calm judgments. Why should not our calm judgments level our sympathies as effectively as our moral sentiments? There may well be a causal connexion between the two kinds of feelings; indeed, it is likely

[1] *Treatise of Human Nature*, pp. 603–4.

that there is. But then each kind is causally connected with many other things as well, so that our knowledge is not much extended by saying that one is derived from the other. Hume's derivation of the moral sentiments from sympathy is no more plausible than James Mill's derivation of them from egoism.

Hume's words suggest that sympathy and the moral sentiments, though they have different objects, are similar feelings. He says that when a man calls another his enemy, he speaks the language of self-love and expresses sentiments peculiar to himself. But if he calls him vicious, he speaks another language and 'expresses sentiments, in which he expects all his audience to concur with him. He must here, therefore, depart from his private and particular situation . . .; he must . . . touch a string to which all mankind have an accord or symphony.'[1] There is nothing here that implies that the sentiments expressed differ in kind, and the most natural interpretation of Hume's meaning is that they are similar, though in the one case the man who expresses them knows they are peculiar to himself, while in the other he expects his hearers to share them. But to most people approval and disapproval seem to be emotions very different from sympathy and antipathy. This is a matter that introspection alone can decide. Nor will most persons agree with Hume when he says that approval and disapproval are weak sentiments. He may never have felt them strongly, but then he was a very exceptional person.

In a passage to which he attaches little importance, Hume reveals his greatest defect as a moral philosopher. He discusses the distinction made by modern philosophers (but not by the ancients) between the natural abilities and the moral virtues. He admits that the quality of our approval of the natural abilities differs from the quality of our approval of the moral virtues. Yet both the abilities and the virtues are beneficial to mankind or immediately agreeable to those who possess or contemplate them. Hume explains the difference between the qualities of our reactions to these two classes of phenomena by the circumstance that, whereas the natural abilities are largely unalterable, the virtues, or at least the actions proceeding from them, can be stimulated by rewards and punishments, by praise and by blame. All this is certainly true. What is curious is that Hume should treat it as if it were unimportant, whereas it is, in fact,

[1] *Enquiry*, Sec. 11, Part 1.

whatever its correct analysis, of the essence of the matter, and of it every adequate theory of morals must take large account.

Before we can profitably discuss Hume's political philosophy, we must notice a distinction he makes between the natural and the artificial virtues. The natural virtues, such as courage, prudence and benevolence, are the products of natural instincts; and every one readily understands both that they are so and that they are beneficial. Prudence and courage are necessary for self-preservation, and benevolence, the product of sympathy, obviously increases human happiness. But there are other virtues which, in Hume's words, 'produce . . . approbation by means of an artifice or contrivance, which arises from the circumstances and necessity of mankind'.[1] He regards justice as a conventional virtue of this kind.

Now, when Hume talks of justice, he means, above all, respect for the existing conventions about property. It is easy to see why these conventions are respected once they are established, for, in every society, thieves, when caught, are punished. What needs explanation is how it is that such conventions come to be established. They are not the immediate products of any natural instinct. It is true that men are benevolent, but benevolence, according to Hume, though it cannot be explained away or derived from egoism, is normally much weaker than men's selfish passions. It cannot therefore explain how the conventions about property first arose. Nor, of course (though Hume does not bother to make this point), could the conventions about property and the respect for them be imposed by the strong upon the weak. For it is the inequality of property which itself divides society into the strong and the weak. The conventions about property must therefore precede the inequality that makes possible the domination of the many by the few. The question, therefore, still remains: how did these conventions arise?

Hume's answer is that 'nature provides a remedy in the judgment or understanding, for what is irregular and incommodious in the affections. For when men . . . have observ'd, that the principal disturbance in society arises from those goods, which we call external, and from their looseness and easy transition from one person to another; they must seek for a remedy . . . This can be done after no other manner, than by a convention enter'd into by

[1] *Treatise*, p. 472.

all the members of the society to bestow stability on the possession of those external goods, and leave every one in the peaceable enjoyment of what he may acquire by his fortune or industry.'[1] In this passage, as he himself points out, Hume is not using the word convention in the sense of contract. 'It is only,' he says, 'a general sense of the common interest . . . which induces them to regulate their conduct by certain rules. . . . In like manner are human languages gradually establish'd by human conventions without any promise.'[2] Hume, a little later, puts his main argument in these words: ' 'Tis certain that no affection of the human mind has both sufficient force, and a proper direction to counterbalance the love of gain, and render men fit members of society, by making them abstain from the possessions of others. Benevolence to strangers is too weak for the purpose. . . . There is no passion, therefore, capable of controlling the interested affection' (Hume means 'love of gain') 'but the very affection itself, by an alteration of its direction. Now this alteration must necessarily take place upon the least reflexion; since 'tis evident that the passion is much better satisfy'd by its restraint, than by its liberty. . . .'[3]

Whenever nature provides us with anything we need in sufficient abundance, we evolve no conventions regulating its use. Property is the product of selfishness, scarcity and reflexion. Now, once the conventions have come into existence, it is obviously convenient, in the long run, that they should be respected even in those cases where respect for them creates unhappiness; for mankind have more to gain by their general observance than to lose by their observance in hard cases. It may sometimes be in the public interest that the conventions should be altered, though Hume takes no notice of this point; but it can almost never, he is careful to insist, be in the public interest that they should be broken. Hume's account of the origins of justice and property is very different from Locke's; he has nothing to say about man's natural right to the product of his own labour. So far, then, Hume's account is much closer to that of Hobbes than to any one else's. But all that he has yet done is to explain how certain conventions and the respect for them have come into existence; he has not yet explained why this respect is a virtue. This last, however, is the easiest part of his task. Though self-interest was the original motive that led to the establishment of

[1] Ibid. p. 489.  [2] Ibid., p. 490.  [3] Ibid., p. 492.

justice, it is sympathy with the public interest that is the source of the moral approval that attends its practice.

All that Hume has established, if his arguments are valid, is that it is in the public interest that there should be some rules of property; but he has not given us reasons for believing that the rules prevailing in any society are more likely to be in the public interest than other rules which could be devised to take their place. He might have argued that, since men must learn by reflexion that some rules are necessary, this same process of reflexion enables them to discover what rules are best suited to their needs. But Hume does not do this. He merely says that '. . . there are, no doubt, motives of public interest for most of the rules which determine property; but I still suspect, that these rules are principally fix'd by the imagination.'[1] He then goes on to explain how the imagination does the fixing; how 'first possession always engages the attention most'; how, when first possession becomes obscure through the passage of time, 'long possession or prescription takes its place, and gives a person a sufficient property in anything he enjoys'; how a natural association of ideas leads us to suppose that what belongs to a father should, after his death, belong to his son. The imagination, according to Hume, is largely governed by the laws of the association of ideas. How then can he think it probable that the rules of property fixed by the imagination are the rules which, on the whole, best promote the public interest? Hume merely makes an assumption and leaves it at that. The weakness of his argument, at this point, is typical of him; it lies not in any confusion of thought or logical inconsistency but in a simple failure to take all the relevant circumstances into account. It was left to Hume's successors to justify or to condemn the existing laws of property on strictly utilitarian grounds.

Hume has only one argument for the inequality of wealth. It is an argument often used for want of a better. Create equality of possessions among men, and their different abilities will soon restore inequality. Or if the equality is forcibly maintained, society is reduced to indigence, for its ablest members have nothing to induce them to make the most of their abilities. The argument implies that equal possessions mean equality of poverty, and that no egalitarian society can be rich. Hume, like most people who use it,

[1] Ibid., Note to p. 504.

does not care to determine just how much inequality it justifies. It is an argument for no more than unequal rewards for unequal labour, and it does not justify any system of property existing in the world. But Hume, living in a society in which only the inarticulate had important grievances, did not give, and did not need to give, thought to such matters.

Another conventional virtue, to which Hume also devotes much attention, and which he considers to be part of justice, is the keeping of promises.[1] Hume's argument to prove its conventional nature does not differ, in any important respect, from what he has to say about property. A man's mere statement about how he intends to act on a future occasion can, of itself, impose no obligation on him, for it cannot provide him with any motive for doing in the future what he now says he intends to do. It is human conventions that create such a motive, for they are the products of an experience teaching us that human affairs are conducted to better advantage, when every man has some security that every other man will do what he says he intends to do. To this end, there are established certain forms of words among men, by which they can give each other this security. These forms once established, whoever uses them 'must never expect to be trusted any more, if he refuse to perform what he promis'd'.

I have given a mere outline of Hume's moral theory, whose details are no longer of great interest. It reduces morals to a branch of psychology; and it is this that is its principal defect in the eyes of many people. With this common verdict, the reader may or may not agree. But whatever the defects of the theory, it is as subtle and plausible as any other system of ethics propounded by a European between the times of Aristotle and Kant. The reader will have observed that it owes almost nothing to Locke, and a great deal to Hobbes. But it is very different from Hobbes's theory, and includes an explicit rejection of much that Hobbes taught. The influence of Hobbes on Hume is as much negative as positive, but it is incomparably greater than that of any other thinker.

Hume's theory, usually in a cruder form than the one given to it by its inventor, dominated English moral philosophy until it began to be affected, well on into the nineteenth century, by the system of Kant. Even Bentham and James Mill, who taught that the standard

[1] He sometimes calls this virtue 'fidelity'.

of morality is independent of men's sentiments, had perforce to borrow several arguments from Hume to show how it is that men come to accept that standard. James Mill, though he derived them both from egoism, made a large use of sympathy and approval to explain the moral behaviour of man. Though many persons attacked Hume, nearly all of them who undertook to construct a moral theory of their own incorporated a considerable part of his with it. And they borrowed very little from Kant, who was heard of in this country long before he was understood. But it was widely known that many of Kant's arguments were directed against Hume, some of whose critics seem to have sheltered under the authority of a name that was still only a name to them. Sir Leslie Stephen, who had the patience to read many of Hume's critics, gives the impression that some of the attacks on him were made with weapons believed by their users to have been borrowed from Kant, though it is now known that they were made in Scotland by the very people who thought they had imported them from Germany.

Yet it would be a mistake to suggest that nearly all utilitarians adopted or else adapted to their own use Hume's theory of morals. Many of them were not moral philosophers and were content to assert that only pleasure and the means to pleasure are good, and that no action is right except the one likely to produce the greatest happiness under the circumstances. They did not attempt to analyse the notions of goodness and rightness or to explain man's moral behaviour. But those utilitarians who went at all deeply into these matters, though they might explicitly reject some part of Hume's teaching, usually borrowed at least as much as they rejected.

## 2. His Political Theory

Hume's political theory is simpler than his ethics, and what originality it has is mostly negative. It is what he rejects rather than what he adds to the ideas current in his day that distinguishes him from his predecessors. He does not talk of natural law and natural rights, and he quietly demolishes the notion of a social contract. Otherwise, except for a few favourite ideas of his own which all his historical studies failed to dislodge from his mind, he follows Hobbes.

Hume's moral theory rests on the psychological assumptions that thy is not a form of egoism and that the moral sentiments are a species of sympathy. But his political theory takes it for granted that man is predominantly selfish and often foolish. It is, he thinks, 'a just political maxim, that every man must be supposed a knave: though at the same time, it appears somewhat strange, that a maxim should be true in politics, which is false in fact.'[1] Men are truly benevolent in the circle of their families and friends, but their benevolence is too weak to have a larger operation. Besides, in their political behaviour men are partisans, and their selfishness is therefore less liable to restraint. Those whose interests are the same will applaud them whatever they do, and this applause will make them indifferent to the opinions of others. Lonely and unsupported man is, Hume implies, easily influenced and restrained by the opinions of other men, but as soon as he acquires a circle of friends he has shelter and comfort against the rest of the world and can even enjoy its hostility. This, I take it, is what Hume means when he says that honour is a powerful restraint on individual man in his dealings with other men but not on the partisan in his dealings with groups to which he does not belong.

Justice and stable government are advantageous to man; he has intelligence enough to know it but not the wisdom to act accordingly. He often prefers the immediate advantage to be gained from injustice to the more lasting but less obvious advantages that are the fruits of a constant respect for justice. How, Hume asks, is this misfortune to be remedied? His answer is that 'this infirmity of human nature becomes a remedy to itself, and that we provide against our negligence about remote objects, merely because we are naturally inclin'd to that negligence'.[2] As men cannot change their natures, the most they can do is to alter the circumstances under which they act, and so provide themselves with motives for behaving justly when they might otherwise not do so. But this can be done only in one way, by making a few men immediately interested in the maintenance of justice and giving them the power to enforce it. These few men are the civil magistrates, who, since they are indifferent to the great majority of those they govern, have no interest in doing injustice to them, but do have an interest in seeing that they act justly to one another, since the existence of the state and their own pre-eminent position inside it both depend upon the

---

[1] *Essay*, VI, 'On the Independence of Parliament'.   [2] *Treatise*, p. 536.

maintenance of justice. 'Here then,' says Hume, 'is the origin of civil government and society . . . Men are not able radically to cure . . . that narrowness of soul, which makes them prefer the present to the remote . . . All they can do is to change their situation, and render the observance of justice the immediate interest of some particular persons . . .'[1] This is substantially the doctrine of Hobbes. The initial assumptions are the same, though they are somewhat qualified: men are predominantly selfish, they are capable of reflexion, and they are passionate and foolish. And the conclusion is not very different: men must, for their own sakes, guard against their own and other people's rapacity and folly, and this they can do only by bringing into existence a new situation, in which they make it some powerful persons' immediate interest to force them to act in their own permanent interests, even when it is to their immediate advantage to do otherwise.

This view, as it is expounded by Hume, does not imply any particular theory about the historical origins of the state, whereas it forms part of Hobbes's account of those origins. But otherwise there is little enough difference between them. It is Hume's opinion that civil government probably first arose because, in time of war, some one man acquired an ascendancy over the others, who soon got used to discipline and felt the advantage of it.[2] All government is, he says, based on opinion. Force is always with the governed, and in the last resort the few can govern the many only because the many feel, however obscurely, that it is to their advantage to be governed.

It is not Hume's doctrine that it is 'on opinion only that government is founded',[3] that distinguishes him from Hobbes. Hobbes's account of the contract and of the sovereign as the bearer of his subjects' wills is a piece of mysticism that contains no element of truth, but in another sense his theory attaches as much importance to opinion as does Hume's. However reluctant any man may be to obey the laws when he stands to gain by disobedience, all other men are of opinion that he should obey; and it is their opinion that makes it possible for the government to enforce obedience with considerable economy and efficiency. Hobbes is even more conscious than Hume of the weakness of governments, and no less

---

[1] *Treatise*, p. 537.     [2] *Essay*, V, 'Of the Origins of Government'.
[3] *Essay*, IV, 'Of the First Principles of Government'.

convinced that their efficiency depends upon the opinion of the governed that they are indispensable. If Hobbes makes much more than does Hume of fear of punishment as a motive for obedience, it is because he thinks that reasonable people can have no sufficient motive for obeying the government unless they are convinced that the unreasonable will be bound to a similar obedience. But the first law of nature, from which Hobbes derives all the others and therefore also the obligation to obey the government, is just the sort of prudential maxim to which Hume alludes when he says that all government is founded on opinion.

Where Hume does differ from Hobbes is in the importance he attaches to the mere force of habit. He distinguishes between opinion of interest and opinion of right. The first is what we have been discussing already, the prevalent (though not, perhaps, explicitly held) opinion that government is indispensable. The second is mere prejudice created by habit, the opinion that those who have long received obedience are entitled to receive it. This, too, need not be a conscious opinion; it may be and often is no more than deference to those who speak with authority. Opinion of right maintains not only the power of governments but also the security of property. Hume thinks that the hope of private advantage (as distinct from the protection that every man enjoys where the laws are properly enforced), fear and affection contribute but little to the stability of governments. Whenever he can do it, without placing a new burden on men's virtues, Hume shifts the emphasis away from the calculating egoism, the vanity and the fear in terms of which Hobbes delights to explain the political behaviour of mankind. What belongs neither to virtue nor to vice can easily be ascribed to habit and to the association of ideas. The political importance of prejudice is a notion which both Burke and the later utilitarians owe to David Hume.

Hume's beliefs that government is necessary, that men have an implicit idea of its utility and that this idea, as a motive for obedience, is powerfully reinforced by mere habit and prejudice, leads him quite naturally to the conservative conclusion that it is best to submit quietly to whatever government we find established in the country in which we live. Habit and prejudice are strongest where society has changed the least. There is therefore a presumption against change and a very strong presumption against violent

D

change. In the most important of his political essays, *Of the Original Contract*, Hume says that though some innovations must take place, violent ones are to be undertaken by no individual and are dangerous even when attempted by the legislature. Men must expect more evil than good from them, for though there are examples to the contrary, 'they are not to be drawn into precedent, and are only to be regarded as proofs, that the science of politics affords few rules, which will not admit of some exception, and which may not be sometimes controlled by fortune and accident'.[1] Hume speaks of 'violent' innovations but we may take it that he means great ones, for he says that they are dangerous even when the legislature attempts them, and what is done by the legislature is presumably peaceably done. This is the conservative doctrine of the man who was not only the least orthodox of the great English philosophers but also a life-long student of history.

There is another argument, from which Burke and Bentham were to derive conservative consequences, to be found in Hume. It is that stability of property is to be maintained, not only to prevent disputes, but also so as not to disappoint the expectations which it has created. 'By the laws of society', says Hume, 'this coat, this house is mine, and ought to remain perpetually in my possession. I reckon on the secure enjoyment of it; by depriving me of it, you disappoint my expectations, and doubly displease me, and offend every bystander.'[2] From this simple argument many consequences can be and indeed often have been drawn. Men are creatures of habit, and habits create expectations. It is therefore important, if men are to be happy, that they should be able to enjoy in the future what they have enjoyed in the past and are enjoying in the present. To deprive them of their property is to deprive them of the means to expected future enjoyments. But to disappoint expectations that are the creatures of habits, is to destroy those habits, and therefore to weaken the bonds that hold society together. Besides, men suffer more from being deprived of what they have long possessed than other men are made happy by being given what they never expected to have. There is a prima facie case against all transfers of property. What all men want is security; and though, if there is insecurity, some may gain what

---

[1] *Essay*, XII, 'Of the Original Contract'.
[2] *Enquiry Concerning the Principles of Morals*, Appendix III.

others lose, they not only gain less than others lose but they cannot be secure in its possession, for the stability of property, on which security depends, has already been shaken for their benefit.

These consequences, suggested or implied by Hume and later developed by Burke and Bentham, are impressive only in isolation. As soon as we call to mind the law of diminishing utility and also the fact that the spoliation of the rich has prevented bloodshed perhaps as often as it has occasioned it, we can estimate Hume's argument at its true value. Arguments *a priori* are nowhere more out of place than in political theory, but it is precisely in this sphere that even the most sceptical of philosophers does not abandon them. He calls his preferences generalizations from experience and he laughs at the intuitionists, but the foundations on which he builds are no stronger.

Hume, indeed, in matters political was no true sceptic. He was a man of calm temper and quiet prejudices. He disliked confusion of thought and empty symbols, but, provided a statement was meaningful, clear and plausible, he was not much disturbed by lack of evidence for its truth. The genuine scepticism of Montaigne, the true freedom from prejudice which is not a kind of intellectual nihilism but is the product of sympathy and imagination, was not his.

Hume's greatest service as a political theorist is his indifference to questions of origin. As an historian he is, of course, as interested in them as anyone else, but he does not wish to draw political conclusions from them. No matter how governments came into existence, the present duty of obedience is always grounded in utility. 'If the reason be asked of that obedience, which we are bound to pay to government, I readily answer, because society could not otherwise subsist. And this answer is clear and intelligible to all mankind. Your answer is', he says to the contract theorist, 'because we should keep our word. But besides, that nobody, till trained in a philosophical system, can either comprehend or relish this answer: Besides this, I say, you find yourself embarrassed, when it is asked, why are we bound to keep our word? Nor can you give any answer, but what would, immediately, without any circuit, have accounted for our obligation to allegiance.'[1] In other words, fidelity, or the duty to keep promises, is as much grounded in

[1] *Essay*, XII, 'Of the Original Contract'.

utility as any other duty. Why, then, derive the duty of obedience from it, when it can be more directly and plausibly derived from utility? Since we have no knowledge of an original contract and much evidence that existing governments acquired their power by force and fraud, is it not wiser to abandon an intricate theory that is difficult to understand and still more difficult to defend? And if we do so, we can also abandon all such obscure notions as that of 'tacit consent', which are only invented to support a theory whose weakness is felt by its own exponents. These arguments, made to look less simple, are to be found once again in Bentham's *Fragment on Government*. There they are used as a base for a hundred unkind attacks on Sir William Blackstone. But Hume is seldom aggressive; he is content to point out errors and to invite his readers to pass another way.

There are two classes of important political thinkers: those whose fertile minds produce many ideas for later generations to elaborate, and the spell-binders. Hume, like Aristotle, belongs to the former class, though he occupies a humbler place in it. It is the measure of Plato's greatness that he not only belongs to both but is first in each of them. As for political thinkers who say more that is true than is false, they do not exist, for political theory is not yet a science.

# CHAPTER III

## FROM HUME TO BENTHAM

FOR a period of over a hundred years, utilitarianism was the dominant political and moral theory in England. This period lasted from the time that Hume's reputation as a philosopher was made until the publication of J. S. Mill's essay in defence of a doctrine that he had himself, without knowing it, more than half rejected. I do not wish to say that all or even most of the writers on politics and morals were utilitarians. The dominance of a theory, unless it is a creed maintained by a church or a state, does not ordinarily involve its explicit adoption by any large number of those who write or think about the subject with which it deals. The utilitarians, properly so called, were always a minority. Their theories were not flattering to mankind and were therefore repeatedly attacked. Something of the unpopularity of Hobbes, from whom they derived so many of their ideas, always remained with them.

But though the utilitarians were always on the defensive, either to recommend themselves to the world or to expose the follies of their critics, they also produced most of the theories and ideas around which political and moral discussion turned. Their vocabulary, their turns of speech, their favourite prejudices and their hatred of nonsense served not only their own purposes but often those of their opponents as well. They were aggressive and self-confident, and always ready to do battle provided the ground were chosen by themselves. For they were sure that, on any other ground, the battle must be unprofitable to all the combatants; it must be a mere war of words. Complacency and their sort of scepticism are natural allies, and they make a formidable combination. Formidable, indeed, but not attractive; and that is why the utilitarian doctrine has always been more influential than popular. When the effects of their actions need not be considered, even fanatics are less annoying than the sceptics who, whatever else they may doubt, are always sure of their own wisdom. And it is the religious who search their hearts. In their devotion to their creed there is often a true humility, and we are bound to respect them even when we know the harm they do.

But the doctrine's very great influence is what nobody can deny. For over a hundred years, the moral and political philosophers of England and Scotland did little more than either elaborate the theories of Hume and of Hobbes (the latter in the more respectable form given them by Hume), or else protest against them and construct the weakest alternatives. The great contemporaries whose theories (if only small though important parts of them are true) destroy utilitarianism at its roots, were all foreigners. But Rousseau, Kant, Saint-Simon and Marx were unknown or mere names in England until the late nineteenth and early twentieth centuries. Rousseau had made too great a reputation in the world to be ignored even by the English, but he was also held responsible for inspiring a revolution. The English therefore condemned his doctrines, discovered a good deal of nonsense in them and took no notice of the rest. Those who had heard of Kant spoke of him respectfully. It was well known that his heart was in the right place, and that on all important questions he was on the side of the angels. But his theories were complicated and his language obscure. Here was a great piece of artillery indeed and the utilitarians used only muskets, but unfortunately there was as yet no one in England who could handle so large a gun. Saint-Simon died in 1825 and Marx only in 1883. They were both original thinkers and very shrewd and severe critics of the societies in which they lived. Time was therefore needed for the intellectual world to get used to them and to recognize their importance.

Thus it was that the utilitarians, for over a century, had no serious competitors. They could even afford not to make use of all the advantages provided by the subtlety of Hume. As we shall see, Bentham and James Mill impoverished more than they enriched the doctrine inherited from him. There are some people, often hard-working and virtuous, who feel uncomfortable except in narrow and barely-furnished rooms.

Nothing, however, would be less just than to accuse all the utilitarians of austerity. When a doctrine becomes dominant, it acquires some of the virtues of the society it dominates. Richness and variety are characteristic of all the great nations of Western Europe, and of none more than England. The fundamental utilitarian assumptions were made, either openly or tacitly, by many men whose theories have little more than these assumptions in common. It was the fashion, in politics and morals, to erect tall structures on slender foundations. Philosophical systems are artificial things, and philosophers who begin with the same assumptions can arrive at the most different conclusions. His fundamental principles, if he is unable to invent them, a moralist may borrow from others, but the system he derives from them will depend upon his experience and his character.

I shall therefore, though I deal only with the most important, have something to say not only about Helvetius and Beccaria, but also about Paley, Burke, Godwin, Paine, Adam Smith, Malthus and Ricardo. All these men, who were among the cleverest thinkers of their day, were indebted either to Hume or Bentham, or to both of them.

Bentham started out on his intellectual career with only a small stock of ideas. These he took mostly from Hume, but also from Helvetius, Beccaria and Priestley. When Bentham, after an undergraduate career at Queen's College, which he thought a waste of time, revisited Oxford in 1768 to record his vote at the University Parliamentary election, he found, in a little circulating library attached to Harper's coffee-house near his old college, a copy of a pamphlet which had only very recently been published, Priestley's *Essay on Government*. In this pamphlet, he found the magic phrase 'the greatest happiness of the greatest number'. If, then, Bentham got no wisdom at Queen's College, he got the piece of it that he valued most very close at hand. He records his experience in these words: 'It was by that pamphlet and this phrase in it that my principles on the subject of morality, public and private, were determined. It was from that pamphlet and that page of it that I drew the phrase, the words and the import of which have been so widely diffused over the civilized world.' The phrase, however, though Bentham found it in Priestley's pamphlet, was not the invention of Priestley. Sir Leslie Stephen, Professor Halévy and Dr. Montague agree in ascribing the authorship to Francis Hutcheson.

## 1. HELVETIUS

Neither Priestley nor Hutcheson is of great importance in the history of moral and political thought; certainly of much less importance than Helvetius and Beccaria. Helvetius, who lived from 1715 to 1771, was the Frenchman who did more than any other man to make popular Hume's philosophy on the Continent. His book, *De L'Esprit* (1758), is an attempt to analyse all human experience into sensations, by which he means exactly what Hume meant by impressions and ideas. It is, with Hartley's *Observations on Man*, Condillac's *Traité des Sensations*, and James Mill's *Analysis of the Phenomena of the Human Mind*, one of the four most ambitious and systematic attempts to work out in detail the implications of Hume's general principles. But Helvetius's more complicated and less subtle gallicized version of Hume's theory of knowledge does not concern us. We are concerned only with two doctrines of Helvetius, of which one was borrowed from Hume and the other is more closely associated with Helvetius himself. Both these doctrines are much older than the eighteenth century, but it was because Helvetius brought them together and attached great importance to them that they later fired the imagination of Bentham. The first of these doctrines, borrowed from Hume but on which Helvetius leant much more heavily than his master had done, is that the chief utility of governments consists in their ability to force men to act in their own best interests when they feel disinclined to do so. This doctrine, expounded with the greatest clarity and force in Hobbes's *Leviathan*, has been called the principle of the artificial identity of interests. In his most interesting but often misleading book, *The Growth of Philosophic Radicalism*, M. Halévy compares this principle with two others, which also assume the predominant selfishness of men: the principle of the fusion of interests and the principle of their natural identity. The former asserts that, though men's selfishness of itself leads to conflicts between them, its operation is to some extent counteracted by that of sympathy. The latter asserts that though each man seeks his own selfish interest, the world is so made that he can only do so by co-operating in peace and amity with other men. The most famous exponent of what Halévy calls the natural identity of interests is Bernard Mandeville, whose book *The Fable of the Bees* was published in 1714. Mandeville gave his book the sub-title *Private Vices, Public Benefits*, and he succeeded in giving it an appearance of paradox by assuming that most natural passions, and especially the pursuit of wealth, are vicious, and then going on to prove that they are necessary to civilized life. The core of Mandeville's argument is that while every want is an evil, it is the multitude of men's wants that obliges them to serve one another and therefore to live in peace and amity; from which it follows that the greater and more varied men's wants, the more their selfish desire to satisfy them will oblige them to co-operate in the production and distribution of the goods by which alone these wants can be satisfied. This argument, divorced from its author's paradoxes, is easily recognized as the most important of the assumptions made by the classical economists. What Mandeville did for the principle of the natural identity of interests, Helvetius did for that of their artificial identity. He did not invent it, but he made the most of it.

The other idea of Helvetius, also not original with him, but to which he ascribed no less importance, is that man's character is entirely the product of his environment. He seems to have imagined that this is a legitimate inference from the phenomenalism he took over from Hume. But Helvetius did not agree with Montesquieu that national character is largely determined by a people's climatic and geographical environment. He thought man's social environment a more important factor in making him what he is than the geography of his country. Now, whereas geography and climate are beyond human control, social environment is not. Man, by acquiring knowledge of what he is and what made him so, acquires an almost unlimited power to reform his species. But there are in society two classes of persons who can do more than any others to reform their fellows; they are the pedagogues and the legislators. It is their business to give men the education and the laws that will enable them to attain happiness. In the eyes of Helvetius, the pedagogue and the legislator co-operate in the same task; they are both of them primarily educators. Divorced from its phenomenalist origins and its utilitarian bias, this doctrine of Helvetius, that good laws make good men, is as old as Plato and Aristotle. But at the time that he expounded it, men were struck by its novelty. In any case, it is an idea not to be found in Hume. But what is still more important to notice is its essential radicalism. The three Englishmen who were the most completely converted to it, Bentham, Godwin and

Robert Owen, were among the most radical critics of the society in which they lived.

## 2. BECCARIA

The doctrine of Helvetius that morals and legislation, well considered, are the same science, was taken up by the Italian philosopher Beccaria, whose book *Dei delitti e delle pene* (Of Crimes and Punishments) first appeared in 1764. It is an attractive and well-written book, and it quickly attained the greatest popularity. It contains the first Italian version of the famous utilitarian phrase, in the words 'la massima felicità divisa nel maggior numero'. 'If we look into history', says Beccaria in an often-quoted passage from the introduction to his book, 'we shall find that laws, which are or ought to be conventions between men in a state of freedom, have been for the most part the work of the passions of the few or the consequences of fortuitous or temporary necessity; not dictated by a cool examiner of human nature, who . . . had this only end in view, the greatest happiness of the greatest number.' Beccaria, like Bentham after him, proposed to make the scale of punishments correspond to the scale of crimes. One of his rules was that punishments should always be so contrived that, with the least possible pain to the culprit, they should produce the greatest deterrent effect; another, that punishment should be certain and immediate; yet another, that judges should never interpret but should confine themselves to applying the law. These are but three principles, among many, which Bentham was to take directly from Beccaria. But whereas the Italian philosopher merely put forward a number of principles which he did not elaborate, the Englishman corrected them, added to them and derived innumerable consequences from them.

Helvetius and Beccaria were undoubtedly, after Hume, the two greatest influences on Bentham's intellectual life. Bentham, as we shall see later, was not primarily a moral or political philosopher. What he has to say to us about the nature of goodness and obligation, law, society and government, is neither new nor ingenious. Indeed, his moral philosophy, such as it is, is so confused and ambiguous as to be scarcely deserving serious study. In this respect, he is not merely greatly inferior to Hume, but is not even the equal of his own disciple, James Mill. He has been compared with a good mathematician who has the most confused notions about the philosophy of mathematics, and who can perform the most complicated operations without being able to define such notions as 'number', 'class' and 'function'. Most mathematicians put up with this deficiency with a good grace, knowing that their calculations will be none the less accurate on account of it. But Bentham was not so easily satisfied, and he involved himself in difficulties of whose exact nature he was not even aware. His real virtues are those of the codifier of law and the technical reformer; and the importance of Helvetius and Beccaria to him is that they showed him the road on which he was to travel.

### 3. Paley

Before the world had heard of Bentham, another utilitarian philosopher had made a great reputation. I mean William Paley, whose account of a utilitarian God promoting the happiness of his entirely selfish human creatures, was intended to reconcile Englishmen inclined to philosophy with the religion by law established in their country. Paley is so much the disciple of Hobbes that his doctrine, strictly interpreted, may appear hardly to deserve to be called utilitarian. He is as much an egoistic hedonist as any man ever was. And yet it would, I think, be a mistake to deny him the name of utilitarian. Bentham himself often uses the language of egoistic hedonism; and so, too, does James Mill, and much more consistently than his master. Nevertheless, these three writers all try to reconcile their egoistic hedonism with the fashionable utilitarian doctrine, that that action is right which leads to the greatest possible happiness, no matter whose. The difference between Paley, on the one hand, and Bentham and the elder Mill, on the other, is that Paley's reconciliation is more mechanical and less plausible. It may be that the cause of virtue is further from his heart; that having, like James Mill, derived benevolence and morality from the selfish passions, he is more ready to keep their origins constantly in view. It is for this reason only that Paley, rather than Bentham or James Mill, deserves to be called a pseudo-utilitarian. Fear plays as great a part in his system as in that of Hobbes.

It is in God that Paley finds the conciliator of egoism and utilitarianism. Though Paley believes that every man desires only his own happiness and can desire no other man's except as a means to his own, he also believes that God desires the greatest happiness of the greatest number of men. Paley's God is the one true utilitarian in the universe, for He desires men's greatest happiness for its own sake. That the happiness of God should depend upon that of His creatures is a maxim that no clergyman will advance, so that Paley, unlike Hobbes, does, after all, ascribe an immense importance to genuine altruism. Though the greatest happiness of the greatest number is desired for its own sake by only one person, that person happens to be omnipotent. He can therefore easily contrive that His creatures shall desire it as a means to their salvation.

No utilitarian, not even Hume, is more conservative than Paley. There are traces of utilitarianism in Burke, who is as conservative as Paley, but his apology for prevailing conditions is much less explicitly utilitarian. Burke was the more emotional and imaginative of the two men, and unlike the philosophic clergyman he was religious by nature. Paley is too brisk and confident when he explains God's business in the world. Could any man, who felt his own weakness and mortality, speak so familiarly of One whom he believed to be his Maker? Men have stood in greater awe of their employers than this clergyman of his God.

Paley's *Principles of Moral and Political Philosophy* appeared in 1786. 'Moral Philosophy,' he tells us, is 'that science which teaches men their duty and the reasons for it.'[1] He believes that when men have noticed that the conduct of other men is beneficial to themselves, a sentiment of approval arises in their minds, and afterwards accompanies the idea or mention of the same conduct, although the private advantage that first excited it no longer exists. Beneficial, for Paley, means productive of happiness, and happiness is but the excess of pleasure over pain. 'Pleasures', he says, 'differ in nothing, but in continuance and intensity.'[2] So far, all that Paley has said is perfectly compatible with utilitarianism, for though he has told us that we begin by approving only what is beneficial to ourselves, this does not exclude the possibility that we later approve what is beneficial to others. For the sort of conduct that benefits one man is usually the same as that which benefits another. If, then, we continue to approve it after the private advantage that first excited it no longer exists, we may well approve it when the advantage is someone else's. Paley, however, indifferent to the implications of what he has said, will not allow that man is charitable. He defines

[1] *Principles of Moral and Political Philosophy*, Vol. I, p. 1.      [2] Ibid., p. 21.

virtue as 'the doing of good to mankind, in obedience to the will of God, and for the sake of everlasting happiness'.[1] He asks his readers the question 'Why am I obliged to keep my word?' 'Because it is right, says one.—Because it is agreeable to the fitness of things, says another.—Because it is conformable to reason and nature, says a third.—Because it is conformable to truth, says a fourth.—Because it promotes the public good, says a fifth.—Because it is required by the will of God, concludes a sixth.'[2]

Paley's conclusion is that all these answers are right, because 'the fitness of things, means their fitness to produce happiness: the nature of things, means the actual constitution of the world, by which some things . . . produce happiness, and others misery: reason is the principle, by which we discover . . .this constitution: truth is this judgment expressed or drawn out into propositions, . . . and such . . . is the divine character, that what promotes the general happiness is required by the will of God; . . .'[3] It can be seen from this quotation that Paley was a man of the world. He tells the adherents of these rival doctrines that they are all right, and leaves it to them to infer that he is himself more right than them all. Bentham would have proceeded in a different fashion: he would have said that all the others were wrong and he alone was right.

But Paley is aware that he has still left the matter short. He has told us that right means 'conforming with the will of God', but he has not told us why we are obliged to do what is right. His final answer to the question, 'Why am I obliged to keep my word?' is, therefore, that 'I am urged by a violent motive resulting from the command of another'.[4] The violent motive is the expectation of a posthumous reward, and the command is God's. 'Private happiness is our motive, and the will of God our rule.'[5] It is our good fortune that we live in a world in which man, the incurable egoist, has everything to fear and everything to gain from a just, omnipotent and benevolent God.

Paley is nothing if not positive. He justifies his conservatism by two arguments, of which one is that 'happiness is pretty equally distributed among the different orders of civil society', and the other that 'the advantages of property are so great that men are willing to tolerate the greatest inequalities provided it is respected'.

[1] Ibid., p. 41.    [2] Ibid., p. 54.    [3] Ibid., p. 55.    [4] Ibid., p. 59.
[5] Ibid., p. 60.

He has a little parable in which ninety-nine strong and healthy men toil all day for a poor wage to produce a heap of superfluities to be spent or spoiled by a feeble and worthless man, by a child, a woman, a madman or a fool. They look quietly on while the fruits of their labour are consumed, but should one of their number touch or take the least particle of these superfluities, the others would set upon him and hang him for a thief. This picture is not quite true to life, if only because there is no judge or executioner brought into it to hang the wrong-doer, but it is the fruit of Paley's imagination. He looks upon it with complacency and reflects that the benefits of property must indeed be great if men will behave in this way.

In considering the nature of civil government, Paley insists on the fact that the governed are many and their governors few. The physical strength, he concludes, resides with the governed. The question which therefore lies at the root of all political speculation is this: What are the motives that induce the many to submit to the few? No single motive, says Paley, is sufficient; but there are three altogether more important than the rest. The first, and most important, is *prejudice*, which Paley defines as 'the opinion of right founded on custom', i.e. the prevalent opinion that those persons who have long exercised a power have the right to do so. Hume expresses the same idea when he says, in the *Treatise of Human Nature*, that most men, if asked whether they had ever promised to obey their rulers, would think strangely of their questioner and would reply that they were born to such obedience. The second motive is *reason*, or the reflexion, of which only a minority are capable, that government is necessary for human welfare and that it entails obedience. The third motive is *self-interest*, which does not so much attach men to their governments as detach them from combinations against them. Absorbed in their own affairs, men find it difficult to co-operate against their governors. Since prejudice is the main source of a government's authority, it follows that 'every innovation in the constitution, or, in other words, in the custom of governing, diminishes the stability of government.'[1] But Paley does admit that it might sometimes be expedient to use force to get rid of one's rulers, and he approves of the Revolution of 1688.

[1] Ibid., Vol. II, p. 126.

In his criticism of the notion of a social contract and of natural rights, except in the sense of rights that men might still possess outside politically organized society, Paley is a typical utilitarian. But what is more interesting is that he uses his utilitarian principles as the major premises of arguments to prove that the system of parliamentary representation existing before the Great Reform Bill was perfect; that judge-made law (i.e. the binding force of judicial precedents) is good; that the old English penal laws, which hanged a man for stealing a sheep as well as for murder, were excellent; that a very great inequality of wealth is beneficial to the community; and that a religious establishment is desirable. His argument for the inequality of wealth is typical of him. One of the most effective ways of increasing happiness is, he thinks, to increase the number of people who can be happy. It is therefore desirable that the population should increase.[1] But the wealthy, marrying later than the poor, have fewer children; on the other hand, Paley is convinced that one class of society are about as happy as another. It is therefore desirable that most people should be poor. Why, then, need any be rich? Paley's answer is that a small proportion of the population of a country can produce all the necessaries required by the whole of it. But this small proportion will produce only enough for themselves, if they have no inducement to do otherwise. The others must provide this inducement by offering them luxuries in return for their necessaries. This is as far as Paley cares to take his argument, but it has consequences that may well have been clear to him. One such consequence is that it cannot be desirable that all the producers of necessaries should receive luxuries in return for them; for in that case a large minority of the people would be wealthy enough to marry late and have small families. It is therefore proper to infer, from what Paley says, that that society is best organized in which most of the producers of necessaries are poor, and the recipients of luxuries are only a small class of land-owners and capitalists. For Paley is just as insistent that idleness leads to vice and unhappiness as he is that poverty does not. Paley, in fact, logical though he is, does not carry his argument to its logical conclusion. He justifies inequality; but he does not say, what on his own

---

[1] Paley believed that most countries, Britain among them, could easily support much greater populations than existed in his day.

premises he should say, that the greater the inequality the better for mankind.

I have devoted some considerable space to Paley for two reasons: because of his great influence while he lived, and also because he is in some respects so like and in others so unlike Bentham. From theoretical principles that are broadly similar, except that Bentham says nothing about God and often speaks as if the greatest happiness of the greatest number were desirable in itself and not because some one omnipotent person desires it, Paley and Bentham arrive, on nearly all practical questions, at very different conclusions. Nor are these differences due to the fact that Paley was a clergyman and Bentham was not. Had Paley been an atheist, and even a pure utilitarian and not an egoistic hedonist as well, he might have arrived at the same conclusions. Like every other fashionable doctrine, utilitarianism can be adapted to suit a great variety of temperaments.

### 4. BURKE

Paley was much more of a utilitarian than Burke. It would, perhaps, be less misleading to say that, whereas Paley made a deliberate effort to reconcile his religious beliefs and his conviction of the absolute selfishness of men with utilitarianism, Burke made no such attempt to systematize his ideas. Whereas Paley was consistently at least a pseudo-utilitarian, Burke sometimes came close to being a genuine one.

The utilitarian bias in Burke, as Halévy has shown in his book on *Philosophic Radicalism*, is exhibited in three ways. The gist of his argument against any except the most careful and moderate reforms, is that an institution's having lasted a long time is itself a proof of its utility, of its conduciveness to human happiness. There are, he argues, forces that tend to disrupt every human institution: disintegration and decay are facts that nobody will deny. If, then, an institution has lasted a long time, it has resisted these disruptive forces and has thereby proved its utility.

The utilitarian bias is also evident in Burke's argument in favour of prescription. One of the most lively sentiments in every man is expectation. Now, every man expects to keep what he has; and the longer he has had it, the keener his disappointment at its loss. Moreover, this expectation is normally stronger than the hope of obtaining something not possessed before. From these premises, Burke arrives at his conclusion that long possession, or prescription, is 'the most solid of all titles, not only to property, but, which is to secure that property, to Government'.

The second of these arguments is to be found in Hume; and even the first is implicit in much that he says. But Hume does not lend particular emphasis to either. As for Burke's third utilitarian argument, in favour of prejudice, it has the same origin as his second. No one knew better than Hume that we must take an immense number of opinions on trust, and that the longest life and the most perceptive mind can enable their possessor to justify or to repudiate only a few of them. Apart from the most necessary of all prejudices, the belief in causality, for which, says Hume, there can, from the nature of the case, be no evidence, there are a host of others, many of them verifiable in principle, but which no reasonable man would refuse as guides to action before he had verified them. There is, nevertheless, an important difference of opinion between Hume and Burke in the matter of prejudice. Hume does, no doubt, agree that many of the opinions we accept on trust can be verified, but his words often suggest that there are others, no less useful, whose truth or falsity can never be established. When he speaks of religion, Hume is careful not to give offence, but there can be little doubt that among men's religious beliefs he would find many useful but unverifiable prejudices. There are some beliefs without which men cannot live at all, and others without which they cannot live happily. Their minds need shelter and comfort no less than their bodies, or the world will be too much for them.

Burke's attitude differs from Hume's in two respects. He thinks that all the great prejudices on which the stability of human societies depends are capable of verification. They can be shown to be true, and they are useful and give comfort only because they are true. The fundamental moral laws and religious doctrines have been so long the possession of mankind that no good purpose can be served by their criticism, since it is impossible to improve upon them or to add to their number. There is no trace either of cynicism or scepticism in what Burke says about morality and religion. But he not only believes that there is no room for improvements in morality and religion, but also that it is dangerous to put this matter to the test. Societies in which first principles are too often examined

E

and may be rejected by every arrogant fool who thinks himself wiser than the rest of mankind are in danger of dissolution. It is not by prejudice alone, but by reverence and humility as well, that men can live in society. This is an attitude that takes us far indeed from Hume, and it explains the deep influence of Burke on such Catholic thinkers as de Maistre and de Bonald.

Burke was not primarily a utilitarian; but in so far as he was one, he was closer to Hume than to any other representative of the school. He did not share Hume's ultimate scepticism, and he was as unlike him as an Irishman can be unlike a Scot; but he borrowed some of his most striking arguments and put them to uses of which Hume might have approved, though he would have taken them more coolly than did Burke. Burke's political theory is also like Hume's in not being set out in propositions, precise and unqualified, which are treated (whatever their authors may say about them) as if they were self-evident. There is a largeness of view about both Burke and Hume, which is not to be found in the writings of Bentham, Paley and James Mill. No doubt, the principles on which Bentham and the elder Mill rest their political and moral theories are supposed by them to be generalizations from experience. But little or no evidence is offered for their truth, and the reader is expected, in practice, to take them as self-evident. Burke and Hume also make unfounded assumptions, but these form part of philosophies that embody a much wider experience. Nor do they, like Bentham and James Mill, place these assumptions simply and squarely at the foundations and then build the most rigid systems upon them.

# CHAPTER IV

## JEREMY BENTHAM

### 1. HIS LIFE AND INFLUENCE

WE now come to the man who, if he did little to establish the principles on which the utilitarian philosophy rests, is certainly, in the opinion of most men, the most typical utilitarian of them all. Jeremy Bentham applied utilitarian principles to the discussion of a great variety of political, legal and administrative problems, with a thoroughness unrivalled by anyone else. It is no wonder that he was the first utilitarian to have disciples, and to create something that deserves to be called a school of thought. He was not so much a moral and political philosopher as he was a theoretical reformer. It was he who devised some of the best arguments in favour of many of the most important reforms undertaken in this country during the nineteenth century. He did for utilitarianism what Sidney and Beatrice Webb were later to do for British socialism; but he was, if I may say so without disrespect, intellectually superior to the Webbs. If the reader is sometimes astonished by the ease with which Bentham arrives at his first principles, by his confident neglect of difficulties, psychological and philosophical, of which he seems scarcely to be aware, and by the confusions and ambiguities of which he is so often guilty when discussing first principles, he cannot but admire the extraordinary clarity and vigour with which he applies those principles to the most difficult and intricate technical questions. There are several intellectual virtues that Bentham lacked, but he was completely the master of those he possessed. To his readers he still gives the impression of an exceptionally vigorous intellect.

Bentham was born in 1748 and died in 1832. In spite of some years wasted in Oxford, he had the good fortune, very early in life, to discover the principles which were to guide his intellectual activities during the rest of it. It was, as we have seen, in 1768 that he came across the formula 'the greatest happiness of the greatest number'. He seems to have had no doubts, thereafter, about what he should do with his life or the utility of what he was doing. Happy, hard-working, benevolent, unimaginative and unmarried, with a mild affection for music, animals and friends, he had nothing to distract him, and he was able to devote an exceptionally long life to the development of his theories. Bentham was quite aware that he had taken his first principles from other men; his primary task was to establish the methods by which they could be applied in practice. In Leslie Stephen's words, 'In Bentham's mind, the difference between this' (i.e. the science of method he wished to establish) 'and the more general formula' (i.e. the greatest happiness of the greatest number) 'was like the difference between the statements that the planets gravitate round the sun, and the more precise statement that the law of gravitation varies inversely as the square of the distance'.[1] His primary task was therefore to discover to what extent and in what way accurate quantitative comparisons of different sums, or 'lots', of happiness could be made. But he was not to confine himself to this task; he was also, throughout his life, to criticize existing institutions and to describe the reforms that would make them as productive of happiness as possible. Bentham devoted most of his time to these secondary tasks; and what he had to say about them has proved of more permanent value to mankind than his account of how lots of happiness can be measured and compared. Nor did Bentham first deal with his primary task and then go on to the others; he did whatever work he thought it most expedient to do at the time, but he never lost sight of his scheme as a whole. Nor, of course, did he regard what I have called his primary task as more important than the others; on the contrary, he undertook it for the sake of the others.

Bentham's first published work was the *Fragment on Government*, which appeared in 1776. This book, about which I shall have more to say later when I deal more specifically with Bentham's theories, is an attack on Blackstone and on the Whig notion of a social compact of which Blackstone was an equally hesitant critic and defender. His *Fragment on Government* brought Bentham to the notice of Lord Shelburne, who sought him out in 1781. Bentham was, for a time, a frequent visitor of Shelburne's at Bowood, where he met Camden, Dunning and Pitt, and above all Dumont, the Genevan who was to do so much to popularize his theories on the Continent. Though

[1] Leslie Stephen, *The English Utilitarians*, Vol. I, p. 179.

Bentham had first met him elsewhere, it was also at Bowood in 1788 that he acquired the friendship of Romilly. Dumont and Romilly may be said to have been Bentham's first disciples.

Bentham's brother Samuel had gone to Russia in 1780, and in 1783 had been sent by Prince Potëmkin to supervise an industrial establishment at Kritchev on the Dnieper. Jeremy left England in August 1785 to stay with his brother, and did not return to this country until February, 1788. It was while he was in Russia that he wrote his *Defence of Usury*, in which he argued that Adam Smith should never, on his own principles, have condemned it. It was also while Bentham was in Russia that Paley, in 1786, brought out his *Principles of Moral and Political Philosophy*. Bentham's friends, seeing that Paley had already expressed many ideas which they knew Bentham shared, urged him to return to England and to establish a great literary reputation in his own language. It was in 1789 that Bentham at last published his *Introduction to the Principles of Morals and Legislation*, his most important philosophical work, in which he laid down the principles he intended should guide him in all his future work.

The French Revolution failed to excite or to disturb Bentham. He laughed at the principles put forward by the revolutionaries to justify their actions. He thought them fallacious, but, unlike Burke, he was not at all sure they were pernicious. He was surprised that people should take seriously the arguments advanced for and against the French Revolution by Paine and Burke, for he was equally contemptuous of Paine's logic and Burke's sentimentality. Bentham was, however, always willing to give good advice. Already in 1788 he had prepared, for the benefit of the French Estates due to meet early the next year, his *Essai sur la Représentation*, in which he advised the French to look to American models. He advocated manhood suffrage (or, at least, a very low property qualification), and also secret voting. But Bentham was not yet a convinced democrat. He knew, however, that many of the French were democrats, and he was anxious to inform them how they could best carry out their principles. In 1789, Bentham produced his *Essay on Political Tactics*, which he sent to the Abbé Morrelet for the benefit of the French Assembly. This essay was politely received, but the advice it contained was not taken. In it, Bentham inquired into the manner in which a deliberative assembly ought to conduct its business if it is to do so efficiently. Bentham's conclusions are derived from his study of British parliamentary practice, and the *Essay* is altogether an admirable example of his work. It is the first really important study on legislative procedure, and Bentham said of the English system which he analysed, that 'in this bye-corner, an observing eye may see the original seed-plot of English liberty: it is in this hitherto neglected spot that the seeds of that invaluable production have germinated and grown up to their present maturity, scarce noticed by the husbandman, and unsuspected by the destroyer'. We now know that, as early as the fifteenth century, the English Parliament conducted its business on quite different principles from those of the French Estates; that it had already become a much more efficient governmental instrument than any of its Continental counterparts. It is to Bentham's credit that he was perhaps the first person to see clearly and to explain what this efficiency consisted in.

In 1790, Bentham produced a third work for the benefit of the French, his *Draught of a Code for the Organisation of the Judicial Establishment in France*. In this work, he criticized a draft proposed by a Committee of the National Assembly, and suggested alterations, many of which are distinctly democratic in character. But Bentham was still not a convert to democracy. It was rather as if he were saying to the French legislators: 'You are democrats. I therefore invite you to be true to your principles, and I, for one, will be interested in the result'. He was interested in the French Revolution as some people were, between the two World Wars, in what has sometimes been called the 'Russian experiment'. As a reward for his good advice, in August 1792, Bentham, along with Paine, Priestley, Mackintosh and Wilberforce, was made a French citizen. Although he was almost as well disposed to the French as Hume had been, he did not set great store by this honour.

It was not the French Revolution but a succession of English Tory governments that converted Bentham to democracy. Indeed, after the massacres of September 1792, Bentham lost interest in France, and he devoted the better part of his energies to a scheme for the erection of a model prison, the *Panopticon*. As early as 1794 his scheme was officially sanctioned by Act of Parliament, but it was not until 1799 that a suitable site was obtained at Millbank, by which time Bentham had already spent several thousands of pounds inherited from his father. Nothing, however, came of the scheme; and in 1811 a committee reported against it on the ground that Bentham and his brother were to make profits from the criminals' labour. The committee agreed that Jeremy and Samuel were men of unimpeachable character, but argued that their successors might not resemble them. In 1813, Bentham received £23,000 as compensation for the final rejection of a scheme originally sanctioned by Act of Parliament, and on which he had spent large sums of money. His experiences in this matter converted Bentham to democracy. He asked himself how it was that a scheme, so obviously excellent and in the public interest, could come to be rejected. It became clear to him that those in authority had not the public interest at heart, and that they were indifferent to it because they were not truly the agents of the public.

Until 1802, Bentham was comparatively unknown. But in that year, Dumont published in Paris his *Traités de Législation Civile et Pénale*, compiled from manuscripts given to him by Bentham. Dumont was an excellent interpreter of Bentham's meaning, and his work was free from the digressions and over-elaborate arguments in which his master delighted. The publication of this work made Bentham's reputation on the Continent and in America, and it was not long before he became equally famous in his own country. In 1809, Dumont was invited to Russia to prepare a Code of Law on Benthamite principles; in 1817, he was performing the same service for his native Geneva; while in 1821 the Portuguese Parliament invited Bentham himself to prepare an 'all-comprehensive' code. A year later he put before the world his *Codification Proposal*, in which he offered to prepare a code of law for any nation in need of a legislator. To this proposal Bentham appended his testimonials. Meanwhile, he continued until his death his life-long labour, his enormous and unfinished *Constitutional Code*. Bentham enjoyed his great reputation and was fully aware that he deserved it. According to Leslie Stephen, 'he is said to have expressed the wish that he could awaken once in a century to contemplate the prospect of a world gradually adopting his principles and so making steady progress in happiness and wisdom'.[1]

Meanwhile, in 1808, Bentham had met James Mill, and it was James Mill who, more than any other man, helped Bentham to

[1] Leslie Stephen, *The English Utilitarians*, Vol. I, p. 230.

draw democratic inferences from his unfortunate experience over the *Panopticon*: Bentham's *Catechism of Parliamentary Reform*, published in 1809, was the first of his several writings in defence of democratic principles. In it he advocated most of the reforms that became the common stock of English Radicalism in the first half of the nineteenth century. Other men had written in favour of these reforms long before Bentham took it upon himself to do so, but the arguments advanced by them had not been strictly utilitarian in character and had involved appeals to principles (e.g. natural rights) that were plain nonsense in the eyes of Bentham. As the apologist of reform, Bentham was in his element. He could discover more and better arguments than anyone else and could illustrate them with great vigour.

## 2. THE *Fragment on Government*

Two of Bentham's better-known works deal with questions that belong properly to the spheres of political and moral philosophy. They are the *Fragment on Government* and the *Introduction to the Principles of Morals and Legislation*. They are, perhaps, the most readable of his writings, though they do not illustrate his powers as well as do some of his more technical discourses.

The *Fragment on Government* was designed by Bentham as an attack on a small part of the Introduction to Blackstone's *Commentaries*, in which Blackstone offers some general definitions. Bentham quotes selected passages from Blackstone and subjects them to a meticulous examination. His criticisms are often trivial and unfair; and it is not in them that the modern reader is likely to be interested but rather in what Bentham has to say for himself.

Already, in the preface, Bentham gives expression to his most cherished conviction that 'it is the greatest happiness of the greatest number that is the measure of right and wrong'.[1] He then goes on to give evidence of his reforming zeal, objecting to Blackstone's 'ungenerous antipathy' to reform, which of itself seems 'to promise a general vein of obscure and crooked reasoning'. Bentham is confident that there is an intimate connexion between some of the gifts of the understanding and some of the affections of the heart. Bentham, indeed, was an ardent reformer and a lover of mankind for nearly forty years before he became a democrat.

[1] *Fragment on Government*, p. 93. (Edition with Introduction by F. C. Montague.)

Bentham next goes on to argue that the principle of utility, which Blackstone entirely neglected, gives us the best criterion for classifying the 'elements of jurisprudence'. He says that 'the mischievousness of a bad law would be detected . . . by the difficulty of finding a place for it in such a [natural] arrangement, while, on the other hand, a technical arrangement' (Bentham means the sort of classification offered by Blackstone) 'is a sink that with equal facility will swallow any garbage that is thrown into it'.[1] In other words, classify the laws according to a rational principle, and the very process will teach you what existing laws ought to be abolished or amended and what new laws made. Hence one reason for the great importance that Bentham attached throughout his life to the codification of law. The other reason was his belief that a logically arranged code of clearly expressed laws must be intelligible to the layman, and so decrease the powers of judges, solicitors and barristers, whose sinister interest it is to maintain a complicated and obscure system, intelligible to none but themselves. But the sinister interests of the class of men whom Bentham often referred to as 'Judge and Co.' are not made much of in the *Fragment on Government*.

Bentham's definition of the state or political society is one that most later utilitarians have adopted. Bentham tells us that 'When a number of persons (whom we may style subjects) are supposed to be in the habit of paying obedience to a person, or an assemblage of persons, of a known and certain description (whom we may call governor or governors) such persons altogether (subjects and governors) are said to be in a state of political society'[2] . . . This definition is very close to, and is indeed the model of, the famous one subsequently offered by Austin in his *Lectures on Jurisprudence*. Bentham, however, did not share the precise and rigid views about government and sovereignty that we associate with the name of Austin. The habit of obedience might be more or less perfect, and Bentham did not pretend to know what degree of perfection was required before the society in which it existed might properly be called a state. Bentham, unlike Austin, does not assert that in every State there must be some person or set of persons whose powers are legally unlimited; he merely says that, unless the powers of the governors are expressly limited by convention, it is absurd

[1] Ibid., p. 119.  [2] Ibid., p. 137.

to talk of the illegality of their actions or to suppose that they can exceed their authority. Bentham does not say, with Hobbes, that the sovereign's power is morally unlimited, nor yet that, if the sovereign limits his power by convention, that convention is never binding. The Hobbesian and the Austinian notions of sovereignty are equally alien to Bentham, though several of the phrases used by Austin in his famous definition are borrowed from the passage just quoted from the *Fragment on Government*. Bentham would not, for instance, deny that a state member of a federal union is a sovereign state.

Bentham assumes that Blackstone never read the third volume of Hume's *Treatise of Human Nature*, from which he says that he himself derived the greatest profit. 'That the foundations of all virtue are laid in utility, is there demonstrated, after a few exceptions made, with the strongest force of evidence: but I see not, any more than Helvetius saw, what need there was for the exceptions.'[1] It may be that there is better evidence that Bentham misunderstood Hume than that Blackstone never read him. For, if Bentham had understood Hume, he would easily have seen what need there was for the exceptions. Hume's evidence for the main rule was, in fact, of precisely the same character as his evidence for the exceptions: namely, the moral behaviour of mankind. Bentham does not quarrel with the facts Hume gives as evidence for the exceptions; he does not even discuss these facts or consider the possibility that they may be evidence against an exclusively utilitarian system of morals. He merely treats Hume's main contention as if it were self-evident, and then blames Hume for supposing that there is evidence which makes it necessary to qualify it. Bentham considers himself as much an empiricist as Hume, but in fact he is often very much the opposite. He treats what he ought to believe are generalizations from experience as if they were self-evident propositions; and he does not trouble to dispose of what might appear to be evidence against them. The truth is that Bentham is not much interested in the logical status of his borrowed principles; and so finds it easy to extract what he wants from Hume, to misunderstand him and still to be grateful to him. He tells us that, when he read the third volume of Hume's *Treatise*, he felt as if the scales had fallen from his eyes. 'I then, for the first time, learnt to call the cause of the people

[1] Ibid., p. 154 note.

the cause of virtue . . . I learnt to see that utility was the test and measure of all virtue; of loyalty as much as any; and that the obligation to minister to general happiness, was an obligation paramount to and inclusive of every other. Having thus got the instruction I stood in need of, I sat down to take my profit of it.'[1] Bentham thinks he has taken over what is essential to Hume's ethical system, rejecting only what is inconsistent with it. But what he does is to reject the qualifications and subtleties that make the system plausible; and because he misunderstands what he is rejecting, he has no misgivings.

One of the first consequences of Bentham's profiting from the instruction of Hume, is that he 'bids adieu' to the original contract. The theory of the original contract was, he thinks, historically useful, because it provided an excuse, at a time when a better was wanting, to justify popular resistance to bad kings. But how, he asks, are the people to know whether the king has broken his contract? If he promised to promote their happiness, then the test for a breach of contract is utilitarian; and the utilitarian argument for resistance would still remain even if there had been no contract. On the other hand, those who assert that the king promises to obey the law, will yet admit that his every illegal action, however petty, does not justify resistance. But the only test that will enable us to distinguish between trivial and serious illegalities is the test of utility. Besides, the duty to keep promises is itself only intelligible because the keeping of promises is to the advantage of society; so that all the arguments of the contract theorists are reduced to arguments from utility. As soon as this is understood, the notion of the social contract, always unhistorical, ceases to be useful. Bentham gives us his own opinion in these words: 'they (the subjects) should obey so long as the probable mischiefs of obedience are less than the probable mischiefs of resistance . . . (and) *taking the whole body together*, it is their duty to obey, just as long as it is their interest, and no longer'.[2] This is the doctrine of Hume in the words of Bentham.

Blackstone had argued, following Montesquieu, that the British Constitution in the eighteenth century was of the mixed type, having monarchical, aristocratic and democratic features in it; and also that it was an example of the separation of powers.

[1] Ibid., p. 154 note.     [2] Ibid., p. 160.

Bentham, in the *Fragment on Government*, differs from Blackstone
on both these matters. Many of Bentham's arguments against the
view that Britain has a mixed constitution are pedantic. For
instance, he argues that Blackstone has distinguished the three
main types of government (monarchy, aristocracy, and democracy)
by determining where the legislative power resides. But the King
of England, says Bentham, when he acts as a monarch (i.e. on his
own authority and through subordinates) has only executive power,
while he no longer, in practice, makes use of his legislative veto.
Such an argument, advanced in George III's reign, clearly takes no
account of political realities. A much better point against Blackstone, that the House of Commons under George III was not
democratic, does not occur to Bentham. He does, however, show
that Blackstone's argument, that the British Constitution is the best
because it combines all the virtues of the three main types, could be
used just as easily to prove that it is the worst, because it combines
all their vices.

Bentham is more happily inspired in his attack on Blackstone's
notion that the separation of powers was exhibited in the British
political system of his day, under which the king could create
peers, get placemen into the House of Commons and dissolve
Parliament.

The limitations of Bentham as a moral philosopher are nowhere
better illustrated than in the fifth chapter of the *Fragment on Government*. He has already told us, earlier in the book, that the 'obligation
to minister to general happiness, (is) an obligation paramount to
and inclusive of every other'. But now, only eighty pages later, he
says: 'That is my duty to do, which I am liable to be punished,
according to law, if I do not do: this is the original, ordinary and
proper sense of the word duty'.[1] And in the note on the same page,
he says: 'One may conceive three sorts of duties, political, moral
and religious; correspondent to the three sorts of sanctions by which
they are enforced: . . .'[2] Bentham then describes the sanctions,
which are punishment in the ordinary sense of the word, punishment expected at the hands of the Supreme Being, and 'various
mortifications resulting from the ill-will of persons uncertain and
variable—the community in general . . .'[3] If any one should persist,
Bentham continues in a note on another page, 'in asserting it to be a

[1] Ibid., p. 234.          [2] Ibid., p. 234 note.          [3] Ibid., p. 234 note.

duty, but without meaning it should be understood that it is on any one of these three accounts that he looks upon it as such; all he then asserts is his own internal sentiment: all he means then is, that he feels himself pleased or displeased at the thought of the point of conduct in question, but without being able to tell why. In this case he should e'en say so: and not seek to give an undue influence to his own suffrage, by delivering it in terms that purport to declare the voice either of God, or of the law, or of the people'.[1] Nothing could better illustrate than this passage to how little purpose Bentham had studied Hume's ethical system, which rests entirely on the internal sentiments on which Bentham here pours scorn. Bentham's definition of duty is similar to those offered by Hobbes and by Paley; and it would appear to belong more properly to psychological hedonism than to utilitarianism. But Bentham, unlike Hobbes and Paley, never understood precisely what view it was to which he was committing himself. Having thus defined duty, he goes on to discuss the question whether the supreme governors of the state have duties. His conclusion is that they cannot have political (by which he means legal) but may have religious and moral duties, for they are liable to the punishment of God and may also become the objects of popular ill-will. To have a duty, to be under an obligation, is, therefore, for Bentham, the same thing as to be impelled to action or inaction from fear of the evil that some other rational being would do to the agent if he failed to do what was required of him. Yet, in the same note in which he tells us this, Bentham also suggests quite another explanation. He says that he would be glad to see the supreme governors make laws 'because I am persuaded that it is for the benefit of the community that they . . . should do so. This is enough to warrant me in my opinion for saying that they ought to do it'.[2] Taken literally, these few lines make nonsense, for they assert that it is because Bentham believes that governmental legislation would benefit the community that he is right in asserting that the governors ought to make laws. Exercising towards Bentham a charity he rarely extended to Blackstone, we may interpret him as meaning that, if he is right in thinking that governmental legislation would benefit the community, then he is right in holding that the government ought to make laws. But, in that case, duty is no longer what Bentham says

[1] Ibid., p. 235 note.    [2] Ibid., p. 235 note.

it is, for it is now implied that duty is the obligation to promote the public good; and the notion of sanctions is left out of the account altogether.

Having defined the word 'duty' to his own satisfaction, without a trace of awareness that he has stumbled on difficulties that need to be explained before his definition can be accepted, Bentham takes leave of his reader, apologizing for the tedious war of words with which he has wearied him. Had there been sense in Blackstone, he would have attached himself to it. Some of his readers may object that to attack nonsense is to waste time, but his real purpose has been to teach the student 'to place more confidence in his own strength, and less in the infallibility of great names: to help him to emancipate his judgment from the shackles of authority; . . . to warn him not to pay himself with words . . .'[1] Bentham was an amiable but not a modest man. He never knew how well he had performed his task, for he had not only deliberately exposed the intellectual failings of Blackstone but had also involuntarily exhibited his own.

### 3. *The Introduction to the Principles of Morals and Legislation*

This book was published thirteen years after the appearance of the *Fragment on Government*, and it is the most important of all Bentham's writings. It opens with an often-quoted passage containing so many ambiguities that it will not be possible to deal with them all. 'Nature', says Bentham, 'has placed mankind under the governance of two sovereign masters, pain and pleasure. It is for them alone to point out what we ought to do, as well as to determine what we shall do . . . They govern us in all we do . . . In words a man may pretend to abjure their empire: but in reality he will remain subject to it all the while. The principle of utility recognises this subjection, . . .' And then, in a note at the bottom of the first page, Bentham tells us what the principle of utility is. It is 'that principle which states the greatest happiness of all those whose interest is in question, as being the right and proper, and only right and proper and universally desirable, end of human action: . .' In another note on the next page, Bentham says that the principle

[1] Ibid., p. 240.

of utility 'may be taken for an act of the mind; a sentiment . . . which, when applied to an action, approves of its utility, as that quality of it by which the measure of approbation or disapprobation bestowed upon it ought to be governed'.

These passages from the first two pages of a book whose one purpose is to make clear the fundamental principles on which the author rests his system, betray the little thought that was devoted to their composition. Bentham was not primarily a philosopher. He was anxious to have done with first principles as quickly as possible and to settle down to more congenial tasks. But the attentive reader cannot help but ask many questions. What does Bentham mean by the sovereign mastery of pleasure and pain? Does he mean that men necessarily seek their own pleasure and avoid their own pain? Or does he mean that to promote pleasure and to avoid pain, whosever they may be, is always their motive? In other words, is he or is he not committed to the egoistic hedonism expounded by Hobbes? What does he mean when he says that pleasure and pain determine what men ought to do as well as what they will do? May we infer from this that all men always do their duty? What was in Bentham's mind when he said that the principle of utility recognizes this subjection? If men always seek their own pleasure and avoid their own pain, how can the greatest happiness of *all* those whose interest is in question be the only right and proper end of human action? What is meant by calling this end universally desirable? On the other hand, if what men always seek is not only their own pleasure but other people's as well, what is the point of saying that it is their duty to do what they will do in any case? There is, no doubt, nothing self-contradictory in the assertion that it is a man's duty to do what he will do in any case. A benevolent and omniscient God would always do his duty and could not do otherwise. Does Bentham mean us to understand that men, though they always seek the greatest happiness of those whose interest is in question, do not always know where to find it, and that it therefore behoves Bentham to show them how they may do so? But it is clear, from what Bentham says elsewhere, that he does not believe that men are always benevolent. On the contrary, he is more often inclined to think them always, or nearly always, selfish. Again, what does Bentham mean by saying that the principle of utility 'may be taken for an act of the mind; a sentiment . . . which, when applied to an action, approves of its utility'? This act of mind or sentiment is said to be approval of utility, and in the same sentence utility is defined 'as that quality of it (an action) by which the measure of approbation or disapprobation bestowed upon it ought to be governed'.[1] Can we understand Bentham to mean that the principle of utility is itself a sentiment: the approval of a habit whereby men approve of actions that cause happiness and disapprove of those that cause unhappiness? That this is not the right interpretation is suggested by what Bentham says about fourteen pages later: 'What one expects to find in a principle is something that points out some external consideration, as a means of warranting and guiding the internal sentiments of approbation or disapprobation.'[2]

All the questions I have put (and most of which I shall not answer because Bentham's words suggest no answer) are perfectly fair questions. By this I mean that they are not questions designed merely to call attention to Bentham's careless manner of speaking, while, with a little good will, the reader can easily get at his meaning. The truth is that it is not possible to make sense of what Bentham is saying. Nothing can be done except to indicate the more important ambiguities with which these short quotations abound. It seems to me that Bentham, without quite knowing what he is doing, is trying to reconcile two couples of irreconcilable doctrines: egoistic hedonism with utilitarianism, on the one hand; and a psychological with an objective theory of morals on the other.

When Bentham tries to tell us what his moral theory is, he succeeds in telling us very little. But when he begins to apply the principles he has failed to define, it is, I think, possible to get some idea of what they are. Though he often makes statements incompatible with them, I think it is fair to say that Bentham usually adheres to the following principles: (i) that nothing is in itself desirable except pleasure and the relief of pain; (ii) that one man's pleasure is in itself as desirable as any other man's; (iii) that the right action is always the one which the prospective agent believes to be, under the circumstances, productive of the greatest happiness;

[1] *Introduction* to *Principles of Morals and Legislation*, p. 2 note. (Oxford 1876 edition.)
[2] Ibid., p. 16.

(iv) that man is predominantly selfish but is capable of benevolence; (v) that laws and punishments ought, in every political society, to be so adjusted that, with the least possible restraint of liberty and infliction of pain, they ensure that men will, from selfish motives, act in ways that will promote other men's happiness as well as their own.

The first six chapters of the *Introduction to the Principles of Morals and Legislation* are, perhaps, the worst in the book. Quite apart from the ambiguities in the first few pages, to which I have already alluded, there are many others; and there are fallacies as well. The first two chapters merely make more elaborate the confusion already created in the first two pages. The third chapter, which classifies the sources of pain and pleasure, is clear enough; but the fourth, which gives us the rules for estimating the value (i.e. measuring the quantity) of pains and pleasures, turns its back on life and parodies reason. Bentham tells us that the value of a lot of pleasure or pain varies with its intensity, its duration, its certainty or uncertainty, its propinquity or remoteness, its fecundity ('or the chance it has of being followed by sensations of the same kind'), its purity ('or the chance it has of not being followed by sensations of the opposite kind') and its extent (or the number of persons who experience it). These are what Bentham calls the seven 'dimensions' of pleasure and pain; and he believes that by operating with them we can assess the value, by which he means the quantity, of any sum of pleasure or pain. He admits that in practice such calculations can seldom be made with accuracy, but he supposes that they are in principle possible. He says: 'It is not to be expected that this process should be strictly pursued previously to every moral judgment, or to every legislative and judicial operation. It may, however, be always kept in view; and as near as the process actually pursued on these occasions approaches to it, so near will such a process approach to the character of an exact one'.[1] In other words, it is only because it is impracticable to do so that we do not make such accurate calculations; but we do in fact make rough ones, and, no doubt, if we had the time and all the facts at our disposal we could make completely accurate calculations. This is what Bentham believes; whereas the truth is that even an omniscient God could not make such calculations, for the very notion of them is impossible.

[1] Ibid., p. 31.

F

The intensity of a pleasure cannot be measured against its duration, nor its duration against its certainty or uncertainty, nor this latter property against its propinquity or remoteness. Of all the 'dimensions' mentioned by Bentham, only two couples are commensurable, duration with extent and fecundity with purity. We can say that a pleasure or pain of a given intensity experienced by a person for two minutes is equal to that same pleasure or pain experienced by two persons for one minute; and we can also say of a pleasure that its fecundity exceeds its purity, if, for instance, there is one chance in four of its being followed by another pleasure and only one chance in five of its not being followed by a pain.

There is no need to labour an obvious and simple point. Bentham ought not to have talked of the 'dimensions' of pleasure and pain; he ought to have realized that when we are said to 'multiply three dimensions' to discover a volume, the three dimensions are all of them linear, and that the numbers, which are all that we in fact multiply, represent units of equal length. He saw an analogy where there was none. *He also confused measurements of quantity with comparisons of effects.* When a man has to choose between two alternative pleasures, one of which is mild but lasting and the other intense but brief, he never can choose the greater, for the simple reason that neither is the greater. What he can do, however, is to choose the one he desires the more intensely. Now it may well be that there are certain psychological laws which, if we knew them, would enable us to say that the intensity of men's desires for pleasures vary in such and such ways with the intensity of the pleasures desired and in such and such other ways with their estimated duration, their certainty and uncertainty, their propinquity and remoteness, their fecundity, their purity and their extent. If there are such laws, then, if we could know them, we could also calculate that a certain lot of pleasure (to use Bentham's phrase) is likely to be more intensely desired by most men than a certain other lot. But this calculation would be of a kind quite different from the one described by Bentham.

It has sometimes been argued in favour of Bentham's felicific calculus that, whatever the theoretical objections against it, men often do estimate the consequences of alternative possible actions and then choose to perform the one which is likely, in their opinion, to produce the greatest happiness. Bentham himself says of his theory: 'Nor is this a novel and unwarranted, any more than it is a useless theory. In all this there is nothing but what the practice of mankind, wheresoever they have a clear view of their own interest, is perfectly conformable to.'[1] It is, of course, quite true that men do compare the consequences of alternative actions, but this does not mean that they calculate quantities of pleasure. What they do is to get what information they can about the alternatives and then make up their minds in favour of one of them. They analyse each of the alternatives, taking into account as many of its constituents as they have the leisure to do, but this taking into account is not itself, except on rare occasions, a calculation of quantities, however rough and ready; it is merely the process of becoming more intimately acquainted with each alternative separately. We choose between alternative consequences largely as we choose between paintings or other objects of art. In both cases, we consider the alternative wholes and their constituent details as carefully as time and temperament permit, but we do not add, subtract, divide or multiply. Or rather, whereas no calculation at all is possible in the latter case, it is so, to some extent, in the former; for we can make quantitative measurements of duration, extent and chance.

We cannot, however, infer from this that the legislator need make little use of the information supplied to him by the statistician. Experience can, in such cases, furnish us with two sets of relevant generalizations; it can, for instance, teach us that most men prefer some pleasures to others, that some pleasures pall more quickly than others, that men of different ages and different social classes have different preferences, that they will prefer a mild and durable pleasure to an intense and brief one under certain circumstances but not others; and experience can also teach us what are the social and economic conditions that will enable most men to have as many opportunities as possible to enjoy the pleasures they prefer. In other words, it is theoretically possible to give men as much of what they want as they have time to enjoy (or, rather, on the utilitarian hypothesis, as much of what is good for them, in the sense of as much as they would want and have time to enjoy, if they were aware of all the relevant considerations). And the relevant considerations are largely those very things which Bentham unwisely called the dimensions of pleasure—duration, intensity, certainty and

[1] Ibid., p. 32.

uncertainty, proximity, fecundity and so on. Men, in establishing their preferences, take these considerations into account (as far as they are in practice able to do so); but the process does not, except to a very limited extent, involve a calculation of quantities of pleasure and pain. Once these preferences are established, they can be studied, their frequencies can be calculated, and together with other statistical information, vital, social and economic, they can serve as a guide to policy. Calculations of this kind are likely to give the most imperfect results; the margin of error is almost certain to be great. But, though their utility must be often doubtful, they are, in principle, possible. An omniscient being could carry them out with perfect accuracy, and if he were also omnipotent and benevolent, would no doubt act accordingly. He could then quite properly be said to be promoting the greatest happiness of the greatest number, provided it were understood that *no measurable quantity of pleasure was in question*. Moreover, if such a being could realize such a policy, there is no reason why a human government should not try to do so. Utilitarianism does not stand or fall with Bentham's felicific calculus. Such a calculus is impossible, not merely in practice but also in theory. But the utilitarian can have recourse to other calculations, which are, in fact, possible, though they must always, human nature and human knowledge being what they are, be most imperfect. That, however, is not in itself a serious objection to a theory of morals.

His first six chapters completed, Bentham leaves behind him the analysis of his fundamental principles; and we may gratefully follow him out of the quagmire on to firmer ground. 'The business of government,' Bentham tells us, 'is to promote the happiness of society, by punishing and rewarding.'[1] Now, Bentham's task, in the rest of the book, is to establish the rules that a government ought to follow if it is to promote as much of this happiness as it can at the cost of the least possible amount of punishment. Every now and again, Bentham uses the language of the felicific calculus, talking of quantities of pleasure and pain and not merely of the number of persons who experience, and the times during which they experience, these pleasures and pains. Nor does he take into account the orders and frequencies of men's preferences. He often talks, in fact, as if he were advising legislators and judges how to make

[1] Ibid., p. 70.

calculations which it is plainly impossible to make. But all the misleading language can be ignored, and Bentham's rules can be treated as if they were rules for making possible calculations. Once this is done, it is easy to see how much that is really valuable his book contains. What Bentham teaches us, often with great vigour and ingenuity, is how to prevent as many offences as possible as efficiently as we can and at the cost of no greater suffering than is required for the purpose.

Bentham begins by analysing the offence for which the culprit is to be punished. His analysis is extremely complicated, but it is necessary to master only a small part of it in order to understand the general character of his theory of punishment. The distinction to which Bentham attaches the greatest importance is that between a man's motive and his intention when he acts. By an intention he means those consequences of a man's action that he expected would follow upon it. By a motive he means the desire for pleasure or for relief from pain that prompted the action. Bentham's definitions are not as simple as the ones I have offered, and there is more than a little about them that is ambiguous. He defines a motive as 'the internal perception of any individual lot of pleasure or pain, the expectation of which is looked upon as calculated to determine you to act in such and such a manner'.[1] He thinks that by using such language he can give greater precision to his ideas. The result is that his readers often cannot guess what he means by the long sentences in which he defines his terms, and can get his meaning only by considering how he uses them. Those definitions of motive and intention which make sense of the general drift of Bentham's argument must be taken to be correct, even if they do not much resemble the ones he offers. We may therefore take it that the motive is the desire for whose satisfaction the act is done, and the intention the expected consequences of it. The expectation, of course, is the agent's, and the actual consequences may be quite different from those expected. The tendency to act from a certain kind of motive Bentham calls a disposition. He makes many other distinctions, not all of them defensible, but these are the only ones of which we need take notice.

These distinctions made, Bentham goes on to say that no motive is in itself either good or bad, for any motive may sometimes lead

[1] *Ibid.*, p. 99.

to actions having bad consequences and at other times to actions having good ones. Lust, cruelty and avarice, he tells us, are called bad motives, but they are in themselves the same motives as sexual desire, desire to inflict pain and reluctance to part with what one possesses. These motives can lead to good consequences as well as to bad ones; and it is only when they lead to bad ones that they are called lust, cruelty and avarice. Motives give birth to intentions and intentions can be either good or bad. The moralist and the legislator are primarily interested in men's intentions, in the goodness and the badness of the consequences that they intend should follow upon their actions. Men's motives concern the moralist and the legislator only indirectly. For although all motives are in themselves morally neutral, some more often than others give birth to good intentions or else to bad ones.

Many people, including Leslie Stephen, have criticized Bentham for saying that the motives from which men act are morally indifferent. It may be, in practice, a rule that serves the legislator and the judge well enough, for they can hardly be expected to discover men's motives. All that matters to them is that men should do some actions and forbear from others; and their only business must therefore be to apply rewards and punishments in such a way that this end is attained. But the morality of the action cannot, these critics say, be independent of the motive from which it is done. Their difference from Bentham may be smaller than they think. What Benthem means when he says that motives are morally neutral is that any kind of desire may be the cause of either good or bad intentions. A man may desire to eat, and to satisfy his hunger he may either get food from his own larder or he may steal it from his neighbour's. The desire in either case is the same, but the two actions prompted by it are quite different. So too, if a man wishes to give pain to another, his desire may lead to a good intention. He may, for instance, intend to punish a criminal. It is only when he desires to inflict pain on some one who does not deserve it that we condemn him. When Bentham says that a motive is morally neutral, he is thinking of a naked desire without taking into account the circumstances in which it arose or the intention to which it gives birth. But when we say that the morality of the action depends above all upon the motive, we always take into account the circumstances. Otherwise, we could hardly distinguish between ingratitude and indifference, malice and the desire to inflict pain, praise and flattery, benevolence and indulgence. Bentham's doctrine has an air of paradox but it is not nearly as offensive as it sounds. And no one could be more anxious than he to maintain that men rightly disapprove of malice, jealousy, envy and all the other vices.

Bentham distinguishes between the various kinds of motives according to the relative frequencies with which they give birth to good and bad intentions. Benevolence, or good will, has the greatest tendency to coincide with utility. It is the only purely social (by which Bentham means altruistic) motive. Next in order of preference come love of reputation, desire for friendship, and religion. Bentham calls them semi-social motives, because they are partly self-regarding and partly altruistic. Of the purely self-regarding motives, such as physical desire, love of power, self-preservation, Bentham says only that they are less likely than the social and semi-social motives to give birth to good intentions, but he does not establish an order of preference among them. He probably thought that the self-regarding motives do not, except malevolence, have a marked tendency to produce bad rather than good intentions or vice versa. The motives that often give birth to bad intentions he calls 'seducing' or 'corrupting', and those that restrain men from giving way to this seduction he calls 'tutelary'. Benevolence and the semi-social motives are usually tutelary. Milder than malevolence, they are also more constant.

After an elaborate analysis of actions, consequences, motives and intentions, of which I have given only the barest outline, Bentham goes on to establish the rules which ought to guide the legislator in deciding what punishments are to be given to offenders. He begins by asserting that 'all punishment is mischief: all punishment in itself is evil. Upon the principle of utility . . . it ought only to be admitted in as far as it promises to exclude some greater evils'.[1] It therefore immediately follows that punishment ought not to be inflicted where it is groundless (i.e. where there is no mischief for it to prevent); where it is inefficacious; where it is too expensive (i.e. where the mischief it would produce exceeds the mischief it would prevent); where it is needless (i.e. where the mischief could be prevented in some other less painful manner).

Punishment seeks to control men's future actions. If we are to

[1] Ibid., p. 170.

interpret Bentham's meaning strictly, then no one can deserve punishment; it can merely be right that he should be punished. Punishment can seek to control the offender's future actions, in which case it is either reformatory or disabling; or else it can seek to control other people's future actions, in which case it is deterrent. It usually seeks to do both. If it gives satisfaction to the injured party, so much the better; but this is not an important part of its purpose.

Bentham gives us nine rules for the infliction of punishments. They are mostly mere rules of common sense, and there is no need to comment on them. Bentham himself thought otherwise, but it is easy to see that, though they involve calculation, they do not involve the felicific calculus dreamt of by him. These rules are: (i) The punishment must be great enough to outweigh the profit of the offence to the offender; (ii) the greater the mischief of the offence, the greater the punishment; (iii) and (iv) are mere corollaries of (ii); (v) punishment should never be greater than the least amount required to make it effective; (vi) the sensibility of the offender must always be taken into account; (vii) the more uncertain it is that the offender will suffer it, the greater the punishment should be; (viii) the more distant it is, the greater it should be; and (ix) if the offence is of a kind likely to be habitual with the offender, the punishment must be increased to outweigh the profit not only of the immediate offence but of the other probable offences he committed with impunity. If these simple rules now appear obvious to us, we must not, for that reason, belittle Bentham's service to mankind in enunciating them. At the time that he wrote, they had for centuries been ignored by the legislators and judges of Europe.

Bentham, anticipating possible criticism of his rules, says: 'There are some, perhaps, who . . . may look upon the nicety employed in the adjustment of such rules as so much labour lost: for gross ignorance, they will say, never troubles itself about laws, and passion does not calculate. But the evil of ignorance admits of cure: and . . . when matters of such importance as pain and pleasure are at stake, and these in the highest degree . . . who is there that does not calculate? Men calculate, some with less exactness, indeed, and some with more: but all men calculate.'[1] Bentham is quite

[1] Ibid., p. 187.

right. All men calculate, for if they did not it would be impossible, not only for others to govern them, but for themselves to live. But the calculations they make, necessary and crude though they are, are not described by Bentham, either in this or in any other of his works.

Much the longest chapter of the *Introduction to the Principles of Morals and Legislation* is devoted to a classification of offences. In it Bentham repeats the arguments, already advanced in the *Fragment on Government*, in favour of what he calls both a natural and a scientific system of classification, which groups offences according to the influence they have upon the happiness of mankind. 'What a state', he asks, 'would botany, for example, be in if the classes were so contrived that no common characters could be found for them?'[1] But that, he thought, was precisely the case with jurisprudence at the time that he was writing. It was for him to create rational order where there was none, to do for jurisprudence what Linnaeus had done for botany. Bentham's classification of offences covers a hundred pages, but as the details of its elaboration involve no important moral or political principles, it is not necessary to consider it.

So much, then, for the second of the two works of Bentham of which posterity still takes the most notice. In these two works he put forward most of the maxims and definitions that he considered fundamental to his whole system; and it is with them that his reputation as a moral and political theorist stands or falls. It is clear that, in both these capacities, Bentham was greatly the inferior of Hume, from whom he borrowed so much, and often without understanding what it was that he borrowed. Two incompatible couples, utilitarianism and egoistic hedonism, a psychological and an *a priori* system of morals, lay quietly side by side in his capacious mind, and their host had not a suspicion that the guests he was entertaining were so strangely assorted. Leslie Stephen was not wrong when, in his book on the English Utilitarians, he said that Bentham knew little of psychology and ethics. Yet Stephen's final verdict was rightly a generous one. 'However imperfect his system might be, considered as a science of society and human nature . . . (his) method involved a thorough-going examination of the whole body of laws, and a resolution to apply a searching test to every law. If that test was not so unequivocal or ultimate as he

[1] Ibid., p. 300 note.

fancied, it yet implied the constant application of such considerations as must always carry weight, and, perhaps, be always the dominant considerations, with the actual legislator or jurist.'[1] Stephen's conclusion was that Bentham's test, though not all-sufficient, is good enough for the purposes to which Bentham put it. I would agree with this verdict, with one most important qualification. The test that is good enough for Bentham's purposes is not the test described by Bentham; it may fairly be said to involve the notion of the greatest happiness of the greatest number only if that greatest happiness is defined quite otherwise than Bentham defined it.

## 4. His Radicalism

After the failure of his *Panopticon* scheme and his meeting James Mill in 1808, Bentham became as thorough-going a radical as Paine had ever been. But to justify his radicalism he used quite different arguments. He had always believed that every man always desires his own greatest happiness; and he had also believed that the only proper end of government is to promote the greatest happiness of the greatest number. On the other hand, he had now learnt, especially since the rejection of his favourite project, that the actual end of every government is the greatest happiness of the governors. He soon concluded that the fundamental problem of government is to make these two ends coincide; to make it the selfish interest of the governors to promote the greatest happiness of the greatest number. The device that can ensure the coincidence of these two ends is democracy. Bentham, however, recognized that the direct participation of the people in government is not practicable in large countries; he therefore advocated every sort of device that would increase the dependence of their representatives on the people. He favoured annual parliaments, the abolition of the monarchy and the House of Lords, the secret ballot, female suffrage, the election of the Prime Minister by Parliament, the appointment of civil servants by competitive examination. All government, for Bentham as for Paine, is a necessary evil; and it follows that every government must be anxiously watched by the citizens lest it should acquire more power than it needs to carry out its limited duties.

The idea that government is an evil, but that it is, unfortunately,

[1] Leslie Stephen, *The English Utilitarians*, Vol. I, p. 271.

a necessary evil, is a very old one. It is suggested by the early Christian belief that coercive government, like slavery and private property, is the consequence of man's fall, of his sinfulness. It stands at the very centre of Hobbes's system, for what is the purpose of Leviathan except to create the fear that casts out fear? Neither Paine nor the French revolutionaries[1] were good Christians, but they shared with the Christian Fathers the belief that liberty is intrinsically good and that man has a natural right to it. If liberty is good, then government must, they thought, be evil; and its only justification can be that, by restraining man's passions, it removes more obstacles to liberty than it creates. The utilitarians arrive at the same conclusion from a different premise. Their argument is taken from Hobbes. Government is evil, not because liberty is good but because pain is evil; its only justification is that its coercive action creates less pain than it prevents.

Bentham was an egalitarian in the same sense as he was a radical and a liberal. Equality is not desirable for its own sake; all that is so desirable is the greatest happiness of the greatest number. This is the one fundamental principle; the limits of liberty and equality are determined by it and by the lessons of experience. That all men should be treated as if they were equal means, for Bentham, no more than this: that no differences between them that are irrelevant to the legislator's fundamental purpose, the promotion of the greatest happiness of the greatest number, ought to be taken into account. Paley was an egalitarian in exactly this same sense. Paley's God, no doubt, would treat all men as equals, and yet allow the greatest inequalities between them. If Paley approved these inequalities and Bentham did not, it was not because their principles were different but only because they differed about a matter of fact. Paley believed that nearly all such inequalities are a means to the greatest happiness of the greatest number, whereas Bentham, especially after he had met James Mill, came to believe that many of them are not.

It may be instructive, before we part company with Bentham, to notice how closely his arguments for radicalism resemble those of

[1] The Jacobins, when they controlled it, were very willing that the state should be strong; however great the sacrifice of individual liberty. But then, the Jacobins were unlike most French revolutionaries. They were a ruthless minority who acquired power largely because they did not share the liberal prejudices of most Frenchmen active in politics.

Hobbes in favour of the absolute power of governments. Every man, says Hobbes, is completely selfish, but painful experience teaches him that he has one great interest in common with all other men: the existence of an absolute sovereign with power to coerce them all. Every man, says Bentham, is almost completely selfish, but painful experience teaches him that he has one great interest in common with all other men: the existence of a government that seeks to promote the greatest happiness of the greatest number and can be trusted to do so only if it is responsible to all the people and jealously watched by them. This argument of Bentham's is hardly consistent with his frequent assertions that the greatest happiness of the greatest number is an ultimate end, for what nobody desires except as a means can hardly be an ultimate end. But we are not to expect from Bentham the degree of consistency that we get from Hobbes.

# CHAPTER V

## THE RADICAL UTILITARIANS

BENTHAM was not the first utilitarian to turn radical, and before we pass on to James Mill and his friends, we must pause to consider the earliest forms of utilitarian radicalism. Priestley, in his *Essay on the First Principles of Government* (1768), had taken up once again what Hume had considered the fundamental problem of politics, the identification of the interests of the governors with those of the governed. Unlike Hume, Priestley believed that no such identity yet existed in England, and that a considerable measure of reform was needed to establish it. Priestley was a very moderate democrat, but the arguments he used in favour of reform are certainly utilitarian in character.

Burke's *Reflections on the French Revolution* moved two men to make a reply to him. The first was James Mackintosh, who, in his *Vindiciae Gallicae*, criticized Burke for his praise of mixed government, of the division of powers and complex political institutions reflecting the complex structure of society. These ideas Burke had got from Montesquieu, one of whose favourite theses it was that simple laws and simple institutions best suit the despotic state. Most of his arguments against Burke, Mackintosh borrowed from Bentham, but whereas Bentham felt only curiosity towards the activities of the French revolutionaries, Mackintosh, until he was thrown off his course by the Jacobin Terror, espoused their cause. He tried to reconcile his utilitarian principles with a defence of the doctrine of the Rights of Man. Mackintosh admitted that the question of the origins of government has no philosophical importance, that what really matters is the end that it promotes, and that this end is happiness. But he held that the language of the Rights of Man still has its use, if it is understood to be a sort of shorthand that needs to be translated at length. 'When I assert,' he says, 'that a man has a right to life, liberty, etc., I only mean to enunciate a moral maxim founded on a general interest, which prohibits any attack on these possessions.' The proper retort to Mackintosh is that this is a mistranslation, for it is certainly not what the American and French revolutionaries meant when they used the language of the Rights of Man.

## 1. PAINE

Far more important than Priestley and Mackintosh was Tom Paine, the greatest English radical of his day. Like Burke, Paine was not a member of the family but was a sort of second cousin to the utilitarians. The arguments that Paine uses in his most famous book are just the kind that seemed excellent to the French revolutionaries, who had many of them read Rousseau but not Helvetius or Hume. Paine's fundamental thesis in the *Rights of Man* is that every man, merely because he is a sentient and a rational being, possesses certain inalienable rights. Some of these, such as the freedom of thought, he can exercise without more ado in the privacy of his own mind; but the others must be secured to him against the encroachments of his fellow-men. He needs a guarantee, and this he can find only in the existence of a government strong enough to force his neighbours to respect his rights. Now, the only way to ensure that the government will do just this and not attempt to do more is to make it democratic and to define its powers in a written constitution.

But in his book *Common Sense* (1776), and also in the second part of his *Rights of Man*, which appeared in 1792, only a few months after the first part, Paine used arguments that are much more utilitarian in character. On the first page of *Common Sense*, he says: 'Some writers have so confounded society with government, as to leave little or no distinction between them: whereas they are not only different but have different origins. Society is produced by our wants, and government by our wickedness; the former promotes our happiness positively, by uniting our affections: the latter negatively, by restraining our vices. The one encourages intercourse, the other creates distinctions. The first is a patron, the last a punisher'.

'Society in every state is a blessing, but government, even in its best state, is but a necessary evil . . . Government, like dress, is the badge of lost innocence. . . . For were the impulses of conscience clear, uniform, and irresistibly obeyed, man would need no other lawgiver; but that not being the case, he finds it necessary to surrender up a part of his property to furnish means for the protection of the rest; and this he is induced to do by the same prudence which in every other case advises him, out of two evils, to chuse the least. Wherefore, security being the true design and end of government, it unanswerably follows, that whatever form thereof appears most likely to ensure it to us with the least expense, and greatest benefit, is preferable to all others.'

It was the opinion of Plato that the first society was the product of men's wants, or rather of their need to co-operate for the satisfaction of these wants, and that this first society was prior to government. This same idea was present in Hume's mind when, in the third Book of his *Treatise*, he rejected the theory that 'men are utterly incapable of society without government'. It is also to be found in Rousseau's *Discourse on the Origins of Inequality among Men*. It is an old idea; as is also the one, to which neither Plato nor Hume would have subscribed, that government is a necessary evil. What is more interesting, however, is that Paine, on this first page of *Common Sense*, when he is setting out his fundamental principles, makes no mention of natural rights. His argument is, at bottom, the same as Bentham's. The end is the happiness of mankind, who will, especially in the economic sphere, be drawn by their own interests into co-operation. But they cannot be relied upon always to co-operate peacefully. Hence the necessity of government, always in itself an evil, because its function is essentially negative and punitive. Paine then goes on to argue that the form of government most likely to carry out this function efficiently and cheaply is democracy. We have, therefore, in the first few pages of *Common Sense* the gist of the utilitarian argument for democracy at least thirty years before Bentham became a radical.

In the second part of *Rights of Man*, Paine resumes and develops the argument he first advanced in *Common Sense*, but this time with a difference. In 1776, Paine had suggested that, men's wants being greater than their power to satisfy them, their own interest had led them first to co-operate in society and later to institute government to preserve the advantages gained in society. But in the second part of *Rights of Man*, he goes further. Nature, he says, 'has not only forced [men] into society, by a diversity of wants, which the reciprocal aid of each other can supply, but she has implanted in [man] a system of social affections, which, though not necessary to its [society's] existence, are essential to his happiness. There is no period in life when this love for society ceases to act. It begins and ends with our being'.[1] It thus appears that, while self-interest alone is strong enough to create and maintain society, a society entirely so maintained would do no more than enable us to satisfy the diversity of our wants. It is through our social affections that we can obtain from society a greater happiness than the mere satisfaction of our physical desires could give us. 'Man,' says Paine, 'is so naturally a creature of society, that it is impossible to put him out of it.'[2] On the other hand, the more perfect the society, the smaller the need for government.

This insistence on the social nature of man is not to be found in Bentham, though he did not deny that there could be society without government. Bentham believed that, whatever the benevolence of men in their dealings with some few of their relatives and friends, they are completely, or almost completely, selfish on all other occasions. If men contrive to live peacefully together in vast societies, this is principally due to two causes: to their knowledge that the means to their happiness is also usually the means to other people's; and to the existence of governments that can restrain them from seeking their own happiness at the expense of other people's. The utility of society and government consists in this: that in the former, men, by co-operation, can reconcile their diverse interests; while the latter possesses a coercive power enabling it to effect this reconciliation whenever it is not the natural product of voluntary co-operation. Paine's social affections, on the other hand, unlike Bentham's benevolence, are not among the mildest of man's sentiments, nor is their usual operation confined to the narrow circle of his relatives and friends. The social affections are with us all our lives, and they are both strong and constant.

## 2. GODWIN

Paine was not, as we have seen, a consistent utilitarian; indeed, the most widely read part of his most famous book, *Rights of Man*, is incompatible with utilitarianism. But Paine had a great influence on another man, who was a consistent utilitarian and also a more extreme radical than himself. William Godwin's *Political Justice*

[1] Ch. i, para. 3.　　　　　　[2] Ch. i, para. 7.

was first published in 1793. At that time, Godwin was already thirty-seven years old. *Political Justice* is therefore not a young man's book, and yet it contains more of the assurance and idealism of youth than any other book written by a utilitarian.

*Political Justice*, when it was first published, made a great stir among intellectuals. But the reaction, which was the inevitable consequence of England's being at war with Revolutionary France, soon destroyed its popularity. Godwin's reputation was, indeed, among the very first victims of the reaction, for he had advocated both anarchy and communism. It was soon the fashion to set Godwin down for a visionary and to assume that the simplest arguments were sufficient to destroy his system.

There is, nevertheless, much to be said for Godwin's *Political Justice*. It is well-written, lucid and full of good arguments. The assumptions that Godwin makes about the nature of man are not further from the truth than those of most other eighteenth-century political and moral writers. His premises are as plausible as theirs and his arguments usually more lucid and often more cogent. It was his misfortune that they led him to the most extreme conclusions just before the reaction that was to kill all sympathy for revolutionary ideas in England, until it came to birth again about twenty-five years later. It was Godwin's destiny to be famous for a year or two, and then to live out the rest of his life almost forgotten. The Privy Council did, however, once think him a dangerous man and considered prosecuting him for seditious libel. He was saved only by the observation of Pitt that a 'three guinea book could never do much harm among those who had not three shillings to spare'. As a matter of fact, four thousand copies of *Political Justice* were sold, and among their purchasers were many working men, who raised subscriptions to cover the cost.

Like most enthusiasts, Godwin got his ideas from only a few sources. He owed most to Jonathan Edwards' *Enquiry into the Freedom of the Will* (1754), Hartley's *Observations on Man* (1749) and d'Holbach's *Système de la Nature* (1770). It was from these three books that Godwin derived his rigid determinism, and his conviction that the notions of 'desert' and 'merit' have no place in a properly constructed political and moral theory. From Helvetius, Godwin adopted the theory that existing social and political institutions have made man what he is; and that man is the creature,

G

not of heredity, but of environment. Man, therefore, is perfectible. By the use of his reason and the discovery of truth he can alter his environment and improve himself, becoming indefinitely better, though perfection itself may always remain out of his reach. But whereas Helvetius looked to better laws and institutions to improve man, Godwin thought that real improvement required the abolition of both laws and governments.

His anarchy and his communism Godwin derived mainly from French sources, especially from Rousseau and from Mably, but also from Ogilvie's *Essay on the Right of Property in Land*, which appeared two or three years before his own *Political Justice*. Rousseau was not an anarchist, but many of his arguments, especially those to be found in his *Discourse on the Origins of Inequality among Men*, are excellent supports of the anarchist case. Godwin was not a disciple of Rousseau, but he was, perhaps, the only utilitarian to be deeply influenced by the Genevan philosopher.

Godwin was a great borrower from Hume, to whom he owed, as did all the other utilitarians, his rejection of the theory of a social contract. It was also to Hume that Godwin owed his conviction that pleasure and the avoidance of pain are the ultimate objects of human endeavour. His utilitarianism, therefore, Godwin gets directly from Hume. Yet his moral theory is quite different from Hume's. He accepts Hume's doctrine that man is the mere recipient of impressions and ideas. But, unlike Hume, he has no desire to introduce the experimental method into morals. He does not reduce morals to a species of social psychology. Nor does he believe that 'Reason is and ought to be the slave of the passions'. On the contrary, he believes that the laws of justice are eternal and immutable, that they are rules of conduct 'originating in the connection of one percipient being with another'.[1] If I have rightly understood Godwin, his fundamental belief is that it follows from the mere fact that percipient beings are in contact with each other, that they ought to conform to certain rules in their behaviour towards one another. Otherwise, it is impossible to understand his meaning when he calls justice eternal. Godwin was not interested in the epistemological implications of his moral theory. He seems to have regarded Hume's account of man's experience as being, in all essentials, satisfactory. He did not understand that, in that case,

[1] *Political Justice*, Bk. II, ch. ii.

there can be no such thing as eternal justice. It is as true of Godwin as it is of Bentham, that he never understood either the theory of knowledge or the moral system of the great Scottish philosopher.

To Paine, Godwin owed one idea only, but one to which both philosophers attribute the greatest importance: that society and government are two different things. Society, they both agree, is necessary and good; and they also agree that all government is evil. But whereas Paine asserts that it is a necessary evil, Godwin doubts its necessity.

Morality, for Godwin, is no more than the system that teaches us to contribute on all occasions, so far as we can, to the well-being and happiness of every intelligent and sensitive existence. That we ought to do so is, apparently, an axiom of reason; it is a proposition whose truth is evident to us as soon as we have understood it. This is not what Godwin says, but it is what is implied by his saying that justice is eternal and that man can find in it a 'principle of deduction in all cases of moral enquiry'. From this premise, that it is always a man's duty to promote the greatest happiness, Godwin arrives at the conclusion that men have no rights but only duties. This conclusion is not quite as paradoxical as it appears. The rights that Godwin denies are merely discretionary powers. He believes that, since, on nearly all occasions when we have the power to choose, we can do more good by choosing one alternative rather than the others, we are never at liberty, except on unimportant occasions, to do what we please. On the other hand, since men have duties to men, it follows that they also have claims against them. When, therefore, Godwin denies the existence of rights, he is thinking not of claims but of discretionary powers.

But it does not follow, according to Godwin, that, because we are hardly ever entitled to do as we please, other men have the duty to constrain us. Men must not be forced to do their duty; they must do it because they themselves understand that it is their duty. Godwin believes that the exercise of private judgment is 'unspeakably beautiful'. While there is any reasonable hope that persuasion will prevail, we must use argument; and we must never use force except to prevent an immediate injury that cannot otherwise be prevented. That man is born with selfish passions unconquerable by reason and which only force or fear can curb, is a belief that Godwin utterly rejects. When men act wrongly, they always believe, he thinks, that they are acting rightly, or else they pass no moral judgment on their actions. They are guilty either of error or of ignorance. But force is not the proper instrument for the correction of error and ignorance.

Nor, when we do use force, can we justify its use on the ground that it is punishment. According to Godwin, there can be, strictly speaking, no such thing as punishment; for, since the will is not free, no man can help doing what he does, and it is absurd to say that he deserves to suffer. This, however, does not mean that men cannot be virtuous and vicious. The virtuous man habitually chooses to do his duty, while the vicious man has another habit; nor do we approve of the former or disapprove of the latter any the less because both virtue and vice have their necessary causes. This argument of Godwin's is not convincing, since desert no more implies the freedom of the will than does virtue.

The idea that no man can deserve to suffer, and that the justification of punishment is to be found only in its utility is common to all the utilitarians. But Godwin differs from the others in denying that punishment can be reformatory. He thinks that punishment degrades both the offender and the judge. 'If he who employs coercion against me,' says Godwin,[1] 'could mould me to his purpose by argument, no doubt he would. He pretends to punish me because his argument is important, but he really punishes me because his argument is weak.' Godwin also differs from the other utilitarians in denying that its deterrent effect can justify punishment, though the argument he uses does not seem to me to be compatible with his utilitarian principles. If he had contented himself with denying that punishment is ever sufficiently deterrent to justify its use, his argument, whether right or wrong, would have been compatible with his utilitarian premises; but the point he makes is that, unless the punishment is justified for some other reason, it cannot be right to inflict it at all, its deterrent effect making no difference. 'The coercion proposed . . .' says Godwin,[2] 'is either right or wrong. If it be right, it should be employed for its own intrinsic recommendations. If it be wrong, what sort of example does it display?' This argument avoids the real point at issue. The advocates of deterrent punishment are quite willing to admit that no man should be made to suffer for no other reason than

[1] Bk. VII, ch. ii.    [2] Bk. VII, ch. v.

that his suffering would serve as an example to others. Before it can be right to punish him, he must at least have committed the offence in question. Their contention is merely that, if he has committed the offence, then the amount of his punishment ought to be partly determined by the extent to which it is likely to deter other people from committing similar offences. Godwin produces not one argument to show that the deterrent effect of a punishment is not likely to be great enough to justify the suffering it occasions.

Indeed, it is clear that utilitarian considerations count for little in Godwin's condemnation of nearly all coercion. He hates coercion so much that he will have none of it, except where it is very obviously necessary to prevent an immediate danger. That is the real and quite irrational motive behind his denial that its deterrent effect can justify punishment. Since punishment ought never, according to Godwin, to be deterrent, it follows that there is no reason at all why it should be made unpleasant. If a man must be prevented from injuring his fellow-men, and if he will not listen to reason, then it is just to imprison him. But his life in prison must be made as pleasant as possible, so that he does not become embittered; prison can be a school of virtue only if it provides the prisoner with opportunities of useful employment and intercourse with pleasant companions. Godwin also approves of banishment, provided it is to an unsettled country, where convicts can build up a new society for themselves without interference from the long-corrupted mother country.

Godwin has often been denounced as a visionary, with almost no understanding of human nature; but it seems to me that what he has to say about punishment and coercion is often true, though he puts an extreme case and uses some unconvincing arguments. Leslie Stephen, in his book on *English Thought in the Eighteenth Century*, treats Godwin as an abstract philosopher whose ignorance of human nature leads him into every kind of absurdity. I think that Sir Leslie Stephen has allowed his sturdy common sense to get the better of him. It is interesting to see that Tolstoy's opinions, in this as in many other matters, are almost the same as Godwin's. Did the world's greatest novelist know nothing of human nature?[1]

[1] Knowledge of human nature is indispensable to the social philosopher, but of itself it takes him only a little way towards the understanding of social problems. Besides, it was the strength of their emotions and not the weakness of their understandings that led Godwin and Tolstoy astray.

Godwin thought that all positive law is pernicious. Every human predicament differs from every other; every case, therefore, is a rule to itself. To try to fit it to the Procrustean bed of the law is not merely to do violence to justice but is also to limit reason. Positive laws are mechanical standards to which men conform to save themselves the trouble of discovering how justice requires them to act in particular cases. 'The true principle which ought to be substituted in the room of law is that of reason exercising an uncontrolled jurisdiction upon the circumstances of the case.'[1] Godwin's attitude to law and to the legal profession is again very like Tolstoy's, as anyone can see who reads the latter's description of the trial of the prostitute Maslova in *Resurrection*. What Godwin does not understand is that positive laws are not all of them attempts to supersede, nor yet to interpret, 'the dictates of an eternal justice'. Abstract principles of justice will not suffice to tell us how we ought to behave in particular cases; we must have a great deal of other information as well. This Godwin does not deny. But he does not understand that this other information cannot be in the possession of every member of society; nor yet, were it all in everyone's possession, would everyone draw similar inferences from it. In order that large numbers of people should be able to live together, it is necessary that certain uniformities of behaviour should exist among them. But they cannot all of them be expected to arrive, independently, at the knowledge of what those uniformities should be. Regulations must be made by some one; there must be, in every society, some people who collect and analyse the relevant information and then propose uniformities of behaviour. It is one thing to say that obedience to rules ought not to be imposed by force; but it is quite another to say that no rules ought to be made.

Godwin looks forward to the disappearance of all government. 'With what delight,' he says in his book,[2] 'must every well-informed friend of mankind look forward to the auspicious period, the dissolution of political government, of that brute engine which has been the only perennial cause of the vices of mankind, and which . . . has mischiefs of various sorts incorporated with its substance, and no otherwise to be removed than by its utter annihilation!' But

---

[1] Bk. VII, ch. viii.  [2] Bk. V, ch. xxiv.

he does not advocate the immediate destruction of government, for the very vices that are the products of government make it necessary that there should be some coercion, and therefore some government to apply it. It is only after much time has elapsed and when at last truth reigns supreme in all men's minds that governments will be unnecessary.

But Godwin will have it that the vices they engender cannot be cured by governments. The progress of truth, which is to say the rational education of mankind, is a task for which governments are peculiarly unsuited.

Governments are the causes of most evils. Some of these evils, on occasions much less frequent than they suppose, they are able to prevent. But to cure any of them is quite beyond their power. The great instrument of governments is force, which, though it can sometimes prevent evil, can never destroy its causes in the minds of men. Force, indeed, must always create some evil, not only because it inflicts pain but also because those who suffer it are debased and made vindictive. It is reason alone that can get at the roots of evil; and governments, expert in the use of force, cannot know how to promote reason. Godwin's final verdict on government is that we should put up with as little of it as is possible until we can get rid of it altogether, for it is always liable to do much evil and can only prevent a small amount.

Godwin was a communist. 'He who looks at his property with the eye of truth,' he says,[1] 'will find that every shilling of it has received its destination from the dictates of reason.' If you have a shilling in your pocket, which your neighbour says he needs, then, if that neighbour is speaking the truth and your own need is not greater, that shilling belongs to him; and if you keep it in your pocket, you are robbing him. But if each man has a claim to his neighbour's superfluities, does it not follow that, if the claim is allowed, the lazy will become parasites on the industrious? Godwin's answer to this objection is that, if property were equally distributed and men lived simple lives, labour would be so gentle a burden as to be a form of relaxation. He estimates that one-twentieth of England's inhabitants could produce all the food and all the other necessaries required by them all; so that, if all luxury were abolished and everybody worked, no one would need to work

[1] Bk. VIII, ch. i.

more than half-an-hour a day. It was possible for men of good will to take this estimate seriously in an unstatistical age.

Godwin, unlike the communists and socialists of to-day, disliked co-operation. All co-operation, because it forces men to suit each other's convenience, restricts their liberty. Some co-operation is unavoidable, but he thinks that, if men take care to reduce their needs to a minimum, they will contrive to satisfy most of them without co-operation. Above all else, Godwin disliked the sort of co-operation which involves cohabitation and marriage. 'So long as I seek to engross one woman to myself and to prohibit my neighbour from proving his superior desert and reaping the fruits of it, I am guilty of the most odious of all monopolies.'[1]

So much, then, for the more important of Godwin's doctrines. Except for some few fundamental principles, he had little enough in common with the utilitarians who preceded him. Nor was he destined to have much influence on his utilitarian successors, with the possible exception of John Stuart Mill. Many of the arguments with which Godwin defends the exercise of private judgment are strikingly similar to those used by the younger Mill in *Liberty*. Both men make the same assumptions: that the prevalence of truth is beneficial to mankind and that it will best prevail in those societies in which no attempt is made to restrain the individual's private judgment. There is good evidence for the truth of the second of these two assumptions, but not much for the first. Apart from John Stuart Mill, two other important European thinkers preached doctrines in important respects similar to those of Godwin. I mean Proudhon and Tolstoy but, so far as I know, there is no reason to believe that they were either of them directly influenced by their English precursor.[2]

[1] Bk. VIII, ch. vi.
[2] Though Tolstoy read *Political Justice*, he did not derive his opinions from it.

# CHAPTER VI

## JAMES MILL

### 1. His Importance

THE radical utilitarianism that had a great influence on the course of English history was the creation, not of Godwin, but of Bentham and James Mill. It repudiated nothing more vigorously than anarchism and communism. It was the creed of men who believed in private property and the efficient punishment of malefactors.

James Mill has been called the disciple of Bentham, although from the first years of their acquaintance he influenced his master almost as much as he was influenced by him. Mill was an admirer of Bentham, but he was also the sterner and more vigorous character; and he could not admire without irritating as well. Yet Bentham's debt to Mill is a great one. It was Mill who helped him to commit himself irrevocably to the democratic cause; and it was Mill who transmitted his doctrines to other minds, giving a more popular and vigorous expression to them than Bentham could have done. Bentham was always a hard worker, and he needed no Scottish disciple, however stern and energetic, to keep him at work. But he had never known how to present his doctrines in a form attractive to the general reader. James Mill was useful to Bentham, as the Genevan Dumont had been, as a man who could stimulate him not only to write but to publish, and who could help him to make what he wrote fit for publication. But Mill was a much abler man than Dumont; and indeed, in some ways, he was abler than Bentham himself. He was the more acute and the more rigorous logician; and he had a better knowledge of economics than his master.

No one denied more energetically than Mill that Bentham had disciples. He said that only two men with any pretension to letters enjoyed the intimacy of Bentham and had the opportunity to learn much from him. Neither of these men, according to Mill (who was one of them), were of the sort who could take any man for a master, 'though they were drawn to Mr. Bentham by the sympathy of common opinions, and by the respect due to a man who had done more than anybody else to illustrate and recommend doctrines, which they deemed of first class importance to the happiness of mankind.'[1] Though Mill would not be a disciple, history has decided that he was one and that he served his master well. Though it may be misleading to talk of a School of Benthamites, it is plausible to do so only because James Mill was so vigorous and influential an exponent of Bentham's doctrines.

Indeed, it was James Mill who made Benthamism both influential and unpopular; and it needed a stern and vigorous Scotsman to do both these things at once. For the Benthamites, or Philosophic Radicals, were certainly not popular. They were too radical and too fond of theory to please the Whigs, who were willing to make some reforms but would not be bullied into accepting simple principles and drawing extreme conclusions from them. The Whig attitude to the Benthamites was best expressed by Macaulay, in his articles in the *Edinburgh Review*, where he castigated them all but none more vigorously than James Mill. Macaulay believed that his blows were damaging but in a dispute about first principles he was no match for Mill. Yet he did not feel at a disadvantage, for there are persons who imagine themselves at home everywhere, however little they know the place in which they find themselves.

The Benthamites were also disliked by such popular radicals as Cobbett and Hunt, whom Mill despised, though they did more than any other men to frighten the ruling oligarchy into passing the first Reform Bill. Mill thought little better of Cartwright and Sir Francis Burdett, but he was not above giving them advice. Among the popular radicals, he made an exception only in favour of Francis Place, who was neither an orator nor a journalist, but a patient organizer always willing to listen to his intellectual superiors.

That the great Reform Bill was passed through Parliament was largely owing to the efforts of three sets of people, who none of them liked the others. The radical agitators, the Whigs and the Benthamites all made their separate contributions to the common victory. But the contribution of the Benthamites, though it was great, was the least important of the three. The Whigs saw the great measure through Parliament, while the agitators frightened their opponents into acquiescence. The role of the Benthamites was to irritate and stimulate the Whigs, and to restrain the popular

[1] *Fragment on Mackintosh*, p. 124. (1870 edition.)

radicals as far as their influence could reach them. For the Benthamites, like all reasonable men who wish well to mankind, hated violent revolution.

But the Benthamites served their country best after the passage of the great Reform Bill. Though Bentham died in 1832 and James Mill only four years later, their doctrines were most influential in the small but powerful circles of practical intellectuals who, in all civilized countries, make the subordinate decisions of policy that are hardly less important than the major ones. If the ideas and the spirit of Bentham were long active in these circles, to which Britain owes so many of her greatest reforms, this was due, above all, to James Mill.

## 2. His Theory of Morals

When we leave Bentham's discussion of first principles to notice the use he makes of them, we pass from darkness into light. It was left to James Mill to describe clearly what his master could only hint at. Mill's theory of morals is to be found in two of his works, in the last nine chapters of the second volume of the *Analysis of the Phenomena of the Human Mind* and in the *Fragment on Mackintosh*. It is the first complete and clearly-stated utilitarian moral philosophy which is very different from that of Hume. Where Paley is summary and Bentham confused, Mill is both elaborate and clear. His reputation has probably suffered on that account, for it is often easy to trace his errors to their source. He puts his inadequate views so vigorously that his reader is left in no doubt that the means are lacking to make a true theory. And if he later introduces the very notions he has excluded, the manoeuvre is too obvious to pass unnoticed.

Mill's theory of morals is part of an attempt to explain all the phenomena of the human mind in terms of the association of sensations and ideas, which are the mere copies of sensations. Since this attempt cannot succeed, Mill is sometimes obliged, though he does not know it, to abandon his own definitions and to use words in their ordinary meanings. But though his definitions and his uses of words do not always coincide, his meaning is usually clear enough. Or if he is confused, it is easier with him than with most men to detect the nature of the confusion.

Mill distinguishes between interesting and indifferent sensations, between those that are pleasant or painful and those that are neither. The idea of a pleasant sensation he calls a desire, and the idea of a painful one, an aversion. Though his theory of the association of ideas cannot explain how men come to conceive of the past and the future, Mill believes that it can, and therefore makes full use of the distinction between them. 'The word desire,' he says, 'is commonly used to mark the idea of a pleasurable sensation, when the Future is associated with it.'[1]

Mill then goes on to distinguish between desire and motive. He says that when the idea of a future pleasant sensation is associated with the idea of our own action as its cause, then we have a motive. But not every motive leads to action, for we can have several motives at the same time, and the action prompted by one of them makes it impossible for the others to produce their effects. That education is best which creates such habits in men that the motives leading to actions having the best consequences are usually victorious.

Like Bentham, Mill makes the morality of an action depend not on the agent's motive but on his intention. The motive of an action is the idea of those of its pleasurable consequences for whose sake it is done, and its intention is all of its consequences expected by the agent. An intention, according to Mill, is immoral whenever a man acts expecting a preponderance of evil consequences or without caring whether there will be such a preponderance or not. For James Mill, as for Bentham, the man of virtue is the good calculator. 'The men, therefore, philosophers they ought not to be called, who preach a morality without calculation, take away morality altogether; because morality is an attribute of intention; and an intention is then only good when the act intended has in the sum of its ascertainable consequences a superiority of good over evil.'[2] Mill says that the rightness of an action is the same thing as its utility. His meaning may, perhaps, be more precisely expressed if it is said that a man acts rightly whenever the expected consequences of what he does are better than those of any other action possible to him.

Mill still has to explain how it is that men come to act morally. For the mere opinion that of several actions possible under the

[1] *Anal. Hum. Mind*, II, ch. xix, p. 153.    [2] *Fragment on Mackintosh*, p. 164.

circumstances one will have better consequences than any of the others is no motive for doing it. Mill's explanation of why men act morally is a simple one. Every man, if left to himself, would seek his own pleasures without regard for other people's. But no man is left to himself and men have to learn by experience to live comfortably together. It is experience that teaches them, out of their innumerable actions, to select one class they call moral and another they call immoral. Those actions are moral which it is important to other men that each man should do but which he has no interest in doing; and those actions are immoral which it is important to other men that he should not do but from which he has no interest in abstaining. Men provide each other with motives for doing moral actions and abstaining from immoral ones. They see to it that good comes to him who does the former and abstains from the latter, and evil to him who abstains from the former and does the latter. They can do this either by punishing and rewarding, or merely by praising and blaming. Experience will decide what means are best suited to the purpose. 'The whole business of the moral sentiments,' says Mill, 'moral approbation and disapprobation, has this for its object, the distribution of the good and evil we have at command, for the production of acts of the useful sort, the prevention of acts of the contrary sort.'[1]

This theory so far combines elements borrowed from Hobbes and from Hume and adds others suggested by Bentham. Unlike Hobbes, James Mill calls that action right which leads to the greatest possible happiness, no matter whose. But like Hobbes, he believes that every man naturally desires only his own happiness and must be supplied artificially with selfish motives for promoting other people's. And in the supply of these motives, he ascribes an important role to the moral sentiments. But his description of these sentiments and of the manner in which they arise in us takes Mill a long way from Hobbes. For he admits that, though the original distinction between moral and immoral actions is due to men's reflection about what it is in their interest that other men should do, the habit of moral action is acquired by all men long before they are capable of justifying it rationally. According to Mill, we acquire the moral habit in this way: our parents praise some actions and blame others, and they reward us for doing the former and

[1] Ibid., p. 250.

punish us for doing the latter; we therefore associate the idea of praise with one class of actions and of blame with another, and to do this is to have the notions of praiseworthy and blameworthy actions. Since we desire the usual consequences of the former and avoid those of the latter, we soon acquire the habit of moral action, which later remains with us even when we are no longer liable to suffer these consequences.

This process, as Mill describes it, would appear to lead mankind away from the selfish hedonism natural to them in their primitive state to what is at least the threshold of true morality. For if, the moral habit once acquired, a man does the praiseworthy actions and abstains from the blameworthy ones, even when he no longer expects either praise or blame, is he not capable of unselfishness, of action prompted by some idea not of a pleasurable sensation to be experienced by himself? But Mill will not let mankind attain virtue at so cheap a price. He has an argument, and a most unplausible one, to show that men are completely selfish after all. The man who does a praiseworthy action, when he knows that he will receive not praise but blame for it, still acts in anticipation of praise. This anticipation is only momentary, but it is so powerful that it can, though immediately succeeded by the expectation of evil, take effect in virtuous action. A momentary idea can, says Mill, have the strongest effect upon us, however quickly other ideas succeed it. To deserve praise is to anticipate it. Mill can give no other meaning to the notion of desert. A man, therefore, who is eager to deserve praise when he knows he cannot get it, must, if only for a moment, expect it and then come to know that his expectation is vain. The absurdity of this argument is evident, even if we accept Mill's premises. To anticipate anything is, in his view, to have an idea of it associated with the idea of its cause. If what a man anticipates is pleasant and its cause is his own action, then, unless there is something to prevent its doing so, his anticipation must produce that action. But in the case in question, there is something to prevent its doing so; there is the subsequent anticipation of evil. And this latter anticipation must either replace the former or, if they co-exist, it must be the stronger, for otherwise it is impossible, within the limits of James Mill's philosophy, to explain what is meant by the statement that the man does the praiseworthy action though he expects to be blamed for it.

Mill's account of sympathy and benevolence is no more satisfactory than his account of virtue. 'The idea', he tells us, 'of a man enjoying a train of pleasures, or happiness, is felt by every body to be a pleasurable idea. The idea of a man under a train of sufferings or pains, is equally felt to be a painful idea. This can arise from nothing but the association of our own pleasures with the first idea, and of our pains with the second. We never feel any pains and pleasures but our own. The fact, indeed, is, that our very idea of the pains or pleasures of another man is only the idea of our own pains, or our own pleasures, associated with the idea of another man.'[1] No man as intelligent as James Mill undoubtedly was ever produced a worse argument than this. The association of ideas, as he conceives it, cannot explain how we come by the notion of any man, ourself or another. But since we do come by the notion of another man, how can it be impossible for us to have an idea of his pleasures or pains? For, on Mill's theory, our idea of another man can be nothing but our idea of a train of feelings not our own. And what could be more absurd than his statement that our idea of another man's pleasure is the idea of our own associated with our idea of him? Who can doubt that when I think of my own pleasure and of another man, I am still far from thinking of his pleasure? I cannot possibly think of a pleasure as another man's, if I continue to think of it as my own. It is Mill himself, though he often warns us to beware of the intricacies of language, who has been caught.

Whenever he feels most open to attack, Mill resorts to his doctrine of the indissoluble association of ideas. Speaking of himself, he says that 'it is Mr. Mill who first made known the great principle of the indissoluble association. It is he, who has shewn, that various mental phenomena, which had puzzled all preceding inquirers, may be satisfactorily accounted for, by application to them of the principle of indissoluble association'.[2] He uses the principle when he wishes to show that something is there, though other people have not noticed it. Whenever, because they have been so often repeated together in the past, the association between two or more ideas is so strong that they always arise in our minds in such close combination as not to be distinguishable, there is an indissoluble association between them. The unreflecting mind, when it has these associated ideas, mistakes the complex whole presented to it

[1] *Anal. Hum. Mind*, II, ch. xxi, p. 175.  [2] *Fragment on Mackintosh*, p. 173.

for a simple one. To illustrate his meaning, Mill offers the analogy of a wheel, on which seven colours have been painted, but which revolves so rapidly that it looks white. In like manner, several ideas, passing quickly through the mind, appear to be one; and the consequence is that men have come to mistake many of their complex ideas for simple ones. Among such complex ideas mistaken for simple ones are most of the notions that the moral philosopher must analyse. It is no wonder, then, that James Mill should believe that the discoverer of the principle of indissoluble association could make the greatest progress in this analysis. He thinks that 'Mr. Mill (has) traced home to their source, not one, but all of the social affections; and (has) shown by distinct analysis that they are entirely composed of pleasurable feelings'.[1]

Now, Mill's analogy can help no one to understand his meaning. It is no more than a manner of speaking to say that the colour white is composed of seven others; it is either an elliptical statement about the physical causes of our sensations of colour or it is a statement about the order in which those sensations succeed one another. When we look at what is white, the colour that we see is as simple as any other. We do not see seven colours in such rapid succession that we cannot distinguish between them and then mistake them for what appears to be an eighth colour but does not in fact exist. If virtue and the social affections are related to our ideas of our own pleasures and pains as white is to the seven prismatic colours, then, whatever their causal connexion with these pleasures and pains, they differ in kind from them. Moreover, James Mill has no right to talk of sensations or ideas succeeding one another so rapidly that they are indistinguishable. For he says that to have a sensation is to know that one has it, and to have two sensations is to know they are two.[2] His own conception of the nature of knowledge forbids any other conclusion. Nothing, on his theory, can ever be indistinguishable from anything else. But what cannot be done in the unaccommodating world is possible in the world of philosophy, where a man can cut the ground from under his own feet and yet stand upon it.

James Mill, like Bentham, takes pride in the fact that his theory provides an objective standard of morality. In what does this objectivity consist? If Mill is saying no more than that he intends to

[1] Ibid., p. 188.  [2] *Anal. Hum. Mind*, I, ch. v, p. 170, and II, ch. xiv, p. 10.

use the word *right* as if it meant *useful*, his statement is unimportant. If he is saying that the English habitually use the two words in the same meaning, his statement is disputable. But even if we suppose it true, we are no nearer to an objective standard of morality. For if *right* means *useful*, it is clear that it cannot mean *morally obligatory*. When, therefore, he has to explain how men come to regard some actions as morally obligatory, Mill has no alternative but to follow the example of Hume and have recourse to the moral sentiments. He does, it is true, insist that men only approve what they believe to be useful. But this is also, though with some qualifications that Mill would reject, the opinion of Hume. Yet Mill believes that his system is superior to Hume's because it provides an objective standard of morality. His purpose in the *Fragment on Mackintosh* is to defend this standard against the man whom he considers the most impertinent of its critics.

## 3. His Political Theory

The elder Mill's political theory is even simpler than his system of morals. Its fundamental principles are expounded in an article on *Government* published in the 1820 edition of the *Encyclopaedia Britannica*.

Government, according to Mill, deals with a particular class of pleasures and pains, those that men derive from one another. Now, the means to happiness are not naturally abundant, and men must work to produce them. But most work is unpleasant; and since all men desire pleasure and avoid pain, they will try, unless they are prevented, to seize the fruits of other men's labour and to do nothing themselves. Mill believes that it is a law of human nature that every man desires as much power as will enable him to make the persons and properties of other men subservient to his pleasures. It is therefore desirable, if the means of happiness are to be produced in the greatest abundance, that every man should retain as much as possible of the fruits of his labour. But this he can only do if all men unite together and delegate to some few of their number the power to protect them all. Those who exercise this protective power are the government.

But how can the many ensure that the few will use this power to protect them? Since it is a law of human nature that every man desires to make other men subservient to his pleasures, there is a constant danger that the governors will abuse their power, making those whom they ought to protect their victims. There exists only one device which can always prevent this abuse of power. This device is representative government, which makes the governors responsible to the governed; for though all the members of a community cannot govern, they can choose the persons who do. Thus it is that James Mill, starting from the same premises as Hobbes, arrives at the conclusion that the best of all governments is a representative democracy. His theory is the same as Bentham's, but expressed more simply and with greater vigour.

Writing for an educated public still hostile to radical ideas, James Mill is careful not to offend too many prejudices. Though Bentham had advocated a unicameral legislature and had quietly assumed that the properly constituted state would be a republic, Mill attacks neither the monarchy nor the House of Lords. He says only that if, as their supporters say, kings and legislators by right of birth are necessary institutions, no representative assembly, whose interests are those of the nation, will wish to abolish them. Such an evasive argument comes very properly from a utilitarian anxious to avoid a controversy more likely to cause offence than to lead to useful results. Even Bentham, a scholarly recluse bearing the reactions of the public very little in mind, had known that to abolish monarchy and aristocracy in England was not practical politics. James Mill, in theory as little as Bentham a friend of mixed government, is writing to convince a hostile public and so makes known to them only those of his opinions he is most anxious they should share.

Nor does James Mill advocate universal suffrage but only a franchise so wide that it will make impossible the predominance of sinister interests. He does not tell us just how wide it should be to effect this purpose. All that he does is to give us a general rule: that no class of persons ought to be unrepresented whose interests are not obviously included in those of other people. To illustrate his rule, Mill takes the example of children. Their interests, he thinks, are included in those of their parents, who love and take care of them. So, too, the interests of women are largely included in those of their men-folk. But Mill does not think this a sufficient reason for refusing the vote to women. Children are not only loved and cared for by their parents; they are also incapable of knowing their own interests. We may therefore conclude from what Mill says that, though other limitations may be justified in particular circumstances, the universally valid rule is that only those classes ought to be unrepresented whose interests, which they are themselves incapable of promoting, are included in those of other people. The always sufficient reason for refusing the vote to anyone is that, while he cannot himself make a rational use of it, there is someone else, whose interest includes his own, who can.

James Mill admits that most people do not know their own interests. But he thinks this no reason for excluding them from the franchise. A narrow ruling class will, he thinks, always act badly, because they will prefer their own interests to those of the public. This is an inevitable consequence of the incurable selfishness of mankind.[1] However wise or foolish an oligarchy may be, they will never promote the greatest happiness of the greatest number, for the interests of the entire community are never included in those of any small class within it. But the ignorance of the multitude can be cured or, rather, it can always be diminished. The best way of promoting the public happiness is to enfranchise the many and to educate them; and, in any case, it is a better way than to leave government to the irresponsible few, whatever their wisdom. It may be difficult and expensive to educate the masses, but it is impossible to prevent a small ruling class from promoting their own happiness at the expense of other people.

The case for representative democracy has seldom been put with such economy and vigour. We may believe, to-day, that ignorance is harder to cure than Mill thought it was, but we would most of us, in Western Europe and North America, agree with him when he says that no irresponsible ruling class can be trusted to govern in the interest of the whole community. Indeed, we have evidence of the truth of this more terrible than Mill ever knew. The greatest oppressors have seized power by exploiting the hatreds of the people but they have not been responsible to them. The power

---

[1] When Mill, in this context, speaks of men's selfishness, he is not thinking of his own analysis of virtue, benevolence and all the social affections into 'indissoluble' associations of a man's ideas of his own pleasures with his ideas of other people as their causes. As Mill himself says, whatever the analysis of the social affections, they remain what they are. When he talks of the selfishness of men's political behaviour, he uses the word in its ordinary meaning as a thing different from benevolence, gratitude, and all the social affections.

of governments and the discipline of organized minorities is such
that there never was a time when oppressors could afford to be so
indifferent to the reactions of their victims. This sort of oppression
of which Mill knew nothing, does not exist in primitive and illiterate
communities. It is to be found only in parts of the world that are
considerably industrialized, where schools are many and political
doctrines imported from the West prevail. It is therefore the
product of the same conditions that make possible modern representative democracy. But this in no way weakens but rather adds
to the strength of Mill's arguments. There was a time when
representative government was impossible everywhere. Men could
not do otherwise than submit to rulers who oppressed them, but
the very conditions that made responsible government impossible
placed some limits on men's power to oppress one another. But
among European peoples to-day, responsible government (however
difficult) is not impossible, while oppressors have opportunities
unknown before.

We may qualify Mill's arguments in many ways and yet find in
them a powerful support for democracy. Natural differences of
ability, which education cannot abolish, are much greater than he
supposed, but it is not easy to distinguish the wise from the foolish.
The small minority of clever men do not form a separate class with
common interests, and it is not possible to segregate them and to
make irresponsible governors of them. There is no argument
against democracy from the stupidity of mankind, unless it can be
shown that most governments are so much wiser than their subjects,
that the latter have less to fear from their selfishness than to gain
from the unfettered exercise of their wisdom. In primitive communities, where knowledge is scarce and the effective use of power
difficult, there is a case against democracy. It can be argued that
what little knowledge is there to be had must be the monopoly of a
small class, since the means are lacking of distributing it more
widely; and that the people, being ignorant, would do well not to
meddle with what they cannot understand. But the same causes,
industrial progress and the accumulation of wealth, which make it
possible to diminish popular ignorance, also increase the power of
governments to oppress their subjects. Representative democracy,
from a doubtful good, becomes the only alternative to the worst of
political evils. Mill, with no experience to guide him, could say

nothing about the defects of the system he advocated. He looked upon it as an almost perfect device; and it was left to his son to criticize it. John Stuart Mill, compared with some others, was a mild critic of the democracy whose coming he foresaw and which is now with us. To-day, we can bring more formidable accusations against it than any he could think of, and yet we have better cause to defend it than any earlier generation.

# CHAPTER VII

## UTILITARIANISM AND THE CLASSICAL ECONOMISTS

THE political theory of Bentham and the elder Mill derives, through Hume, from Hobbes. Like all the other utilitarians they assume that, outside the narrow circle of his family and friends, most of a man's actions of which other men need take notice are designed to obtain some advantage for himself. Hobbes had said nothing to suggest that the public happiness is itself desirable, but he had shown that men can turn each other's selfishness to good account, that every man can find it his interest to live in a society in which all men, himself included, are often obliged to do what they do not want or to refrain from what they do. In the state of nature men interfere with one another, and this interference makes their lives intolerable. They therefore set up a political society, which substitutes a milder, more orderly and economical inter-ference for the repeated, brutal and incalculable shocks to which they previously were exposed. Like a house in which travellers shelter from the storm, society protects men much more than it limits their freedom. When Hobbes talked of an absolute sovereign, he meant only that the extent of his powers must be determined by himself; he did not mean that the sovereign must control all the activities of his subjects. Within the wide limits of his country's laws, each man governs himself. When Hobbes lived, governments made few laws and men still oppressed each other more than they were oppressed by their governments.

But Hobbes gave mankind no advice about the proper extent of a sovereign's power. He prescribed no rules to guide the sovereign in deciding when it was his own and his subjects' interest that the laws should be silent. It was Mandeville, in his *Fable of the Bees*, who first taught modern Europeans that there exists a natural harmony of interests in the economic sphere. The greater the variety of men's wants, the easier for every man to find it his private interest to produce what will satisfy some of these wants.

The more acquisitive men are, the more intent on pleasure and refinements of pleasure, the easier it is for them to co-operate. As society grows richer, its members are drawn closer together, each of them dependent for his happiness on an always greater number of the others. But the more men find it their interest to work peacefully together, the less it is necessary to oblige them to do so. Mandeville did not isolate men's activities as producers and distributors of material wealth, and say that with these activities governments ought not to interfere. But though he did not draw this conclusion it is implied by his theory.

Mandeville's argument, differently put so that it might convince without annoying, was adopted by Hume and by his friend and admirer, Adam Smith. Hume advocated a greater freedom of trade than existed in his day, and exposed some of the fallacies to which governments were still attached. But it was Adam Smith who described the economic processes whereby the natural harmony of interests is assured. The processes that he described are not the inventions of governments; they arise naturally in all societies as men learn to use their labour and skill more effectively for the satisfaction of their wants.

The classical economists, especially the three most famous of them, Adam Smith, Malthus and Ricardo, were utilitarians. They believed that the proper end of government is the greatest happiness of the governed. They were most of them practical men. They did not write books on economics merely because they were interested in describing how men produce and distribute material wealth. They were great controversialists in their day, and what they wanted above all was to give advice to governments. They called the science, whose creation is ascribed to them and to the French physiocrats, political economy. The advice they gave was mostly negative, but the principle behind it was utilitarian. They said to the government: don't do what we tell you not to do and men will be the happier for your abstinence; you need only look at the methods whereby they produce and exchange goods and services (and we have taken the trouble to describe these methods for you) and you will see that we are right. The classical political economy, which prevailed in this country from 1776 until the middle of the next century, was the theory behind the advice given by utilitarians to the successive governments of their country.

As they all gave different advice, they quarrelled about the theory and so were obliged to take more notice of each other than the government took of them. But for all that, their first object, as Professor Cannan has shown, was practical.

## 1. ADAM SMITH

In his *Theory of the Moral Sentiments*, Adam Smith, as became the disciple of Hume, had allowed a large role to sympathy. But in the *Wealth of Nations* he assumes that man, the producer and distributor of material wealth, is completely selfish. Nevertheless, the general economic interest is secure, because, though it is the object of no man's endeavour, it is the natural result of the division of labour and the mechanism of exchange. These two devices ensure that each man does what he is best fitted to do, and that he is more than compensated for the unpleasantness of his work by the utility of the objects he can acquire as a result of it. 'The real price of everything,' he tells us, 'what everything really costs to the man who wishes to acquire it, is the toil and trouble of acquiring it . . . Labour was the first price that was paid for all things.'[1] His theory is that all economic activity is the endurance of present pain in the hope of future pleasure to be got by consuming the fruits of one's labour or what is exchanged for them. The division of labour and the market ensure, between them, that as much as possible of what is useful is produced at the least cost in terms of labour. Whatever impedes the division of labour and the free operation of the market is therefore injurious; for the division of labour ensures that a given amount of work, and therefore also of pain, produces as much as possible of what is useful, while it is owing to the market that useful things are produced in the order of their utility and get to the people who want them

Even if we accept the psychological and utilitarian assumptions on which it rests, Adam Smith's argument is plausible only when one all-important qualification is made. What he says may be true, provided that natural resources, however scarce, are available to everyone on the same terms as to anyone else. As this has never been the case in any society we know of, all that Adam Smith is entitled to say is that the division of labour and the free market

[1] *Wealth of Nations*, Bk. I, ch. iv.

produce the greatest amount of happiness compatible with the existing system of property. Adam Smith was, of course, quite aware that the unequal distribution of property enables the owners of scarce resources to charge a rent for their use, which they can spend to buy the produce of other men's labour without needing to produce anything themselves. But he did not allow this fact to weaken his belief in the natural harmony of interests.

Even if we suppose (though they are not to be found in the *Wealth of Nations*) that there are solid utilitarian arguments for the inequality of property, there are still passages enough in that work to disturb our faith in the natural harmony of interests. Adam Smith says that with the progress of civilization real wages will increase and profits decrease, which suggests that there may be a conflict of interests between labourers and capitalists. It does not follow that there is one, for the incomes of individual capitalists may continue to rise though the return on each unit of their capital falls. And even if their combined share of the national income should come to be a smaller fraction of it, which it need not do though the rate of interest falls, its absolute amount may be much greater. These are matters that require proof, if the doctrine of the natural harmony of interests is to be saved. But Adam Smith is content to say nothing about them. He also tells us that rents will increase with real wages, so that (given the system of property, and its justice unquestioned) there is an apparent harmony of interests between landowners and labourers. And in another place he says that labourers seldom know their own interests and that landowners are lazy and improvident. The capitalists, on the other hand, are the best informed, most intelligent and most industrious class in the community. In the system of Adam Smith, it is they that are the real makers of progress. It is a curious harmony of interests which appears to increase the rewards of the ignorant and the lazy more quickly than those of the intelligent and industrious. Smith's position can perhaps be defended, but its truth is not obvious. It may be that the capitalists, even though the balance of advantages should turn against them, have more to gain than to lose from the uncontrolled progress of material civilization. But it does not follow that they can do nothing to redress the balance. Could they not improve their relative position by acquiring control of the government and having laws made in their favour? Is it certain that, if they could do so, the general happiness would be diminished? What, after all, does a natural harmony of interests amount to? It is clear that Adam Smith never asked himself these questions. It is not enough to show (what he never did) that every class has something to gain from the community's economic progress; it must also be proved that neither the community as a whole nor any class within it has less to gain by leaving that progress to itself than by seeking to control it. For anything that either Adam Smith or any other economist knew to the contrary, it might be true both that if one class prospers all must do so and that the greatest prosperity of any one class is incompatible with the greatest prosperity of them all. But if this were so, it would be misleading to talk of a natural harmony of selfish interests. Though the greatest happiness of the whole community depended on leaving men's economic activities uncontrolled, every class might stand to gain by using the state to control them in its own exclusive interest.

Adam Smith did not attempt to reconcile his later admissions with the original assumption with which they are not obviously compatible. M. Halévy attributes this failure to his noticing these apparent symptoms of disharmony long after he had made the assumption. As they successively occurred to him, Adam Smith made a note of each of these symptoms, but he never realized that, taken together, they are a serious threat to the position from which he started. He therefore saw no reason why he should abandon or defend that position. But since he retained it, he was led, though unaware of what he was doing, to minimize the importance of every admission that might make it untenable. Halévy compares these admissions with 'foreign bodies that the organism is always trying to eliminate'.[1] He assumes that the theory could not possibly assimilate them, but he goes too far. Halévy would be right if it followed, with no need for further evidence, that where some people stand to gain less than others, it is always their interest not to leave matters alone. He knows just as little as any classical economist what conditions must prevail before there can be a natural harmony of selfish interests.

---

[1] *The Growth of Philosophic Radicalism*, p. 103.

## 2. MALTHUS

The next important economist after Adam Smith was Malthus, whose *Essay on Population* first appeared in 1798, twenty-two years after the *Wealth of Nations*. It had been a favourite idea in the eighteenth century, especially in France and America but also in Britain, that the cause of depopulation is luxury. Rich men, it was thought, waste the substance of the community and spread the vices that cause disease and death. We have already noticed one utilitarian clergyman, William Paley, who rejected this idea and put forward the opposite one that poverty increases population, while he defended luxury, saying that it provides work for the poor and keeps them out of mischief. Malthus, another utilitarian clergyman, also rejected the popular theory, but for reasons very different from Paley's. Paley had agreed with those whose theory he rejected that most countries could support much larger populations than inhabited them; he had merely denied that luxury is the cause of depopulation. But Malthus also denied that most countries, and in particular the countries of Western Europe, were under-populated. Population, he said, has a natural tendency to increase at a geometrical ratio, while the means of subsistence will normally increase at no more than an arithmetical ratio. There exists, therefore, in every old-established country a constant pressure of population on the means of subsistence. This is so whether or not there are great inequalities of property. Malthus admitted that in newly discovered continents, before natural resources are fully developed, the means of subsistence may increase fast enough to keep pace with this natural growth of population. But in older countries, where all the better land is already cultivated, this cannot happen. Malthus therefore concluded that, whatever the distribution of property, the greatest part of the inhabitants of all old countries must be wretchedly poor, receiving a subsistence just sufficient to keep them alive. Those born in excess of the number that the resources of the community can maintain are condemned to a premature death by famine or disease. Malthus called misery and vice the positive checks that keep down the population to the level of subsistence; and he also admitted that there is another, which he called moral or preventive, consisting in voluntary abstinence from procreation. But in the first edition of his *Essay*, he did not attach great importance to this moral check.

It may be that when he published the first edition of his *Essay*, Malthus was so anxious to refute the theory that luxury is the cause of depopulation, that he forgot his obligations as a clergyman. He had said vice was a positive check on population. But if population must always grow faster than the means of subsistence, it follows that whatever is needed to check its growth is useful; and if useful, then good. What is called vice is therefore not vice at all, but ought rather to be called virtue. Such a conclusion cannot be avoided if the utilitarian assumptions and the facts alleged by Malthus are both true. But it is a conclusion that a clergyman must, at all costs, avoid. Besides, Malthus was naturally of a benevolent, if rather conservative, temper. In later editions of his *Essay*, he qualified his doctrine, making it less startling, more plausible and more humane. The moral check, he said, is not yet sufficiently effective, but it may well become so if the proper remedy is applied. And this proper remedy is *education*. Now education, if it can teach people to limit the size of their families, can ensure, not merely that population grows no faster than the means of subsistence, but that it grows more slowly. It can therefore provide, not only an effective substitute for misery and vice, but a remedy for poverty itself. Malthus, in the later editions of his *Essay*, looked forward to the day when the population of England might be two or three times as great and yet the labouring classes much better off than they were in his day.

Malthus, like Bernard Shaw, had no eye for the charms of poverty. He looked forward to its abolition, but was no less anxious that the rich should not be plundered. He thought that the ignorance of the poor, and not the luxury of the rich, is the true cause of misery. Educate the poor and they will not only desire to enrich themselves but will discover the means of doing so. Those who saw in luxury the cause of depopulation implied that there is a natural divergence between the interests of the rich and the poor. Malthus's reply denies the implication and asserts that education alone can put the labouring poor in the way of prosperity. The Poor Laws, he thought, merely aggravated the pauperism they were intended to alleviate. Popular education and savings banks, the encouragement of knowledge and of prudence, were his sovereign remedies.

Otherwise men might safely be left to themselves, without interference from their governments.

Initiative and prudence are, so Malthus thought, the most useful social virtues. But they are virtues that flourish only in a stable society, where men can make calculations about the future without fear that the assumptions on which these calculations rest will cease to hold good. He was a supporter of every institution that promotes social stability. Of these, the two most important, in his opinion, are marriage and private property. He believed that they both involve inequality, since property will not encourage initiative and prudence unless a man has the right to enjoy the fruits of his labour and to pass on to his children, after his death, the unconsumed part of them. But though Malthus taught that inequality is indispensable, he also said that it is the main interest of society to improve the lot of the labouring poor. It was their enrichment that would most rapidly increase the public happiness.

## 3. RICARDO

Adam Smith, who borrowed it from France, introduced the word distribution into English economic theory. But his main interest as an economist was not to discover how the produce of a nation is divided among the classes that make it up. What he most wanted to do was to describe the advantages of the division of labour, and the laws that determine prices. He was interested in wages, profits and rent as the three constituents of prices. It was Ricardo who, according to Professor Cannan, was the first English economist to declare that the main business of his science is to discover what determines the distribution of the nation's produce. Now, the laissez-faire economist who, in an adolescent capitalist society, pays most attention to prices and to the division of labour, can avoid too close an acquaintance with the facts most disturbing to his utilitarian faith. But as soon as his chief interest becomes the distribution of incomes his position is more difficult. Yet Ricardo remained true to the common doctrine that the uncontrolled is the best of all possible economies. But his description of it is depressing to read. Like Dr. Pangloss he reached the point where optimism and pessimism are scarcely to be distinguished. His most gloomy prophecies have turned out to be false.

Ricardo described an economy in which real wages tend to fall, profits are progressively reduced until capital accumulation ceases, and only the landlords prosper. There was information enough at hand to enable him to reach quite different conclusions, but he made his own choice and predicted economic stagnation. His great book, the *Principles of Political Economy and Taxation*, was published in 1817, after men had become familiar with Malthus's theories about population and the nature of rent. Ricardo made use of these theories to determine the shares of the national revenue going to landlords and labourers, so that what was left was profits. This method, apparently so convenient, has one great disadvantage. It suggests that the incomes of capitalists are residuary in some sense in which rents and wages are not. Whatever increases rents, or rents and wages together, will then appear to reduce profits. But the hire of capital is a price that enters into costs of production on much the same terms as the wages of labour and the rent of land. Ricardo treated the national revenue as if it were the gross income of a tradesman, who first pays his landlord and his employees and then keeps what is left.

According to Malthus and to Sir Edward West, who arrived simultaneously at more or less similar conclusions, rent is a sort of premium paid by the cultivators to the owners of the more fertile soils. It arises because fertile land is scarce and can produce more than enough to maintain those who cultivate it. When population increases, there is a greater demand for necessaries, land that is less fertile is brought into cultivation and the prices of necessaries rise. Costs of production on the more fertile lands remain the same, but it is the costs on the least fertile that determine prices. The result is that the rent of every piece of land, which is equal to the difference between costs of production on it and on the least fertile land under cultivation, must rise. This simple theory of rent was adopted uncritically by Ricardo. It is only true when three conditions hold good: when the greater demand for necessaries is met by bringing more land into cultivation, when the amount of labour and capital employed on a given quantity of land is not increased, and when there are no great technical improvements that increase productivity. Population might increase and its wants be satisfied by the improved cultivation of a smaller quantity of land; or if some less fertile land were brought into cultivation its crops, more efficiently raised, might be greater than were formerly grown on more fertile soils. Improved cultivation leads, no doubt, to increased rents. But this sort of increase, which is compatible with lower prices, higher real wages and higher profits, did not attract Ricardo. What he needed, to establish his theory, was an increase in rents, together with rising prices, stationary or even falling real wages and declining profits. Ricardo knew, as well as anyone, that great technical improvements had been made and that more were to be expected. He knew also that the amount of capital sunk into land was much greater than it had been and would, in all probability, still increase. He admitted that these factors must moderate the trends he described, but that they might more than offset them he would not acknowledge. And even this admission was an afterthought. Of the currents, whose flow and counterflow the economist must study, he chose to take special notice of some and to assume that they are stronger than the others.

Having decided that rents will rise because the cost of producing necessaries must do so, Ricardo found no difficulty in showing that money wages will also rise. Labour has, he thought, a natural price, which is the amount 'necessary to enable the labourers, one with another, to subsist and to perpetuate their race without increase or diminution.' This amount consists of a certain quantity of the necessaries of life, so that if the prices of those necessaries rise, the subsistence wage must rise with them. Now, since the increase in rents has already absorbed the increase in prices, this rise in wages must be at the expense of profits. As more and more land is brought into cultivation, money wages steadily rise until profits are so small that people no longer find it worth their while to save. At this point, economic progress ceases.

In the system of Ricardo, as in that of every other economist of his day, the ultimate cause of economic progress is the accumulation of capital. This accumulation increases the demand for labour, wages rise above the natural level, labourers marry earlier and produce larger families, and wages fall once again to the subsistence level. Ricardo admitted that the natural price of labour, the subsistence wage, is itself liable to change. But he believed that over long periods, whose length he would not estimate, it remains unchanged. A rise in the demand for labour increases its supply, just as a fall reduces it, so that the current rate of wages oscillates round the natural price of labour. Ricardo did not deny that the natural price of labour had increased over the centuries. Nor did he positively assert that it would increase no more. But he also spoke of a natural tendency for real wages to fall. How are we to reconcile these apparently contradictory statements? We can do so only in this way. We must suppose Ricardo to have meant that, whereas wages tend always to remain at the subsistence level, this tendency, in the earlier periods of economic progress, is more than offset by the accumulation of capital. The natural price of labour, the subsistence wage, just sufficient, according to prevailing notions, to satisfy essential needs, will rise very slowly. But in later periods, when land that is less and less fertile is brought into cultivation, capital accumulation, so far from making possible a slow rise in real wages, does not even suffice to prevent their fall. This fall, though it is resisted by the strong tendency of wages to remain at the subsistence level, is due to the much greater costs of production on less fertile land. In the progressive economy, as depicted by Ricardo, the three important factors are the accumulation of capital, the constant pressure of a growing population on the means of subsistence, and the ever more extensive cultivation of less fertile land. Each of these factors has its appropriate effect: the first tends to increase real wages and the demand for labour, the second to keep real wages at a constant level, and the third to increase money wages, while reducing their real value and causing a rapid fall in the rate of profit. In the early stages of capitalist accumulation, the first factor operates more strongly than the other two, but in the end it is the third that is strongest, and it eventually puts a stop to the economic progress caused by the first.

Ricardo could not say when the course of progress would come to an end. He could not even know that real wages had slowly begun to fall. He could say only that there was a beginning and an end, but the distance covered and that still remained to cover he could not estimate. The natural price of labour, the subsistence wage fixed by custom, might rise in the future as it had in the past, and it might, by the time capital accumulation ceased, have reached a point much higher than its present one. The terms laid down by Ricardo for mankind did not exclude these possibilities. But though he did not deny these things with his lips, pessimism was closer to his heart. To illustrate his arguments, he chose examples in which real wages are made to fall; and he preferred to be guided by his own examples than to look for statistics.[1] He did not even believe, as Malthus did, that education might teach the labouring poor to have smaller families and so relieve the pressure of population on subsistence.

Under the hand of Ricardo, the rock on which the classical economists built their system seems to crumble away. The impetus on which progress depends will, he thinks, eventually spend itself, and by the time it is spent, it will have done most for the idle, less for the industrious and least for the intelligent. Ricardo's capitalist is like the steward of an estate, who exerts himself to increase its produce only to find that his shiftless master takes an always greater share of it. He continues to exert himself in the hope that his reward, though a smaller part of the whole produce, may yet be larger than it was. But eventually he abandons even this hope and tries to increase his reward at the expense of his labourers, who stubbornly resist his efforts. In the end, knowing that greater exertion must enrich others at his expense, he does no more than is just sufficient to maintain the produce of the estate.

But though he believed that uncontrolled progress must end in stagnation, Ricardo remained true to the doctrine of laissez-faire. Though the pursuit of their selfish interests might bring fewer blessings to mankind than Mandeville and Adam Smith had hoped, it was still the truest wisdom to leave men to their own devices. Though the best is worse than we expected, it is the most that we can reasonably hope for. In this diminished sense, the natural harmony of interests still holds good. But whether, reduced to these proportions, it deserves so grand a name is another question.

We can easily imagine how attractive the wilful pessimism of Ricardo must have been to Marx. He also believed that the capitalist economy is progressive and that its progress must come to an end. But in the place of stagnation he put revolution, and he prophesied a final harmony of interests so perfect that governments would wither away. If he loaded Ricardo's picture with still darker colours, it was because he needed a greater contrast with the glory he reserved for mankind.

[1] As Professor Cannan has shown in his excellent book *Theories of Production and Distribution* (1776–1848).

I

# CHAPTER VIII

# JOHN STUART MILL

## 1. HIS IMPORTANCE

IF Hume was the greatest of the utilitarians, John Stuart Mill comes next after him. They had this in common, that neither owed a pure allegiance to the doctrine. Otherwise, the two men could hardly have been more different. Hume nearly always knew what he was about; he was as completely in control of his arguments as any philosopher, discussing the most difficult subjects, has ever been. But Mill was not, in this sense, a master. He was often bewildered by the intricacies of his own thought, unaware of the implications of what he had said and of what still remained to be proved. He could abandon a doctrine the most completely when he thought he was defending it with the greatest warmth. But he was much more than a philosopher who was often confused. He had a mind exceptionally hospitable to good ideas, whatever their source, and sometimes capable of inventing them.

John Stuart Mill was educated by his father, and the stories of his extraordinary intellectual achievements in early childhood have often been repeated. He was more thoroughly educated than it is good for any man to be, and his knowledge had so long a start of his understanding that the latter could never catch up with it. He was also physically weak and emotionally inhibited. He had neither the wilful energy of his father, nor the cool temperament of Bentham and Hume.

John Stuart Mill was born in 1806. In 1823, already more learned than most highly educated men, he was appointed a clerk in India House. Thirty-three years later, in 1856, he became Chief of the Office at a salary of £2,000 a year. But he was opposed to the direct rule of India by the English Crown and Parliament, and so in 1858, at the age of fifty-two and after thirty-five years spent in an office, he retired. He had still fifteen years to live, but his health was broken and he could no longer work as he once had done. His two largest books, his *Logic* and his *Political Economy*, had both been completed long before his retirement. Of the three essays, on which his reputation as a moral and political philosopher chiefly depends, only one, *Liberty*, was completed before his retirement, though his wife's death delayed its publication until 1859.

Sir Leslie Stephen, who liked robust talent, thought that Mill was something of a prig. But his autobiography does not create this impression, unless a man, whatever his modesty, who takes himself too seriously, is to be called a prig. Mill was an exceptionally good man, gentle, candid and generous. He was also tender and affectionate, and, unlike the other great utilitarians, contrived to fall deeply in love. The many virtues of a not very happy but truly modest man have touched the hearts of most people who have studied his writings, though others, more difficult to please, have found him unimaginative and unmasculine. Mill lacked gaiety and ease. He was too gentle to express contempt for other men and too solemn to laugh at them.

Mill's *Liberty* was published in 1859, his *Utilitarianism* and his *Considerations on Parliamentary Government* (now known as *Representative Government*) in 1861. These three essays, written by a sick man in his premature old age, exhibit all his defects as a thinker, his lack of clarity, his inconsistency and his inability either to accept wholeheartedly or to reject the principles inherited from his father and from Bentham. Mill's good qualities serve to accentuate his defects, for his candour causes him to admit one circumstance after another that cannot be reconciled with the assumptions he starts with. Perhaps the most defective of the three essays is *Utilitarianism*, in which Mill seems to lose control of his arguments at every turn. It is the product of an intelligent and honest but almost exhausted mind. The essay on *Liberty* is much better, though it is not exempt from the author's usual faults. *Representative Government*, less abstract than the other two essays, is therefore not liable to the same reproach, though it is, to the political philosopher, the least interesting of the three.

For all their defects, *Liberty* and *Utilitarianism* are important works. The very candour that obliges Mill to admit so much that is inconsistent with the principles handed down to him by his father and Bentham throws a strong light on the inadequacies of the utilitarian theory. Bentham and the elder Mill had elaborated a narrower and less plausible doctrine than Hume's; and its narrowness

was precisely what most recommended it to them. But what
had served to concentrate and direct their energies, left their heir
frustrated and dissatisfied. He felt the need to take into account
many things that his father could safely ignore because they meant
nothing to him. But the younger Mill did not know how to break
the bonds that held him; he did not even understand that it was
necessary to do so. If he was unable to turn a blind eye to facts
which experience and other men's books had brought to his notice,
he was equally incapable of framing new hypotheses to account for
them. In this, he was certainly unimaginative. And this was also
his great misfortune as a philosopher. He should have had a
narrower or else a more inventive mind. He could have had either
without coming any nearer to the truth than he did, but his reputation as a philosopher would have been more enviable. As it is, he
was less solid and less assured than his father, while he lacked the
powerful imagination that has enabled some philosophers, out of
the most varied materials, to build a great system, which, however
small its resemblance to the real world, yet appears coherent.


## 2. *Liberty*

Bentham, during the latter part of his life, like James Mill and
his utilitarian friends, had looked upon democracy as the certain
cure of all political evils. These evils, they thought, were the
effects of the activities of sinister interests, and democracy would
make these activities impossible. Hume had set mankind a problem
in political arithmetic: how can the interests of the governed be
equated with those of the governors? Bentham and James Mill
were convinced that they knew the answer, and they neither of
them lived long enough to discover their error. Bentham died in
1832, when Britain took her first timid step towards democracy;
and four years later James Mill, too, was dead. In those days,
democracy only existed in America, and no careful study of it
could yet be obtained in England. But by the time the younger
Mill wrote his *Liberty* much more was known about democracy,
and there were already men in Europe who were alive to its defects.
The first and ablest of foreign students of the United States, de
Tocqueville, had published his *Democracy in America* in 1835, but
it was not till several years later that his work was widely known in

England. Mill, when he read it, was soon convinced that some of the evils described in it were already in existence in his own country. He was too much of a realist to believe that democracy could be avoided, and he was too much his father's son to deplore its coming. His object, in *Liberty*, is to warn men of democracy's attendant evils and to show them how they can be diminished.

The rule of all, says Mill, is not the rule of each man by himself, but the rule of each by the others. The will of the people is the will of the majority; and this majority may desire to oppress. Precautions are as much needed against this form of oppression as against any other. Moreover, quite apart from the oppressions of governments, there is the tyranny of opinion, which is, perhaps, even more dangerous. 'Wherever there is an ascendant class, a large portion of the morality of the country emanates from its class interests, and its feelings of class superiority.'[1] This is no less true when the ascendant class is a majority.

Men, says Mill, are naturally intolerant whenever their feelings are strong. If we now have religious freedom, it is because we are less concerned with religion. Nor, according to Mill, are the English greater lovers of liberty than other peoples. They and their cousins in America are inheritors of the same traditional suspicion of governments; they are therefore more willing than other people to defend the individual against the encroachments of organized power. But the tyranny of opinion is perhaps stronger among them than elsewhere. This was also the belief of de Tocqueville and of Stendhal, but Mill was the first Englishman to doubt his fellow-countrymen's love of liberty.

Mill's object in this essay is, he tells us, to assert and defend the principle that 'the sole end for which mankind are warranted, individually or collectively, in interfering with the liberty of action of any of their number, is self-protection. That the only purpose for which power can be rightly exercised over any member of a civilised community, against his will, is to prevent harm to others. His own good, either physical or moral, is not a sufficient warrant.'[2] But Mill makes it clear that he regards this principle as quite compatible with his utilitarianism. 'It is proper to state,' he says, 'that I forego any advantage which could be derived to my argument from the idea of abstract right, as a thing independent of utility.'[3]

[1] *Liberty*, ch. i, ¶ 6.    [2] Ibid., ch. i, ¶ 9.    [3] Ibid., ch. i, ¶ 11.

Mill's position, therefore, as he states it in the first chapter of the essay, is this: In a civilized society, no sane adult is responsible to other persons for any part of his conduct that concerns only himself, for it is not in the real interest of society that he should be so responsible. This is Mill's position, as he originally states it; but it is not the position he defends in the remainder of his essay. Indeed, he gives us only one reason for believing that it is desirable, *on utilitarian grounds*, that men should not be answerable to society for what concerns only themselves. He says that interference with the individual for his own sake is likely, more often than not, to be ill-judged. This is to imply that when we try to prevent one man from harming another, we are more likely to succeed than when we try to prevent him from harming himself. Otherwise, Mill quietly assumes that the utilitarian grounds exist and he leaves the matter there. Though he has foregone any advantage to be derived from the idea of abstract right, he does not hesitate to put the burden of proof on whoever would deny his principle. What he is himself concerned to do is not to show that there are good utilitarian grounds for the non-interference he advocates, but to determine the limits of the interference which he regards as permissible. It is in this sense that Mill, in his *Liberty*, in untrue to his professed utilitarian principles. He leaves undone all those things that a utilitarian ought to do, but what he does is as well worth doing as anything he ever attempted.

In the second chapter of the essay, Mill deals with the liberty of thought and discussion. He assumes, in fact though not explicitly, that it is to the advantage of mankind that knowledge should increase among them and should be possessed by as many of them as possible. The notion that some beliefs, whether true or false, are salutary and for that reason ought to be protected, he utterly rejects. The opinion that they are salutary is, he says, as much open to doubt as any other. Mill's argument will easily convince anyone who accepts his initial tacit assumption, that it is, in the long run, to man's advantage to know the truth. But it will not convince anyone who makes the opposite assumption. If I believe very strongly that certain beliefs are salutary, I may be willing to admit not only that they are false but also that I may be wrong in believing they are salutary; but if my belief is strong, I shall think it right to act upon it, though I can still conceive of the possibility of my being mistaken.

Most of our actions are inspired by probable opinions; enforcements and suppressions of belief are actions like any others. If it is said that they alone of all actions are never justified, this is an assertion that is not self-evident but stands in as much need of proof as any other.

Mill is, I think, wrong when he says that 'all silencing of discussion is an assumption of infallibility'.[1] It may be true that men who often silence discussion come, in the end, to believe that they are always right. History and our experience both teach us that nothing persuades a man of his infallibility more effectively than the power, long exercised, of silencing others.

But this is not nearly enough to establish Mill's point. It does not prove that those who exercise the power only occasionally and under the guidance of a powerful tradition make any such assumption. A man may admit his fallibility and may yet, believing the matter to be of the utmost importance, enforce his own opinion and suppress that of others, having no other ground for his action than his belief that he is very probably right and that disaster will follow if another opinion prevails.

Mill thinks he has disposed of this objection when he says that 'there is the greatest difference between presuming an opinion to be true because, with every opportunity for contesting it, it has not been refuted, and assuming its truth for the purpose of not permitting its refutation'.[2] This is his answer to those who say, in the words he has himself put into their mouths, that 'there is no greater assumption of infallibility in forbidding the propagation of error, than in any other thing which is done by public authority on its own judgment and responsibility'.[3] Like most of us, when we speak for our opponents, Mill gains an easy victory. But he also misses the point. He makes his objectors say that even the most ordinary governmental action implies an assumption of infallibility. He then easily shows that it does not, and that to act on an opinion is not to assume it cannot be false. And finally he takes it for granted that ordinary governmental action differs, in this respect, from the suppression of opinion supposed to be pernicious. An objector, better advised than those imagined by Mill, might put his case differently. He might say: granted that many opinions are pernicious (since all actions, bad and good, proceed from opinions), it does not follow, because men are fallible and may

[1] Ibid., ch. ii, ¶ 3.     [2] Ibid., ch. ii, ¶ 6.     [3] Ibid., ch. ii, ¶ 5.

mistake good for evil, that they are entitled to prevent actions alone and never the opinions from which those actions proceed. There are, no doubt, a number of reasons which make it more expedient to control men's actions than their opinions. It is easier to control actions than opinions, and it is also easier to show that they have pernicious consequences. Moreover, a government can supply men with motives for not doing what their pernicious opinions might otherwise cause them to do. Economy is the true utilitarian explanation of why it is better to control men's actions than their beliefs. But it does not follow that governments ought never to control men's opinions, or that, if they try to do so, they claim to be infallible.

Whatever theoretical reservations we may wish to make, we are most of us, who have been educated in this country, inclined to believe that it is better, in almost every case, to leave men's opinions alone. We live in an exceptionally tolerant society, and most of us are practical sceptics. Many different opinions, most of which (though we know not which) we know must be false, have been presented to us for our inspection. Our beliefs do not greatly excite us and we are seldom inclined to act upon them in order to do other people good which they think evil. Should we, contemptuous of other people's opinions, seek to put our peculiar beliefs into practice, there exist, apart from the state, several benevolent institutions to protect even our children and domestic animals from the consequences. But this is not so in all human societies, and in them the liberal philosophy of John Stuart Mill seems less obviously true. Where opinions are many, unexciting and seldom acted upon in defiance of the hostility of the probable victims of such action, tolerance is a harmless virtue. But where opinions are few, exciting and acted upon regardless of the consequences, it is not always unwise (though it may be difficult) to keep errors and half-truths out of the minds of foolish enthusiasts.

If we happen to live in a civilized, tolerant and humane society, we can afford to assume, with Mill, that more will be lost than gained by the suppression of pernicious opinions. We can then admire the arguments with which he fortifies our favourite prejudices. He describes, better than any one has done before or since, the conditions that must exist in any society if knowledge is to grow inside it and to be shared by as many of its members as possible. We must tolerate error, says Mill, because our acquaintance with it will deepen and make more lively our knowledge of the truth. We must avoid even the mildest tyranny of opinion, because clever men, the discoverers of truth, are often timid and even a slight persecution will silence or make hypocrites of them. Should a few great thinkers dare to defy persecution, men of smaller abilities, even if they are brave, will not do so, for they have less independence of thought and cannot resist their environment. The truth on any great practical question is too large for any one mind to contain it, and the adjustment of partial truths to each other takes place, not in the isolation of single minds, but 'by the rough process of a struggle between combatants fighting under hostile banners'.[1] No doubt the struggle does not enlighten the combatants; 'but it is not,' says Mill, 'on the impassioned partisan, it is on the calmer and more disinterested bystander, that this collision of opinions works its salutary effect'.[2] It is in this second chapter, full of the most excellent liberal arguments, that Mill comes closest to the position taken up by Godwin in *Political Justice*. But Mill, unlike Godwin, advocates anarchy only in the realm of ideas.

It is in the third chapter of *Liberty*, in which he discusses 'individuality, as one of the elements of well-being', that Mill, without knowing it, abandons utilitarianism. In it he makes the un-utilitarian complaint 'that individual spontaneity is hardly recognized by the common modes of thinking as having any *intrinsic* worth, or deserving any regard on its own account'.[3] He then mentions with approval the doctrine of 'self-realization' preached by William von Humboldt. 'It really is of importance,' says Mill, 'not only what men do, but also what manner of men they are that do it.'[4] And he asks, 'what more or better can be said of any condition of human affairs than that it brings human beings themselves nearer to the best thing they can be?'[5] Nothing could be less utilitarian than the spirit of this question. It did not matter, in the least, to Bentham and James Mill what men are like, whether they are highly developed individuals or 'ape-like imitators', provided only that they are happy, that they have as much pleasure as possible and as little pain. The younger Mill does, as a matter of fact, undertake to show that the highly-developed individual is useful to society;

[1] Ibid., ch. ii, ¶ 36.   [2] Ibid., ch. ii, ¶ 39.   [3] Ibid., ch. iii, ¶ 2.
[4] Ibid., ch. iii, ¶ 4.   [5] Ibid., ch. iii, ¶ 10.

but he does so only for the benefit of people who, unlike himself, cannot see that such individuality justifies itself. He ends the chapter with a complaint. 'The greatness of England,' he says, 'is now all collective; individually small, we only appear capable of anything great by our habit of combining . . .'[1]

The last two chapters of the essay discuss the proper limits to the authority of society over the individual. It has often been objected against Mill, that his criterion is difficult to apply and does not leave much liberty to the individual. As he himself admits, since no one is completely isolated, almost any action is liable to harm or to benefit other people. A man can do nothing seriously harmful to himself, without injury to at least some other persons, whose welfare depends upon his being able to act in ways in which the harm he does himself prevents him from acting. But Mill is not much impressed by the admissions he has to make. It may well be true that we cannot say of any class of actions that they never injure other people, and that we cannot, therefore, say that people ought never to be prevented from doing them. But this in no way invalidates Mill's criterion, nor does it make it less easy to apply than any other. Few moral theories assert that actions of any given type are always right or always wrong; and Mill has as much right to be vague as any other moralist in a matter in which greater precision is not possible. As for the objection that Mill's criterion leaves almost no liberty to the individual, it is not well founded; for though any kind of action may sometimes injure other people nearly as much as or more than it injures the agent, it does not follow that the actions which injure them not at all, or so little as not to be worth regarding, are few. Indeed, we all know they are many, and that people love to interfere with what does not concern them. We may argue, then, that Mill's criterion is not strictly consistent with his utilitarian principles, but we cannot say that it is impossible to apply it or unimportant to do so.

Mill is, indeed, quite aware that the strict application of his criterion must deprive many people of powers they now possess, for it must curtail the authority of husbands over wives and of parents over children. Mill also explains that the case for laissez-faire in the economic sphere has nothing to do with his defence of individual liberty. His criterion does not exclude the most extreme

[1] Ibid., ch. iii, ¶ 16.

socialism, though it does, of course, exclude the sort of totalitarian government with which we are familiar to-day. At the end of his essay, Mill gives us three rules for the limitation of state interference, even in those spheres in which men's actions clearly affect other people as much as themselves—that is to say, in those spheres in which his liberal criterion does not exclude interference. No government should, he thinks, interfere with its subjects' actions, though they affect other people as much as themselves, whenever one or more of three conditions hold good: when the action is likely to be better done by private persons than by the government; when, though private persons usually do it less well than the officers of government, it is still desirable that they should do it as a means to their own education; and whenever there is a danger of adding unnecessarily to the government's power. By this last condition, Mill probably means to warn us against granting to governments powers, which they may need for useful purposes not otherwise to be achieved, but which will enable them to grow so strong that they can abuse their powers with impunity. Mill also warns us against the dangers of a powerful bureaucracy. These must, he thinks, always be great, however benevolent the bureaucrats. 'For the governors,' he says, 'are as much slaves of their organisation and discipline as the governed are of the governors.'[1] These are Mill's arguments in favour of private enterprise. He puts them shortly at the end of his essay, and it is a pity that he found no time to develop them. By temperament and by experience he was admirably suited to make the fine distinctions on which the reconciliation of liberty and efficient government must always depend.

When Mill wrote his essay on *Liberty*, democrats were ardent believers in democracy. They were full of confidence in themselves and in their final victory. Mill's essay is therefore a warning to enthusiasts. It assumes that democracy will come and that when it comes it will be strong. It is a plea to the powerful not to abuse their powers. It is addressed, as a work written in English must be, principally to the English-speaking peoples, a group of nations exceptionally vigorous, self-confident and politically experienced. It is precisely among them that democracy is to-day most firmly established, and it is to them that an essay, which warns men of the dangers *from* and not *to* democracy, is still the most useful. The

[1] Ibid., ch. v, ¶ 21.

English-speaking peoples do not now praise democracy as they did when it was a novelty, but they are not tempted to abandon it. Its ways are their ways, much more so to-day than when Mill was alive. If democracy is in danger among them, it is not so much from internal collapse as from foreign war. Mill's warnings still apply in a large part of the world inhabited by the richest and the strongest nations.

We are all busy, nowadays, describing the evils of bureaucracy, remembering, no doubt, how well we managed our lives before governments took so many of our cares upon them. We tell each other daily that we are not sufficiently alive to dangers about which we never stop talking. Perhaps it was because he knew his own people that Mill was content to say so little about bureaucracy. But his warnings against the tyranny of opinion are always necessary, though it may be that Englishmen and Americans need them less to-day than their ancestors did a hundred years ago. Mill was thinking of the respectable middle class to which he himself belonged, and of the America described by de Tocqueville and still dominated by rural Puritanism. The less censorious and better-humoured working classes have now a greater influence in this country, while both here and in America the towns, always more tolerant of novelty, set the fashions for the villages. The present danger in this country is not so much that those who have unpopular and valuable opinions will be ill-treated as that no one will take any notice of them. From the enormous variety of opinions, experiences and tastes collected for our benefit in free and easily accessible libraries, museums and galleries, we take refuge in the narrow circles of our intellectual friends, among whom a few familiar ideas and prejudices circulate.

In his essay on *Representative Government*, Mill again gives expression to his distrust of democracy. But he thinks that, whatever its defects, it is still the best form of government. He admits that it is unsuited to many peoples, since it requires greater abilities and greater self-control from all the members of the community than does any other form of government. It is only, he thinks, at a comparatively late stage in their development that a people become capable of representative government. But once they are capable of it, it is not only more suited to them than any other kind, it also makes them better men than they used to be. Mill returns again to the idea of self-improvement for its own sake, an idea that never fails to attract him though it is the negation of the utilitarian principles he professes. He thinks it the great merit of representative democracy, not that it makes men happier (though he believes it does so) but that it makes them more intelligent, more virtuous and more responsible than they would be without it. 'One of the benefits of freedom is,' he says, 'that under it the ruler cannot pass by the people's minds, and mend their affairs for them without amending them.'[1] 'Evil for evil,' he thinks, 'a good despotism in a country at all advanced in civilization, is more noxious than a bad one; for it is more relaxing and enervating to the thoughts, feelings and energies of the people.'[2]

Here again, because of what we know has happened since Mill's death, we must qualify his opinions. He had not our means of knowing how bad a bad despotism can be. Though it may not relax men's minds, it corrupts and debases them. It puts fear and reckless enthusiasm in the place of all the social affections that hold a community together; and when that fear and enthusiasm are gone, there is nothing left. In their secret hearts, men are ashamed of being treated like dumb animals, to be praised, threatened or whipped whenever it suits their masters. When this shame is intolerable and they dare not protest, they are diminished in their own eyes and the injury done to them is the greatest that governments can do to men. An evil despotism destroys man's self-respect as a good one can never do. But when Mill talked of a bad despotism, he had nothing worse in mind than some of the small German and Italian states and Imperial Russia. They were bad enough, but their power to compel and to humiliate was small indeed compared with what more recent governments have possessed.

Though Mill praises representative government because it educates the governed, he does not ignore the arguments which had appeared convincing to his father and to Bentham. He also believes that the rights and interests of every man are, in most cases, best defended by himself, and that therefore every man ought to have some influence with the government on whose actions his welfare largely depends. The more free and active each citizen, the more prosperous the state. The radical utilitarian doctrine, that freedom is the means to prosperity, and prosperity the means to

---

[1] *Representative Government*, ch. iii, ¶ 6.     [2] Ibid., ch. iii, ¶ 7.

happiness, is never neglected by the younger Mill. But it is only one half of his argument for representative democracy.

*Representative Government* is a much longer essay than *Liberty*, and it is full of good arguments. But to the political philosopher it is the less interesting of the two. It raises fewer theoretical problems, and, with the exception of a few chapters, it is a treatise on political institutions. But *Liberty* is incomparably the best and the most eloquent of all Mill's works. Among modern writers, only Machiavelli, Hobbes and Rousseau have dealt with a political subject in a way that makes a more powerful and immediate impression on the reader's mind.

### 3. *Utilitarianism*

Mill wrote this essay to defend his father and Bentham from the attacks made upon them. His defence is not a good one. He was too much impressed by the attack to know how to meet it. With so many concessions made to the enemy, what should have been a defence reads like an apology. Mill was in the difficult position of a man whose loyalty is stronger than his faith, who cannot be blind and yet dare not see too much. Such people do not construct the most impressive philosophical systems, nor do they strike the hardest blows, but when they have the intelligence and honesty of Mill, their predicament is always instructive.

Mill begins his essay by distinguishing between what he calls the 'intuitionist' and 'inductive' schools of morals. His own opinion, he says, is that questions of ultimate ends are not amenable to direct proof. Whatever can be proved to be good, must be so by being shown to be a means to something admitted to be good without proof. He then goes on to say that he has no intention of adopting the view of the intuitionists, that the principles of morals are self-evident. Though direct proof is impossible, 'considerations may be presented capable of determining the intellect either to give or to withhold its assent to the doctrine; and this is equivalent to proof'.[1]

What exactly does Mill mean? If he believes, as he appears to do, that the greatest happiness principle is not self-evident, he has, as a philosopher, no alternative except to offer his readers evidence

[1] *Utilitarianism*, ch. 1, ¶ 5.

of its truth. And this is, in fact, precisely what he does try to do. The whole of his essay is devoted to the task; and therefore all its arguments rest upon the assumption that questions of ultimate ends are amenable to proof. Hume certainly thought they were; and there is nothing incompatible with this belief in his dictum that 'Reason is and ought to be the slave of the passions'. But Mill is guilty of a confusion. If you say that an end is ultimate, you merely say it is desired for its own sake and not as a means to something else. But the question of whether or not it is so desired is as much amenable to disproof or proof as any other matter of fact. All that Hume meant by his dictum, is that reason cannot tell us what we ought to desire for its own sake. But if we wish to discover what men do so desire, we must observe their behaviour; and if any one denies our conclusions, we must then point to the evidence. Though reason does not prescribe ultimate ends, it enables us to discover what they are. Whoever accepts the view that morals is an experimental science must believe at least two things: that the statement that men ought to desire something for its own sake is, when fully analysed, merely a statement about their desires and feelings; and that questions of ultimate ends are therefore always amenable to proof. Hume does sometimes use language that suggests he does not hold the second of these beliefs, but this is only his careless manner of expressing himself. He is, in fact, quite aware of what is implied by his attempt to introduce the experimental method into morals. But John Stuart Mill, making a similar attempt, is not so well aware of what he is doing. Hence his curious statement that something cannot be proved, though considerations equivalent to proof can be brought to induce men to accept it.

Mill admits that some pleasures are higher than others. He tells us that if one of two pleasures is, 'by those who are completely acquainted with both, placed so far above the other that they prefer it, even though knowing it to be attended with a greater amount of discontent, and would not resign it for any quantity of the other pleasure which their nature is capable of, we are justified in ascribing to the preferred enjoyment a superiority in quality, so far outweighing quantity, as to render it, in comparison, of small account'.[1] Mill's words suggest that the superiority is in the thing preferred and does not merely consist in its being preferred.

[1] Ibid., ch. ii, ¶ 5.

An argument very like Mill's is used by Socrates in the ninth book of the *Republic*. He there distinguishes between three classes of men: lovers of wisdom, lovers of honour and lovers of gain. Each class, when asked which sort of life is the pleasantest, will praise their own and prefer it to the others. How, then, is the question to be decided between them? What criterion can be used in such a case? No other, according to Socrates, than experience. The lover of wisdom has, he thinks, the greatest experience of all the pleasures that are in question. He has tasted them all, while the lovers of honour and of gain know nothing of the pleasures to be derived from the pursuit of knowledge. He has taken the measure of their lives, while they know nothing of his. He alone is competent to judge; and his verdict is final.

Such an argument may convince when we are trying to discover which of three engines is best suited to our purpose. It is an argument we can use, when we have no better one, to help us choose the most efficient of several alternative means to the same end. But used as Socrates and Mill use it, it carries no conviction at all. No man has ever known the pleasures experienced by another; he can only say that, among his own, he prefers some to the rest. If Socrates preferred philosophy to sensuality and praise, it was because he was the sort of man that nature made him. His love of wisdom and his passion for exposing pretentious ignorance caused him to attach the highest value to pleasures that to other men may appear insipid. We most of us derive our greatest happiness from doing what we can do best. But there are men who can rise superior to the prejudices created by pride in their own talents. Montaigne was as full of curiosity as any man and as convinced as Socrates of his own ignorance, but he did not therefore suppose that his favourite pleasures were the supreme good. He even thought it unworthy of a man of honour that he should be at pains to get the better of an argument.

To justify his preference for the verdict of 'those most competent to judge', Mill says that comparisons between qualities of pleasure are not different in principle from comparisons between quantities. He says 'there is no other tribunal to be referred to even on the question of quantity. What means are there of determining which is the acutest of two pains, or the intensest of two pleasurable sensations, except the general suffrage of those who are familiar with both? Neither pains nor pleasures are homogeneous, and pain is always heterogeneous with pleasure.'[1] This argument does not establish the point that Mill wishes to make. The fact that people prefer some pleasures to others is no evidence that those they prefer are either superior in quality or greater than the others, unless it is first assumed that people normally prefer what is superior or greater to what is inferior or less. But though the argument does not serve Mill's purpose, it does what he never intended; for it cuts away the foundations of the Benthamite felicific calculus. If pleasures and pains are not homogeneous, then the calculation and comparison of their quantities is in principle impossible; all that we can calculate is the frequency and order of men's preferences. So that, already by the tenth page of an essay written in its defence, Mill has made two wide breaches in his father's and Bentham's system. He has asserted that some pleasures are qualitatively superior to others, and he has implied that the felicific calculus is impossible.

It has been said that, when Mill admits that some pleasures are higher than others, he is untrue to his own doctrine that nothing is good but pleasure. For if one pleasure is higher than another, that in respect of which it is higher is not pleasure but some other thing, which must therefore be admitted to be good. This simple argument is, perhaps, not as conclusive as it looks. If a man were to say that nothing is beautiful except colour and then to place the colours in an order of beauty, it would not follow that he was admitting that anything but colour could be beautiful. The difference between one colour and another is not a difference of degree, nor yet is it a difference in respect of anything except colour. So, too, the higher and the lower pleasures, though different in kind, may yet differ only in respect of pleasure. If this were so, it might then be true both that nothing is good but pleasure and that some kinds of pleasure are superior to others, though neither more intense nor of longer duration. There is, perhaps, no reason for supposing any such thing; but if Mill chooses to take up this position, better arguments than those used hitherto must be found to dislodge him from it.

Mill's theory of pleasure is his theory about the ultimate end of human action. This end is, he thinks, a life 'exempt as far as

[1] Ibid., ch. ii, ¶ 8.

K

possible from pain, and as rich as possible in enjoyments, both in point of quantity and quality.' It is also the standard of morality, for morality consists of those rules of conduct whose general observance will secure, as far as possible, this sort of life to all mankind. 'In the golden rule of Jesus of Nazareth,' says Mill, 'we read the complete spirit of the ethics of utility. To do as you would be done by, and to love your neighbour as yourself, constitute the ideal perfection of utilitarian morality.'[1] This is not the sort of language that would come naturally to the lips of Bentham or James Mill. But it is typical of their greatest disciple. *Do as you would be done by* is a prudential maxim, whose ablest English exponent is Thomas Hobbes. *Love your neighbour as yourself* is a rule of a quite different order, though its observance may have much the same visible effects. No one better than the younger Mill could feel the essential difference between the two rules. If he puts them together, it is to lend nobility to the utilitarian doctrine, and not to prove that Christianity is sensible.

Having explained the nature of the good life, Mill then goes on to define moral obligation. It is, he says, the internal sanction of duty, and he carefully distinguishes it from the external sanction, which is no more than the hope of favour and the fear of displeasure from our fellow-men or from God. The internal sanction of duty is, he says, 'a feeling of our own mind, a pain more or less intense, attendant on violation of duty'.[2] Now this feeling is 'all encrusted over with collateral associations, derived from sympathy, from love, and still more from fear; from all the forms of religious feeling, from the recollections of childhood and of all our past life; from self-esteem, desire of the esteem of others, and occasionally even self-abasement'.[3] It is this extreme complexity, according to Mill, that leads men to attribute a mystical character to moral obligation, whose binding force consists in 'a mass of feeling which must be broken through in order to do what violates our standard of right'.[4]

What Mill is describing is not the rightness of an action, but the peculiar emotion men often feel when they are considering how they should act. The right action, for the younger Mill as for his father and Bentham, is the one which the prospective agent believes will lead to the happiest consequences. It is not in his account

[1] Ibid., ch. ii, ¶ 18.   [2] Ibid., ch. iii, ¶ 4.   [3] Ibid., ch. iii, ¶ 4.
[4] Ibid., ch. iii, ¶ 4.

of right action but of the feeling of moral obligation that Mill parts company with his father and Bentham. The external sanctions of duty, to which both the elder utilitarians devote so much attention, are described in a few words, and it is on the internal sanction that the younger Mill lavishes his descriptive powers. He says not one word to suggest that the feeling of moral obligation is merely the indissoluble product of past associations of men's selfish desires and expectations. Sympathy, love and the religious emotions, as well as fear, memory and self-esteem, are the joint creators of this rich and powerful emotion, to which men have attributed a mystical character. So different is his emotional experience from his father's that he even finds room in his analysis for self-abasement. Whatever the true account of the matter, his description is certainly more plausible than either Bentham's or the elder Mill's. More seriously even than its author, he took Hume's excellent advice, that in moral philosophy over-simplification is the great danger. It is when, without knowing it, he moves furthest from Bentham and his father, without feeling the need to excuse either himself or them, that the younger Mill is at his best.

So far, so good. But Mill still has to explain how it is that we come to feel morally obliged to behave in accordance with the greatest happiness principle. He admits that the conscience can be educated in almost any direction. There is almost nothing that we cannot be taught to be ashamed of or to feel morally obliged to do. But he thinks that there is nevertheless a natural tendency in the human mind to associate the feeling of moral obligation with actions that normally produce the greatest happiness. Associations of it with other principles are wholly of 'artificial' creation, and they yield, by degrees, to the dissolving force of intellectual analysis. On the other hand, there is a 'powerful natural sentiment' which reinforces the attachment of the feeling of moral obligation with the utilitarian principle. This powerful sentiment is the desire to be 'in unity' with our fellow-creatures; in other words, it is the social instinct. Mill, however, does not explain how it is that the social instinct attaches the feeling of moral obligation to the utilitarian principle. He just assumes that it must be so, that the point is too obvious to be worth discussing. But it appears obvious only to those who accept the utilitarian philosophy. Mere observers of human behaviour are not so easly convinced. There are, for instance, many sociologists who would agree that the social instinct, whatever it is, attaches the moral sentiments to certain rules of conduct 'useful' to the society in question; but there are few of them who would define 'useful' as 'conducive to the greatest happiness'.

So far, except for some ambiguities and a few plausible arguments of his own, the younger Mill's moral system is closer to Hume's than to his father's and Bentham's. The one concession he has made to the Benthamite form of utilitarianism is his statement 'that actions are right in proportion as they tend to promote happiness, wrong as they tend to produce the reverse of happiness'.[1] But in the fourth chapter of the essay, he abandons Hume and produces arguments whose weakness would have been noticed by no one more quickly than by the great Scottish philosopher. Mill wishes to prove that happiness is desirable, and he says: 'The only proof capable of being given that an object is visible, is that people actually see it . . . In like manner, I apprehend, the sole evidence it is possible to produce that anything is desirable is that people actually do desire it . . . No reason can be given why the general happiness is desirable, except that each person, so far as he believes it to be attainable, desires his own happiness. This, however, being a fact, we have not only all the proof which the case admits of, but all which it is possible to require, that happiness is good: that each person's happiness is a good to that person, and the general happiness, therefore, a good to the aggregate of all persons.'[2]

The passage just quoted has often been attacked. Nobody but Mill ever supposed that *desirable* stands to *desired* as *visible* to *seen*. Visible means 'capable of being seen' and desirable 'worthy of being desired', so that while a thing's being seen proves it is visible, its being desired is no evidence that it is desirable. And it is equally clear that there is no argument from each person's happiness being his good to the general happiness as the good of all.

Mill's next object is to prove that nothing but happiness is desirable. He begins by admitting that many things besides happiness are in fact desired. Why, then, are they not desirable? Is it because they are no more than means to happiness, which alone is desired for its own sake? No such simple solution will satisfy Mill. 'Utilitarian moralists', he tells us, ' . . . not only place virtue at the very head of the things which are good as means to the ultimate

---

[1] Ibid., ch. ii, ¶ 2.                    [2] Ibid., ch. iv, ¶ 3.

end, but they also recognize as a psychological fact the possibility of its being, to the individual, a good in itself, without looking to any end beyond it; and hold that the mind is not in a right state, not in a state conformable to Utility, not in the state most conducive to the general happiness, unless it does love virtue in this manner . . '[1] Once virtue is loved in this way, it becomes a part of man's happiness. How this can be is explained by Mill a few pages later on, when he says: 'I believe that . . . desiring a thing and finding it pleasant, aversion to it and thinking of it as painful, are phenomena entirely inseparable, or rather two aspects of the same phenomenon; in strictness of language, two different modes of naming the same fact; that to think of a thing as desirable (unless for the sake of its consequences), and to think of it as pleasant, are one and the same thing; and that to desire anything, except in proportion as the idea of it is pleasant, is a physical and metaphysical impossibility.'[2] The gist of this argument seems to be: nothing is desired for its own sake except happiness. Some things, like virtue, which were originally desired because they are a means to happiness, are now often desired for their own sake. But to desire a thing for its own sake is to find it pleasant. Therefore virtue, once merely a means to happiness, is now also a constituent of it; and it is a means all the more efficient because it is also a part of the end. This argument depends upon a simple confusion to which both Butler and Hume had pointed in their refutations of Hobbesian egoism. It may be true that, whenever we desire something, we take pleasure at the thought of obtaining it; but we have this pleasure before we obtain what we desire. This pleasure is, strictly speaking, the companion and not the object of desire. But apart from this pleasure, there need be no other in question. To take pleasure at the thought of being virtuous is not the same thing as to desire virtue because it is pleasant. Mill, failing to make this distinction, found it possible to assert that to desire something is to think of it as pleasant. This assertion is false; but even if it were true, Mill's argument would be none the better. For, if to desire something is to find it pleasant, to desire virtue is still not to desire pleasure. To desire virtue is, then, to find virtue pleasant, but to desire pleasure is to find pleasure (and not virtue) pleasant, so that virtue is no nearer to becoming

[1] Ibid., ch. iv, ¶ 5.       [2] Ibid., ch. iv, ¶ 10.

a constituent of happiness. No juggling with words and no false psychology can effect a reconciliation in such a case.

In the last and fifth chapter of the essay, Mill discusses the connexion between justice and morality. This chapter is, perhaps, the best of the five. Taking etymology for his guide, Mill supposes that the primitive notion of justice (for instance, among the Jews of the Old Testament) was simply conformity to law. The distinction between morality and legality, the notion of an 'unjust law', belongs to a more developed society. It is only to be found among the Greeks and the Romans at a fairly advanced stage in their development. But though the distinction between law and morality is nowadays clear, the connexion between the two is still close. 'It is a part of the notion of Duty in every one of its forms,' says Mill, 'that a person may rightly be compelled to fulfil it. Duty is a thing which may be exacted from a person, as one exacts a debt.'[1]

Mill distinguishes between justice, in the narrow sense, which is merely doing what the law enjoins, and justice, in the larger sense, which is doing all one's duties to assignable persons, that is, to all persons who have a right to expect us to act in any particular way. He also talks of general duties that imply no rights in assignable persons. He offers as an example our duty to be charitable though no person may have a right to assistance from us. These general duties fall outside the sphere of justice, for the 'two essential ingredients in the sentiment of justice are', says Mill, 'the desire to punish a person who has done harm, and the knowledge or belief that there is some definite individual or individuals to whom harm has been done.'[2] 'The sentiment of justice . . . is . . . the natural feeling of retaliation or vengeance, rendered by intellect and sympathy applicable to those injuries . . . which wound us through, or in common with, society at large. This sentiment, in itself, has nothing moral in it; what is moral is the exclusive subordination of it to the social sympathies . . . For the natural feeling would make us resent indiscriminately whatever anyone does that is disagreeable to us; but when moralised by the social feeling, it only acts in the directions conformable to the general good.'[3]

There is a certain resemblance between Hume's account of the psychological origins of justice and this theory of Mill's. But Mill's real debt is not to Hume but to Alexander Bain, to his book

---

[1] Ibid., ch. v, ¶ 14.    [2] Ibid., ch. v, ¶ 17.    [3] Ibid., ch. v, ¶ 21.

on the *Mind* and to the chapter in it entitled 'The Ethical Emotions or the Moral Sense'. Although Mill, like Hume, assigns an important role to sympathy, he does so at an earlier stage in the process. Hume had said that no emotion is strong enough to control man's self-love and to make him just. If self-love is to be controlled, it must turn upon itself and set limits to its own action. This it does, whenever a man takes a little thought and understands that his strongest passion is better satisfied by its restraint than its liberty. Self-love is the original motive that brought justice into existence, and sympathy is needed only to explain how it became a virtue. It is sympathy with the public interest that makes us approve the practice of justice, and it is this approval that makes it a virtue.

Mill's account puts a much greater burden on sympathy. Justice, for him, is not an unnatural thing, begotten by reflexion out of self-love, and later crowned a virtue by sympathy. Justice owes to sympathy its existence and not only its moral dignity. It is the natural feeling of vengeance applied, not by intellect alone but by sympathy as well, to the injuries done to any man. It is in this way that Mill associates our selfish and our unselfish feelings in the generation of justice, for what intellect does, among other things, is to teach us that by defending others we defend ourselves. Justice is the product of two sentiments, each as natural as the other: the instinct of self-preservation and the feeling of sympathy. The part of intellect, which is Mill's name for what Hume calls reflexion, is, we must suppose, to enlighten both these sentiments. Mill, even at his best, is not free from ambiguity, but if this is his meaning, he is probably nearer the truth than is Hume.

Mill's final purpose is to explain the difference between our emotional reactions to the unjust and the inexpedient; for, on strict utilitarian premises, the former can be only a special case of the latter. He says that certain kinds of conduct are much more generally useful than others. They form, as he puts it, the 'very groundwork' of our existence in society. Our desire to safeguard this groundwork gathers around it feelings so much more intense than those to which we are liable on less important occasions, that 'the difference of degree . . . becomes a real difference in kind'.[1] Hence the need we feel, to make an absolute distinction between what is

[1] Ibid., ch. v, ¶ 25.

right or wrong, on the one hand, and what is expedient or inexpedient, on the other.

There is not much left of Benthamite utilitarianism when John Stuart Mill has completed his defence of it. What is left is, strictly speaking, not utilitarianism at all, but a kind of naturalistic ethics that it would be misleading to call a variety of hedonism. Yet in Mill's strange concoction there still are to be found remnants of the parental creed, floating on the surface, separate from one another, solid and insoluble. But for all its faults, Mill's essay, in which he continually turns away from what he professes to describe, is still worth the closest study; not only because it enables the student to exercise the destructive faculties indispensable to the philosopher, but also because it contains much that is plausible and suggestive. There is little to be gained by unravelling the tangled threads of Bentham's fundamental arguments. But the case with Mill is different; the study of his confusions and errors is nearly always profitable.

# CHAPTER IX

## THE UTILITARIANS

THE utilitarian doctrine, established by Hume on foundations laid by Hobbes, is the greatest English contribution to moral and political philosophy. If it is no longer thought adequate as an explanation of men's moral and political behaviour, this is certainly not because any other philosophy has taken its place. Utilitarianism is destroyed and no part of it left standing. But it has not had a successor. There is to-day in England no one system that enjoys anything like the predominance once enjoyed in intellectual circles[1] by utilitarianism. A number of theories, mostly of continental origin, are cherished by small groups of Englishmen, but none of them deserves to be called predominant. We are all democrats, perhaps, and it may be that we are also, in some senses of that word, all socialists. But democracy and socialism, as they are talked of in contemporary England, are not political and moral philosophies; the principles from which they can be (and are) derived are too many and too different from one another. We have to-day no distinguishable group of English philosophers, all preaching more or less the same doctrine and providing the intellectuals with most of their commonplaces when they discuss morals and politics. But the utilitarians were once in England what the Marxists were for a few decades in Germany, the social and political thinkers whose ideas had the widest currency though they were also the most vigorously attacked. The utilitarians were the doctrinaires of England, no less native to the country of their origin than the German Marxists.

I have already, in discussing the theories of the more important utilitarians, criticized the assumptions on which they rest. Hedonism in general, and utilitarianism as an instance of it, are doctrines that have been often attacked. Most of the traditional arguments, as well as others discovered by himself, have been clearly

[1] I believe that, in using this phrase, I deceive no one. By that time there were already intellectuals in the world. Clever men had already discovered that the difference between themselves and the rest of mankind was much greater than Galileo, Descartes and Newton supposed.

stated by Professor Moore in his book *Principia Ethica*. Not all
Professor Moore's arguments are equally convincing, the effective-
ness of several depending upon the assumption that his interpretation of the doctrine he is attacking is the correct one. For instance,
he proves that egoism, a doctrine to which not only Hobbes but
also several of the utilitarians adhered, is self-contradictory. Yet
it is self-contradictory only if goodness is some such quality as
Professor Moore thinks it is. In that case, it is absurd to say that
anything is good for only one man and not for all other men as
well. If Professor Moore's account of goodness is the true one,
nothing can be good for any particular man any more than it can
be round or red only for him. And this, of course, must be so,
even if the good thing in question should be the state of his own
mind. But if good is defined as Hobbes defined it, as whatever is
the object of desire, there obviously can be private goods, in the
only sense required to save Hobbes's theory from self-contradiction.
Again, in his argument against John Stuart Mill's assertion that,
though only pleasure is good, some pleasures are superior to others,
Professor Moore says: 'If you say, as Mill does, that the quality of
pleasure is to be taken into account, then you are no longer holding
that pleasure *alone* is good as an end, since you imply that something
else, something which is *not* in all pleasures, is also good as an end.'[1]
He illustrates the point he wishes to make by substituting the notion
of colour for pleasure. If we suppose that colour alone is good, we
can, according to Professor Moore, have no reason for preferring
one colour to another. But this is true only if we suppose that it is
abstract colour alone that is good. There is, however, no reason
for believing that the natural interpretation of the statement,
'colour alone is good', is the one put upon it by Professor Moore.
It might more naturally be taken to mean that there is nothing good
about anything except its colour; and this interpretation does not
exclude the possibility that some colours should be better than others.
This is true whatever *good* may mean, provided only that it does not
mean *pleasant*. Now, since Mill defined goodness in terms of desire
and said that to desire a thing is to find it pleasant, it is clear that he
did consider goodness the same thing as pleasure. But that is not
the point Professor Moore makes against him. He argues that,
whatever good may mean, to say that only colour is good is to

[1] *Principia Ethica*, p. 80.

imply that no colour can be better than another. If it can be proved that Mill, already committed to definite views about both goodness and pleasure, ought not to have said that one sort of pleasure is better than another, the proof must be different from Professor Moore's. For his proof implies what is false: that the statements 'only pleasure is good' and 'some pleasures are better than others' are incompatible. But though Professor Moore places to his own credit some unnecessary dialectical victories, most of the arguments in *Principia Ethica* are, I think, convincing. And if that is so, then utilitarianism, however qualified to make it look more plausible, is an untenable theory.

The utilitarians have been called rationalists, even by the people who have most successfully pulled their arguments to pieces. The compliment is deserved, and the collapse of their system does not seriously detract from its value. What reason has set up, reason can best destroy. Everyone who seeks to convince by argument has a common ground with the utilitarians. But everyone who seeks to convince by argument also necessarily exposes a large surface to hostile attack. He tries to make his meaning clear; and because clarity is more easily attained than truth, he must expect to be the sooner corrected the more readily he is understood. The utilitarians were more listened to than revered. This did at least mean that their reputations never stood in the way of truth. But in more recent times, in political and moral philosophy, more particularly since Hegel and Marx, the rule has been: tout comprendre, c'est ne rien pardonner.

It is interesting that the utilitarians, the most English of all schools of political and moral philosophers, should have been such unrelenting rationalists, deriving so much from so few and such simple assumptions. For the defect of which the English are most proud is that they are not logical. They say they do not like consistency, or even the appearance of it, when it is only to be had at the expense of truth. And this, as experience teaches us, is the price usually paid for it. Better a muddle that touches reality at many points than a coherent system which, if it touches it at some, must, owing to its rigidity, miss it at all the others. Better a variety of practical rules, none of them too clearly expressed and not necessarily compatible with one another, than an apparently well-constructed doctrine which has, among other disadvantages, this one, that it makes it easier for other people to prove that we have not lived up to our own principles. The Anglo-Saxon ideal is supposed to be something like the philosophy of the American Supreme Court, which has at its disposal any number of unrelated precedents enabling it to interpret a reticent constitution in whatever way it thinks best. But in moral and political philosophy, the English have had as steady a preference for logic and simplicity as any other European people. Indeed, if the student of politics and morals wishes to escape for a little from implacable logic and the most self-confident simplicity, he must turn away from the English, whether utilitarians or contractualists, and seek refuge in the more muddled, emotional and extravagant writings of Frenchmen and Germans. It is from Rousseau, Kant, Saint-Simon and Marx, seldom lucid and sometimes mere purveyors of nonsense,[1] that he can learn many things that are true, though badly expressed, and that escaped the notice of the high-and-dry intellectual utilitarians.

Though his own views may fail to convince, Kant has shown that the simple psychology of the eighteenth-century moralists does not explain the facts. The desire for pleasure, prudence and egoism, even if sympathy is added to them, are not the stuff of which to make a plausible theory of morals. Whatever men may be doing when they are acting morally, they are not seeking pleasure, nor are they being selfish, prudent or sympathetic. Morality curbs egoism, is often indifferent to pleasure and usually overrides prudence. These are the undeniable facts vouched for by our daily experience. That society could not hold together without morality is also a fact, but it does not follow that morality is a kind of social insurance, in which each individual finds his account. To treat the moral laws prevailing in any society as if their function must be to create a harmony between otherwise divergent interests, is a serious fault of method. It implies an assumption that the true answer to the problem investigated by the moral philosopher must be of a certain kind, but the utilitarians had no good reason for making this assumption. Many of them made no serious attempt to answer the questions they pretended to ask, such as: what is morality? and, what is the State? They did not analyse the moral

---

[1] I use this word in the technical and inoffensive sense habitual among philosophers. There is, of course, nonsense and nonsense, some of it a credit to the heart and even the head of its author. Though the truth should lie far removed from both their systems, there will always be a world of difference between Kant and Hegel.

behaviour of men in the attempt to discover what it is they are doing when they behave morally. Nor did they study their political behaviour or the institutions maintained by and determining that behaviour. What they did was to attempt answers to quite other questions of which the most important was: under what circumstances will each man's efforts to be as happy as possible promote the greatest happiness of all men? They did not distinguish, as they ought to have done, between the analysis of social phenomena and the solution of practical problems; and they were too much inclined to believe that to attempt the latter was to achieve the former. The utilitarians who came closest to making a genuine attempt to answer, not only questions about how what they thought desirable could be achieved, but also others that belong more properly to moral and political philosophy were Hume and John Stuart Mill. They did not, like Bentham, confuse the analysis of moral and political phenomena with the solution of practical problems. But in their case, too, the careless attempt to find compatible answers to quite dissimilar questions led to false assumptions or to serious distortions of truth.

In the sphere of ethics, Hume took notice of two questions: what are the characteristics of moral and immoral actions? and, what is the function of morality? He gave a separate answer to each, understanding what Bentham and James Mill never seem to have done, that one would not do for both. His answer to the first was his description of the moral sentiments and their operation; his answer to the second, the bare statement that these sentiments are so directed that they induce men to do what will increase happiness, and abstain from what will diminish it. But for the truth of this statement, the greatest of experimental philosophers never troubled to produce one shred of evidence. So little was he aware of the difficulty confronting him, that he thought it enough to appeal to the common sense of mankind. The younger Mill, when it suited him, also made assumptions equally convenient and unsupported. He did not like that men should interfere with each other except to prevent harm to others. But, though he was a utilitarian, he never troubled to show that this non-interference would promote happiness. He also believed in 'self-realization'. But he never explained to his readers how he conceived this 'self-realization'. Did he mean by it whatever a man would become if other men interfered with him as little as possible? This is the only meaning of the word which makes it obvious that liberty, as Mill defined it, is the condition of 'self-realization'. If, for instance, 'self-realization' is taken to mean 'as good or valuable a life as the individual is capable of living', it is no longer obvious that the liberty described by Mill is what makes it possible. Plato also believed in 'self-realization', and in the *Laws* he advocated a secret police. And what is the connexion between 'self-realization' and 'happiness'? Mill did not even ask this question. He did not do what, as a utilitarian, he should have done. However subtle or shrewd a philosopher may otherwise be, there is always a simplicity that shapes his thoughts and prevents him from asking questions inconvenient to his own theories.

The utilitarians, even those who most often claimed to be experimental philosophers, were all dogmatists. They supposed, when they gave the matter a thought, that the principles from which they started were generalizations from experience. But in fact they were nothing of the kind. The truth is that only one of them, Hume, knew what was implied by the claim to have introduced the 'experimental method' into morals. He described the method well enough, but, as we have seen, he never used it. As he was a man of the world and an historian, his assumptions were more plausible than those of Bentham and the elder Mill. But they were not scientifically tested. What could better show how little Hume understood the difficulties of his task than his belief that one man could accomplish it? He never thought it necessary to warn his readers that his own theory was the product of one man's experience, and that no one had yet made a real study of the facts that theory was supposed to explain. His assumptions are of the kind that intelligent and experienced men might think plausible as they discussed them of an evening over their port. They sound sensible, but there is no real evidence that they are true.

In the political field, the great error of the utilitarians was their individualism. By this I do not mean their belief that nothing is desirable except the happiness of individuals. For that is a judgment of value as much entitled to respect as any other. I mean only their assumption that the general structure of society can be adequately explained in terms of men's desires and purposes. Society, government and morality are not means to individual ends; they are not contrivances made by men to suit their purposes. They are the effects of human actions done with a view to other effects. Had not men behaved as they did, these things never would have come into existence, but they were not the ends of the actions that produced them. It is only very recently that we have come to understand even a little about the societies in which we live. The social and political institutions that surround us were not made by us, nor is it true that they continue to exist because we understand and find them good. Society is not made by men, though social laws are nothing but laws of human behaviour. Because it is true that society is nothing except men and their habits and laws, and that all social institutions are the products of human activities, it does not follow that men make societies. For to make is to contrive for a purpose, and implies a conscious end and a knowledge of means. It is only because we use words that suggest purposes to describe nearly all the consequences of human activities that it comes natural to us to describe social and political institutions as if they were made by men. We do, of course, have our theories about these institutions and we have our purposes; and so also did our ancestors. However ignorant the theories and foolish the purposes, they determine human behaviour and so affect social institutions. Men are always trying to adapt their institutions to their desires, and to some extent they succeed. But all this makes it no less true that these institutions are not the realizations of human purposes, and that they affect these purposes just as much (and perhaps much more) than they are affected by them.

The utilitarians, above all men, were determined not to be the dupes of words, and they destroyed more nonsense than any other modern school of philosophers. With occasional lapses, they wrote with unusual lucidity. Yet it may be that language got the better of them just when it was most necessary that they should be its masters. The political vocabulary constantly implies purposes where none exist, and the utilitarians used it without taking sufficient notice of this fact. A man does not cease to be the dupe of words because he writes clearly, if what he says is an error suggested by the ambiguities of ordinary language. Marriage, property, government and law are all institutions having social functions and satisfying human needs; nothing is easier than to talk of their 'purposes' and to imply that men established them for good and sufficient reasons. It is easy to see that if we were to lose them we should be much worse off than we are. What is less obvious is that many of the desires they satisfy were created by them, so that it is at least as true that we want them because we have them as that we have them because we want them.

These are considerations too obvious not to have occurred to such clever men as the utilitarians. Hume, when he destroyed the theory of the social contract, suggested that governments had arisen as a matter of convenience, with no one understanding quite what had happened, and that later they were accepted because every one felt they were indispensable. He supposed that, if government was created by covenant, it must have been in the same way as language, which developed among men and was accepted by them because it occurred to nobody to do otherwise. Besides, the whole theory of association of ideas, as it was used by the utilitarians, implies that the individual is as much the creature as the creator of society. James Mill tried to show that all the social affections are produced by the association of ideas, whose operation so modifies the native character of men that it can scarcely be recognized under the second nature evolved from it. But though the utilitarians understood these things and made the most of them when it suited their purposes, they did not understand their full significance for political theory. The experience that determines the associations of ideas which make a man's character is itself a social product; neither its nature nor its causes are likely to be understood by that man, and yet because of them he is what he is. All that James Mill, or any other exponent of the theory of the association of ideas, can know is man as he is. Their opinions about how he came to be such are mere conjectures, having no scientific value. What, indeed, could be less scientific than to construct the notion of man, in abstraction from society, and then to explain society in terms of his desires? No doubt, since man is the only political animal, there must be something about him that explains this unique quality. But what this something is, is one of the last questions that political theory, sustained by a wealth of knowledge not yet at its disposal, can answer. To talk of instincts instead of purposes and desires is to come no nearer to the truth; it is merely to substitute empty words for error.

In discussing the 'individualism' of the utilitarians, I have been discussing only their method of explaining social phenomena. I have not been arguing that the state does not exist for the sake of individuals, nor yet that individuals exist for the sake of the state. These two statements are, in my opinion, equally misleading. To convert them into questions and to attempt answers is to lose time that could be wasted more agreeably. Does the state exist for the sake of individuals? It is clear that they never contrived it, and that without it they would not be what they are. They would not have the purposes they now have were it not that they are citizens. Do individuals exist for the sake of the state? This question, like the other, invites no answer. The state is not a person and can have no end, and it is unlikely that we exist for its sake. If these questions are worth asking, they must be addressed to God, who alone can answer them. It may be that He brought states into existence to make men happy and virtuous; or it may be that He liked the look of states and created men to make them possible. Here are two possibilities that the philosopher can contemplate, but he ought not to pretend he knows which is the more likely to be true.

I ought, perhaps, to add, so as to avoid misunderstanding, that the writers who have said, either that the state exists for the sake of individuals or the opposite, have often subscribed to one or two of four opinions, all of them plausible though not all compatible with each other. But none of these opinions (nor any combination of them) implies that individuals exist for the sake of the state or the state for their sake. These four opinions are: (a) nothing is intrinsically good except some experience or activity of an individual; (b) the state (i.e. the association of many individuals standing in determinate relations to one another) is intrinsically good; (α) there exist universally valid moral laws; (β) every moral code is the product of a given society, and it has no validity outside that society except to the extent that other societies are like it. Philosophers who have held opinion (b) have sometimes also believed that the state is a mind having purposes of its own, and that it can never be right for the individual to disobey the laws of his state. To make these conclusions appear more plausible, these philosophers have often asserted (β) as well as (b). But it is clear that neither (b) nor (β), nor both together, can imply, either that the state has purposes of its own, or that it can never be right for the individual to disobey the laws. On the other hand, what the utilitarians and many other

English philosophers have often asserted is also badly argued: that because the state is only an association of individuals, it cannot be good in itself but only as a means to the happiness, welfare or virtue of individuals. It may be that nothing is good except what is individual; but if this far from self-evident proposition should be true, it certainly is not proved to be so by the bare assertion that the state is not a person or a mind. Indeed, the proposition, though it may be true, is not as plausible as the other three. For we know that men's devotion to societies and institutions is usually out of all proportion to their belief in their utility. They love them for what they are and not only for the good they do to individuals. It is the crudest psychology to suppose that patriotism, or any other group loyalty, is the desire to promote the welfare of individuals. If we care for our fellow countrymen more than for other men, it is because they share our loyalties. We prefer our compatriots because we love our country; and we do not love our country for their sakes. Patriotism and philanthropy are as often at war as at peace, and they seldom collaborate. Civilized men like to reconcile the two, and they even pretend to derive the former from the latter. But in more primitive societies, it is the group and its institutions, the living together after a certain fashion, that men most value. And they value it for what it is, without so much as asking themselves how it affects the happiness, welfare or virtue of individuals. Those therefore who say that nothing is good but what is individual are committed to the opinion that what most people have always valued much more than the welfare of the immense majority of persons whom they know (not to talk of the ones that they don't know) has in fact no intrinsic value.

The first political thinker of modern times who, for at least as long as it took him to write one essay, left these two superfluous questions (does the state exist for the sake of individuals, or the opposite?) quite out of account was Rousseau. In his *Discourse on the Origins of Inequality among Men*, he gives an account of the birth and development of society, an account which he admits is conjectural but which implies a conception of the relation of man to society much closer to the truth than the one preferred by the utilitarians. According to this account, the use of reason and language go naturally together, and neither is possible outside society. From this it follows that, until man becomes a social animal, he literally does not know what he is doing. He is urged by his emotions and desires to actions of whose further consequences he knows nothing, and yet these consequences are the emergence and development of a society that profoundly modifies his character. It is true that a social contract is described in the *Discourse*, but it is also implied that the developments leading up to it and its own further consequences are alike outside the control of the men in whose actions they are manifest. Rousseau sets no store by the details of his account and is content to suppose that something of the kind may have happened. It was Marx who coined the phrase: 'It is not the consciousness of men that determines their being, but their social being that determines their consciousness.' The truth, thus clumsily expressed, was illustrated a century earlier by Rousseau, at considerable length and in less misleading language.

This essay, though perhaps the most original of Rousseau's political writings, is only a small part of them. In the *Social Contract* and elsewhere, Rousseau was untrue to the principle implied in the *Discourse*. It was Saint-Simon, who, among modern thinkers, first put its true value on the principle that human societies develop in accordance with laws unknown to their members, whose characters, beliefs and purposes are profoundly affected by that development. Saint-Simon, a careless and often obscure writer, never succeeded in stating the principle without at the same time suggesting much that is false. In one passage, he tells us that 'the supreme law of the progress of the human spirit dominates and carries everything along with it; men are only its instruments. Though this force issues from us, it is no more in our power to put ourselves out of the way of its influence or to control its operation than to alter the primitive impulse that makes our planet turn round the sun.'[1] Here is a passage that is as obscure as extravagant. What is this supreme law? If it is a law of the development of society, why call it a law of the human mind or spirit? The use of the word *progress* adds a touch of optimism that science can very well do without. And why should it be assumed, without qualification, that men have no power to control their future? To call men instruments is to suppose a purpose beyond them. It is not possible, by selecting quotations, to separate the dross from the gold in Saint-Simon's writings. The two are inextricably mixed together.

[1] *Organisateur*, IV, p. 119.

Like Marx, Saint-Simon was incapable of speaking without saying a great deal more than was true or even than he meant. And he had the added misfortune of writing in French, a language in which nonsense hardly ever sounds impressive. But the meaning of the passage I have quoted is, I think, clear enough. It implies at least this much: that societies develop according to laws that are not made by men; and that this development, though it accords with human nature, is not to be explained in terms of human desires, beliefs and purposes. It also implies a great deal more that is false. But many of these false implications are denied by Saint-Simon elsewhere, while the principle I have tried to enunciate pervades his whole theory and affects all his thought about political and social matters. 'The natural course of events' says Saint-Simon in another passage, 'brings to birth the institutions adapted to each phase in the development of society (nécessaires à chaque âge du corps social)'.[1] Or, in other words, these institutions are not human contrivances. From such premises as these, Saint-Simon argued to the conclusion that the method of the social sciences must be historical. Their purpose is to trace the development of social institutions and to determine their functions at any given stage of that development. It is not the purpose of these sciences to guess at the motives that lead individuals to obey governments and to accept conventions. Saint-Simon was never interested in the great problem that has exercised so many political theorists, both before his time and since; he was not interested in political obligation. He set an example from which we have not yet sufficiently profited. For surely, the beginning of wisdom for political theorists, if their study is ever to become scientific, is to understand that the problem of political obligation is not theoretically important. The true answer to it, though sometimes cleverly disguised, is always a platitude. It cannot be a case of the duty to keep promises, for the great majority never promised obedience. And if we say, with the utilitarians, that subjects ought not to disobey unless they believe that disobedience will prevent more evil than it occasions, we make a statement as useless as it is true. Or, rather, it is a statement that has only a negative utility; for if we believe it is true we shall not be tempted to say anything so astonishing as, for instance, that subjects must always obey their governments because the state is its own end.

[1] *Physiologie Sociale*, X, p. 190.

Though the problem of political obligation, taken in the abstract, is theoretically unimportant, this does not mean that it matters little whether or not subjects obey their governments. Of the decisions that men can take, few are of greater importance than the resolve to disobey or overthrow government. And this decision, because of the dangers involved and the uncertainty of its consequences, is as difficult as it is important. But it does not follow, because a problem is always important and difficult in practice, that the political theorist, considering it in its generality and apart from the circumstances that on any particular occasion make it important and difficult, need hesitate in asserting that there is no true answer to it except a platitude. In the past, every attempt to justify a fancy answer has led the philosopher to perverse or absurd opinions in matters of theory, such as that men must somehow have done what (e.g. given a consent) they apparently never could have done, or that the state is its own end, or that it exists for the sake of the good life or the common good. Even the utilitarians, whose answer was scarcely a fancy one, were not content to make a general and harmless statement about political obligation. They, unfortunately, went on to say or to imply that the state exists because it is an instrument needed by men to promote their own greatest happiness. It is not until we come to Saint-Simon and Marx that we find the problem of political obligation quite neglected, and the account of the individual's relation to the state he belongs to in no way modified so as to prove that his duty of obedience is or is not thus and thus limited.

If we compare the utilitarian theories with those of Saint-Simon, we immediately notice two things: the indifference of the utilitarians to history and the little importance they attach to faith. In both these respects they belong to the eighteenth rather than to the nineteenth century. Hume was an historian, but he made only a small use of history to illustrate and support his political theories. Bentham and James Mill, like Voltaire, regarded history as no better than the record of the crimes and follies of mankind. They even took Voltaire's aphorism more seriously than its author had done. That history could teach the political theorist anything worth while was what never occurred to these two men, who condemned *a priori* reasonings and vulgar prejudices, and who always believed that their fundamental principles were generalizations from experience. Indeed, the political writings of even Hobbes and Locke (except when they are engaged in controversies of a semi-theological character), no less than those of the utilitarians, are remarkable for the small interest they exhibit in history and in the comparative study of societies. Even the extravagant and un-worldly Rousseau, at his most theoretical in the *Social Contract*, devoted a larger proportion of his few pages to comments on the contemporary world and antiquity.

When I say that the utilitarians attached little importance to faith, I do not refer only to their indifference to religion. I mean, rather, that they had no idea of how much men's behaviour is affected by their beliefs. Hume, it is true, said that all government rests on opinion, but he meant only that, if people did not think it their interest to do so, they would not obey their rulers. He never understood that, quite apart from religion, there exists in every society a whole system of prevalent beliefs and prejudices, peculiar to that society, without which it is impossible to explain the behaviour of its members. Men are selfish, generous, cowardly, brave, jealous, stupid and intelligent from one end of the earth to the other, and we learn nothing at all about the development of any society or its difference from another by contemplating the vices and virtues common to mankind. But it is the beliefs and prejudices that have no direct connexion with the general psycho-logical characteristics of men (and that must be acquired, because they cannot be inherited, by any particular man), in which the political theorist is interested. It is they that are intimately connected with the institutions prevailing in a given society. It is, perhaps, the great merit of Saint-Simon that he understood this better than any man had done before him.

The individualism of the utilitarians, their explanation of social phenomena by a human psychology supposedly prior to society, also made them indifferent to social classes. They conceived of society as composed of a number of competing individuals and not of rival groups. They did not, of course, deny the existence or political importance of classes, nor did they fail to mention them when it would have been unnatural not to do so. But they found no place for them in their general theory of society. It seemed obvious to them that, as the result of competition, some must be rich and some poor; and since this must be so in the free economy of which alone they approved, they thought it no less desirable than inevitable. But the social and political consequences of this fact did not, except on occasion, interest them. They were out to destroy sinister interests, they objected to monopolies, and they, most of them, had no respect for aristocracy; but that the political and class structures of society are so closely bound up with one another that a change in the one can hardly occur without a change in the other, is an idea that meant almost nothing to them. They neither denied the fact nor understood its importance for the political theorist. That combination of ingenuity and indifference to fact, which is Hume's great defect as a moral and political philosopher, is nowhere more conspicuous than in his account of property. Bentham and James Mill, highly critical of aristocracy, hoped that democracy would make predominant the educated middle class to which they themselves belonged. They had their strong social preferences but no real understanding of the political importance of classes. They had read Plato and Aristotle but had failed to learn the most obvious lesson taught by them. It is again in Saint-Simon that we get the first modern account of how, as political systems succeed one another, the relations of the social classes to each other are altogether changed. He thought that, already in the twelfth century, with the enfranchisement of the communes and the emergence of the 'industrial' class, there began the great process that was to destroy the medieval world and to form, beneath the decayed remnants of the old, the strong and healthy structure of a new society. Only the last of the great utilitarians, John Stuart Mill, lived in a Europe already so much alive to Saint-Simon's ideas that it was impossible for an intelligent man to neglect them. It is the younger Mill of whom alone we can say that he was often willing to sacrifice logic to truth.

I have said enough about the defects of the utilitarians, defects from which the younger Mill, not only because he lived later, but also for temperamental reasons, suffered less than the others. They were common to the great majority of eighteenth- and early nineteenth-century political thinkers, most of whom lacked the great intellectual qualities of the utilitarians. As destroyers of nonsense, Bentham and James Mill had not the tact, elegance and economy of Hume. But they were shrewd and vigorous critics. It is to the English utilitarians, much more than to any continental writers, that we owe our liberation from the political vocabulary inherited from the middle ages. They did, for political and moral philosophy, what the Cartesians did for the theory of knowledge. They made some simple definitions that define nothing, and they left a great deal too much out of account. But they also resolutely set aside much that political theorists are the better for discarding, and no serious student of the social sciences will think little of this service. It is a great and indispensable, and always a difficult, service; for men are most attached to nonsense in those studies that touch closest to their lives. Where the undergrowth is thick and strong, only the sharpest instruments and strongest arms can make the place clean.

It was given to the utilitarians to clear the ground but not to lay out the garden. And they have this grievance against their successors, that the garden is still barely visible and the ground almost as encumbered as it was a hundred and fifty years ago. If it should happen that they laboured in vain, the fault will be not theirs but ours. A number of good ideas were born in the nineteenth century, mostly in France. But who can say that in the social studies there are now discernible the orderly progress and the large measure of agreement which alone are evidence that a new science has come into the world?

# UTILITARIANISM

BY
JOHN STUART MILL

# CHAPTER 1

## GENERAL REMARKS

THERE are few circumstances among those which make up the present condition of human knowledge, more unlike what might have been expected, or more significant of the backward state in which speculation on the most important subjects still lingers, than the little progress which has been made in the decision of the controversy respecting the criterion of right and wrong. From the dawn of philosophy, the question concerning the *summum bonum*, or, what is the same thing, concerning the foundation of morality, has been accounted the main problem in speculative thought, has occupied the most gifted intellects, and divided them into sects and schools, carrying on a vigorous warfare against one another. And after more than two thousand years the same discussions continue, philosophers are still ranged under the same contending banners, and neither thinkers nor mankind at large seem nearer to being unanimous on the subject, than when the youth Socrates listened to the old Protagoras, and asserted (if Plato's dialogue be grounded on a real conversation) the theory of utilitarianism against the popular morality of the so-called sophist.

It is true that similar confusion and uncertainty, and in some cases similar discordance, exist respecting the first principles of all the sciences, not excepting that which is deemed the most certain of them, mathematics; without much impairing, generally indeed without impairing at all, the trustworthiness of the conclusions of those sciences. An apparent anomaly, the explanation of which is, that the detailed doctrines of a science are not usually deduced from, nor depend for their evidence upon, what are called its first principles. Were it not so, there would be no science more precarious, or whose conclusions were more insufficiently made out, than algebra; which derives none of its certainty from what are commonly taught to learners as its elements, since these, as laid down by some of its most eminent teachers, are as full of fictions as English law, and of mysteries as theology. The truths which are ultimately accepted as the first principles of a science, are really the last results of metaphysical analysis, practised on the elementary notions with which the science is conversant; and their relation to the science is not that of foundations to an edifice, but of roots to a tree, which may perform their office equally well though they be never dug down to and exposed to light. But though in science the particular truths precede the general theory, the contrary might be expected to be the case with a practical art, such as morals or legislation. All action is for the sake of some end, and rules of action, it seems natural to suppose, must take their whole character and colour from the end to which they are subservient. When we engage in a pursuit, a clear and precise conception of what we are pursuing would seem to be the first thing we need, instead of the last we are to look forward to. A test of right and wrong must be the means, one would think, of ascertaining what is right or wrong, and not a consequence of having already ascertained it.

The difficulty is not avoided by having recourse to the popular theory of a natural faculty, a sense or instinct, informing us of right and wrong. For—besides that the existence of such a moral instinct is itself one of the matters in dispute—those believers in it who have any pretensions to philosophy, have been obliged to abandon the idea that it discerns what is right or wrong in the particular case in hand, as our other senses discern the sight or sound actually present. Our moral faculty, according to all those of its interpreters who are entitled to the name of thinkers, supplies us only with the general principles of moral judgments; it is a branch of our reason, not of our sensitive faculty; and must be looked to for the abstract doctrines of morality, not for perception of it in the concrete. The intuitive, no less than what may be termed the inductive, school of ethics, insists on the necessity of general laws. They both agree that the morality of an individual action is not a question of direct perception, but of the application of a law to an individual case. They recognise also, to a great extent, the same moral laws; but differ as to their evidence, and the source from which they derive their authority. According to the one opinion, the principles of morals are evident *à priori*, requiring nothing to command assent, except that the meaning of the terms be understood. According to the other doctrine, right and wrong, as well as truth and falsehood, are questions of observation and experience. But both hold equally that morality must be deduced from principles; and the intuitive school affirm as strongly as the inductive, that there is a science of morals. Yet they seldom attempt to make out a list of the *à priori* principles which are to serve as the premises of the science; still more rarely do they make any effort to reduce those various principles to one first principle, or common ground of obligation. They either assume the ordinary precepts of morals as of *à priori* authority, or they lay down as the common groundwork of those maxims, some generality much less obviously authoritative than the maxims themselves, and which has never succeeded in gaining popular acceptance. Yet to support their pretensions there ought either to be some one fundamental principle or law, at the root of all morality, or if there be several, there should be a determinate order of precedence among them; and the one principle, or the rule for deciding between the various principles when they conflict, ought to be self-evident.

To inquire how far the bad effects of this deficiency have been mitigated in practice, or to what extent the moral beliefs of mankind have been vitiated or made uncertain by the absence of any distinct recognition of an ultimate standard, would imply a complete survey and criticism of past and present ethical doctrine. It would, however, be easy to show that whatever steadiness or consistency these moral beliefs have attained, has been mainly due to the tacit influence of a standard not recognised. Although the non-existence of an acknowledged first principle has made ethics not so much a guide as a consecration of men's actual sentiments, still, as men's sentiments, both of favour and of aversion, are greatly influenced by what they suppose to be the effects of things upon their happiness, the principle of utility, or as Bentham latterly called it, the greatest happiness principle, has had a large share in forming the moral doctrines even of those who most scornfully reject its authority. Nor is there any school of thought which refuses to admit that the influence of actions on happiness is a most material and even predominant consideration in many of the details of morals, however unwilling to acknowledge it as the fundamental principle of morality, and the source of moral obligation. I might go much further, and say that to all those *à priori* moralists who deem it necessary to argue at all, utilitarian arguments are indispensable.

It is not my present purpose to criticise these thinkers; but I cannot help referring, for illustration, to a systematic treatise by one of the most illustrious of them, the *Metaphysics of Ethics*, by Kant. This remarkable man, whose system of thought will long remain one of the landmarks in the history of philosophical speculation, does, in the treatise in question, lay down a universal first principle as the origin and ground of moral obligation; it is this:—'So act, that the rule on which thou actest would admit of being adopted as a law by all rational beings.' But when he begins to deduce from this precept any of the actual duties of morality, he fails, almost grotesquely, to show that there would be any contradiction, any logical (not to say physical) impossibility, in the adoption by all rational beings of the most outrageously immoral rules of conduct. All he shows is that the *consequences* of their universal adoption would be such as no one would choose to incur.

On the present occasion, I shall, without further discussion of the other theories, attempt to contribute something towards the understanding and appreciation of the Utilitarian or Happiness theory, and towards such proof as it is susceptible of. It is evident that this cannot be proof in the ordinary and popular meaning of the term. Questions of ultimate ends are not amenable to direct proof. Whatever can be proved to be good, must be so by being shown to be a means to something admitted to be good without proof. The medical art is proved to be good by its conducing to health; but how is it possible to prove that health is good? The art of music is good, for the reason, among others, that it produces pleasure; but what proof is it possible to give that pleasure is good? If, then, it is asserted that there is a comprehensive formula, including all things which are in themselves good, and that whatever else is good, is not so as an end, but as a mean, the formula may be accepted or rejected, but is not a subject of what is commonly understood by proof. We are not, however, to infer that its acceptance or rejection must depend on blind impulse, or arbitrary choice. There is a larger meaning of the word proof, in which this question is as amenable to it as any other of the disputed questions of philosophy. The subject is within the cognisance of the rational faculty; and neither does that faculty deal with it solely in the way of intuition. Considerations may be presented capable of determining the intellect either to give or withhold its assent to the doctrine; and this is equivalent to proof.

We shall examine presently of what nature are these considerations; in what manner they apply to the case, and what rational grounds, therefore, can be given for accepting or rejecting the utilitarian formula. But it is a preliminary condition of rational acceptance or rejection, that the formula should be correctly understood. I believe that the very imperfect notion ordinarily formed of its meaning, is the chief obstacle which impedes its reception; and that could it be cleared, even from only the grosser misconceptions, the question would be greatly simplified, and a large proportion of its difficulties removed. Before, therefore, I attempt to enter into the philosophical grounds which can be given for assenting to the utilitarian standard, I shall offer some illustrations of the doctrine itself; with the view of showing more clearly what it is, distinguishing it from what it is not, and disposing of such of the practical objections to it as either originate in, or are closely connected with, mistaken interpretations of its meaning. Having thus prepared the ground, I shall afterwards endeavour to throw such light as I can upon the question, considered as one of philosophical theory.

# CHAPTER 2

## WHAT UTILITARIANISM IS

A PASSING remark is all that needs be given to the ignorant blunder of supposing that those who stand up for utility as the test of right and wrong, use the term in that restricted and merely colloquial sense in which utility is opposed to pleasure. An apology is due to the philosophical opponents of utilitarianism, for even the momentary appearance of confounding them with any one capable of so absurd a misconception; which is the more extraordinary, inasmuch as the contrary accusation, of referring everything to pleasure, and that too in its grossest form, is another of the common charges against utilitarianism: and, as has been pointedly remarked by an able writer, the same sort of persons, and often the very same persons, denounce the theory 'as impracticably dry when the word utility precedes the word pleasure, and as too practicably voluptuous when the word pleasure precedes the word utility.' Those who know anything about the matter are aware that every writer, from Epicurus to Bentham, who maintained the theory of utility, meant by it, not something to be contradistinguished from pleasure, but pleasure itself, together with exemption from pain; and instead of opposing the useful to the agreeable or the ornamental, have always declared that the useful means these, among other things. Yet the common herd, including the herd of writers, not only in newspapers and periodicals, but in books of weight and pretension, are perpetually falling into this shallow mistake. Having caught up the word utilitarian, while knowing nothing whatever about it but its sound, they habitually express by it the rejection, or the neglect, of pleasure in some of its forms; of beauty, of ornament, or of amusement. Nor is the term thus ignorantly misapplied solely in disparagement, but occasionally in compliment; as though it implied superiority to frivolity and the mere pleasures of the moment. And this perverted use is the only one in which the word is popularly known, and the one from which the new generation are acquiring their sole notion of its meaning. Those who introduced the word, but who had for many years discontinued it as a distinctive appellation, may well feel themselves called upon to resume it, if by doing so they can hope to contribute anything towards rescuing it from this utter degradation.[1]

The creed which accepts as the foundation of morals, Utility, or the Greatest Happiness Principle, holds that actions are right in proportion as they tend to promote happiness, wrong as they tend to produce the reverse of happiness. By happiness is intended pleasure, and the absence of pain; by unhappiness, pain, and the privation of pleasure. To give a clear view of the moral standard set up by the theory, much more requires to be said; in particular, what things it includes in the ideas of pain and pleasure; and to what extent this is left an open question. But these supplementary explanations do not affect the theory of life on which this theory of morality is grounded—namely, that pleasure, and freedom from pain, are the only things desirable as ends; and that all desirable things (which are as numerous in the utilitarian as in any other scheme) are desirable either for the pleasure inherent in themselves, or as means to the promotion of pleasure and the prevention of pain.

Now, such a theory of life excites in many minds, and among them in some of the most estimable in feeling and purpose, inveterate dislike. To suppose that life has (as they express it) no higher end than pleasure—no better and nobler object of desire and pursuit—they designate as utterly mean and grovelling; as a doctrine worthy only of swine, to whom the followers of Epicurus were, at a very early period, contemptuously likened; and modern holders of the doctrine are occasionally made the subject of equally polite comparisons by its German, French, and English assailants.

When thus attacked, the Epicureans have always answered, that it is not they, but their accusers, who represent human nature

[1] The author of this essay has reason for believing himself to be the first person who brought the word utilitarian into use. He did not invent it, but adopted it from a passing expression in Mr. Galt's *Annals of the Parish*. After using it as a designation for several years, he and others abandoned it from a growing dislike to anything resembling a badge or watchword of sectarian distinction. But as a name for one single opinion, not a set of opinions—to denote the recognition of utility as a standard, not any particular way of applying it—the term supplies a want in the language, and offers, in many cases, a convenient mode of avoiding tiresome circumlocution.

M

in a degrading light; since the accusation supposes human beings to be capable of no pleasures except those of which swine are capable. If this supposition were true, the charge could not be gainsaid, but would then be no longer an imputation; for if the sources of pleasure were precisely the same to human beings and to swine, the rule of life which is good enough for the one would be good enough for the other. The comparison of the Epicurean life to that of beasts is felt as degrading, precisely because a beast's pleasures do not satisfy a human being's conceptions of happiness. Human beings have faculties more elevated than the animal appetites, and when once made conscious of them, do not regard anything as happiness which does not include their gratification. I do not, indeed, consider the Epicureans to have been by any means faultless in drawing out their scheme of consequences from the utilitarian principle. To do this in any sufficient manner, many Stoic, as well as Christian elements require to be included. But there is no known Epicurean theory of life which does not assign to the pleasures of the intellect, of the feelings and imagination, and of the moral sentiments, a much higher value as pleasures than to those of mere sensation. It must be admitted, however, that utilitarian writers in general have placed the superiority of mental over bodily pleasures chiefly in the greater permanency, safety, uncostliness, etc., of the former—that is, in their circumstantial advantages rather than in their intrinsic nature. And on all these points utilitarians have fully proved their case; but they might have taken the other, and, as it may be called, higher ground, with entire consistency. It is quite compatible with the principle of utility to recognise the fact, that some *kinds* of pleasure are more desirable and more valuable than others. It would be absurd that while, in estimating all other things, quality is considered as well as quantity, the estimation of pleasures should be supposed to depend on quantity alone.

If I am asked, what I mean by difference of quality in pleasures, or what makes one pleasure more valuable than another, merely as a pleasure, except its being greater in amount, there is but one possible answer. Of two pleasures, if there be one to which all or almost all who have experience of both give a decided preference, irrespective of any feeling of moral obligation to prefer it, that is the more desirable pleasure. If one of the two is, by those who are competently acquainted with both, placed so far above the other that they prefer it, even though knowing it to be attended with a greater amount of discontent, and would not resign it for any quantity of the other pleasure which their nature is capable of, we are justified in ascribing to the preferred enjoyment a superiority in quality, so far outweighing quantity as to render it, in comparison, of small account.

Now it is an unquestionable fact that those who are equally acquainted with, and equally capable of appreciating and enjoying, both, do give a most marked preference to the manner of existence which employs their higher faculties. Few human creatures would consent to be changed into any of the lower animals, for a promise of the fullest allowance of a beast's pleasures; no intelligent human being would consent to be a fool, no instructed person would be an ignoramus, no person of feeling and conscience would be selfish and base, even though they should be persuaded that the fool, the dunce, or the rascal is better satisfied with his lot than they are with theirs. They would not resign what they possess more than he for the most complete satisfaction of all the desires which they have in common with him. If they ever fancy they would, it is only in cases of unhappiness so extreme, that to escape from it they would exchange their lot for almost any other, however undesirable in their own eyes. A being of higher faculties requires more to make him happy, is capable probably of more acute suffering, and certainly accessible to it at more points, than one of an inferior type; but in spite of these liabilities, he can never really wish to sink into what he feels to be a lower grade of existence. We may give what explanation we please of this unwillingness; we may attribute it to pride, a name which is given indiscriminately to some of the most and to some of the least estimable feelings of which mankind are capable: we may refer it to the love of liberty and personal independence, an appeal to which was with the Stoics one of the most effective means for the inculcation of it; to the love of power, or to the love of excitement, both of which do really enter into and contribute to it: but its most appropriate appellation is a sense of dignity, which all human beings possess in one form or other, and in some, though by no means in exact, proportion to their higher faculties, and which is so essential a part of the happiness of those in whom it is strong, that nothing which conflicts with it could be, otherwise than momentarily, an object of desire to them. Whoever supposes that this preference takes place at a sacrifice of happiness—that the superior being, in anything like equal circumstances, is not happier than the inferior—confounds the two very different ideas, of happiness, and content. It is indisputable that the being whose capacities of enjoyment are low, has the greatest chance of having them fully satisfied; and a highly endowed being will always feel that any happiness which he can look for, as the world is constituted, is imperfect. But he can learn to bear its imperfections, if they are at all bearable; and they will not make him envy the being who is indeed unconscious of the imperfections, but only because he feels not at all the good which those imperfections qualify. It is better to be a human being dissatisfied than a pig satisfied; better to be Socrates dissatisfied than a fool satisfied. And if the fool, or the pig, are of a different opinion, it is because they only know their own side of the question. The other party to the comparison knows both sides.

It may be objected, that many who are capable of the higher pleasures, occasionally, under the influence of temptation, postpone them to the lower. But this is quite compatible with a full appreciation of the intrinsic superiority of the higher. Men often, from infirmity of character, make their election for the nearer good, though they know it to be the less valuable; and this no less when the choice is between two bodily pleasures, than when it is between bodily and mental. They pursue sensual indulgences to the injury of health, though perfectly aware that health is the greater good. It may be further objected, that many who begin with youthful enthusiasm for everything noble, as they advance in years sink into indolence and selfishness. But I do not believe that those who undergo this very common change, voluntarily choose the lower description of pleasures in preference to the higher. I believe that before they devote themselves exclusively to the one, they have already become incapable of the other. Capacity for the nobler feelings is in most natures a very tender plant, easily killed, not only by hostile influences, but by mere want of sustenance; and in the majority of young persons it speedily dies away if the occupations to which their position in life has devoted them, and the society into which it has thrown them, are not favourable to keeping that higher capacity in exercise. Men lose their high aspirations as they lose their intellectual tastes, because they have not time or opportunity for indulging them; and they addict themselves to inferior pleasures, not because they deliberately prefer them, but because they are either the only ones to which they have access, or the only ones which they are any longer capable of enjoying. It may be questioned whether any one who has remained equally susceptible to both classes of pleasures, ever knowingly and calmly preferred the lower; though many, in all ages, have broken down in an ineffectual attempt to combine both.

From this verdict of the only competent judges, I apprehend there can be no appeal. On a question which is the best worth having of two pleasures, or which of two modes of existence is the most grateful to the feelings, apart from its moral attributes and from its consequences, the judgment of those who are qualified by knowledge of both, or, if they differ, that of the majority among them, must be admitted as final. And there needs be the less hesitation to accept this judgment respecting the quality of pleasures, since there is no other tribunal to be referred to even on the question of quantity. What means are there of determining which is the acutest of two pains, or the intensest of two pleasurable sensations, except the general suffrage of those who are familiar with both? Neither pains nor pleasures are homogeneous, and pain is always heterogeneous with pleasure. What is there to decide whether a particular pleasure is worth purchasing at the cost of a particular pain, except the feelings and judgment of the experienced? When, therefore, those feelings and judgment declare the pleasures derived from the higher faculties to be preferable *in kind*, apart from the question of intensity, to those of which the animal nature, disjoined from the higher faculties, is susceptible, they are entitled on this subject to the same regard.

I have dwelt on this point, as being a necessary part of a perfectly just conception of Utility or Happiness, considered as the directive rule of human conduct. But it is by no means an indispensable condition to the acceptance of the utilitarian standard; for that standard is not the agent's own greatest happiness, but the greatest amount of happiness altogether; and if it may possibly be doubted whether a noble character is always the happier for its nobleness, there can be no doubt that it makes other people happier, and that the world in general is immensely a gainer by it. Utilitarianism, therefore, could only attain its end by the general cultivation of nobleness of character, even if each individual were only benefited by the nobleness of others, and his own, so far as happiness is concerned, were a sheer deduction from the benefit. But the bare enunciation of such an absurdity as this last, renders refutation superfluous.

According to the Greatest Happiness Principle, as above explained, the ultimate end, with reference to and for the sake of which all other things are desirable (whether we are considering our own good or that of other people), is an existence exempt as far as possible from pain, and as rich as possible in enjoyments, both in point of quantity and quality; the test of quality, and the rule for measuring it against quantity, being the preference felt by those who in their opportunities of experience, to which must be added their habits of self-consciousness and self-observation, are best furnished with the means of comparison. This, being, according to the utilitarian opinion, the end of human action, is necessarily also the standard of morality; which may accordingly be defined, the rules and precepts for human conduct, by the observance of which an existence such as has been described might be, to the greatest extent possible, secured to all mankind; and not to them only, but, so far as the nature of things admits, to the whole sentient creation.

Against this doctrine, however, arises another class of objectors, who say that happiness, in any form, cannot be the rational purpose of human life and action; because, in the first place, it is unattainable: and they contemptuously ask, what right hast thou to be happy? a question which Mr. Carlyle clenches by the addition, What right, a short time ago, hadst thou even *to be*? Next, they say, that men can do *without* happiness; that all noble human beings have felt this, and could not have become noble but by learning the lesson of Entsagen, or renunciation; which lesson, thoroughly learnt and submitted to, they affirm to be the beginning and necessary condition of all virtue.

The first of these objections would go to the root of the matter were it well founded; for if no happiness is to be had at all by human beings, the attainment of it cannot be the end of morality, or of any rational conduct. Though, even in that case, something might still be said for the utilitarian theory; since utility includes not solely the pursuit of happiness, but the prevention or mitigation of unhappiness; and if the former aim be chimerical, there will be all the greater scope and more imperative need for the latter, so long at least as mankind think fit to live, and do not take refuge in the simultaneous act of suicide recommended under certain conditions by Novalis. When, however, it is thus positively asserted to be impossible that human life should be happy, the assertion, if not something like a verbal quibble, is at least an exaggeration. If by happiness be meant a continuity of highly pleasurable excitement, it is evident enough that this is impossible. A state of exalted pleasure lasts only moments, or in some cases, and with some intermissions, hours or days, and is the occasional brilliant flash of enjoyment, not its permanent and steady flame. Of this the philosophers who have taught that happiness is the end of life were as fully aware as those who taunt them. The happiness which they meant was not a life of rapture; but moments of such, in an existence made up of few and transitory pains, many and various pleasures, with a decided predominance of the active over the passive, and having as the foundation of the whole, not to expect more from life than it is capable of bestowing. A life thus composed, to those who have been fortunate enough to obtain it, has always appeared worthy of the name of happiness. And such an existence is even now the lot of many, during some considerable portion of their lives. The present wretched education, and wretched social arrangements, are the only real hindrance to its being attainable by almost all.

The objectors perhaps may doubt whether human beings, if taught to consider happiness as the end of life, would be satisfied with such a moderate share of it. But great numbers of mankind have been satisfied with much less. The main constituents of a satisfied life appear to be two, either of which by itself is often found sufficient for the purpose: tranquillity, and excitement. With much tranquillity, many find that they can be content with very little pleasure: with much excitement, many can reconcile themselves to a considerable quantity of pain. There is assuredly no inherent impossibility in enabling even the mass of mankind to unite both; since the two are so far from being incompatible that they are in natural alliance, the prolongation of either being a preparation for, and exciting a wish for, the other. It is only those in whom indolence amounts to a vice, that do not desire excitement after an interval of repose; it is only those in whom the need of excitement is a disease, that feel the tranquillity which follows excitement dull and insipid, instead of pleasurable in direct proportion to the excitement which preceded it. When people who are tolerably fortunate in their outward lot do not find in life sufficient enjoyment to make it valuable to them, the cause generally is, caring for nobody but themselves. To those who have neither public nor private affections, the excitements of life are much curtailed, and in any case dwindle in value as the time approaches when all selfish interests must be terminated by death: while those who leave after them objects of personal affection, and especially those who have also cultivated a fellow-feeling with the collective interests of mankind, retain as lively an interest in life on the eve of death as in the vigour of youth and health. Next to selfishness, the principal cause which makes life unsatisfactory is want of mental cultivation. A cultivated mind—I do not mean that of a philosopher, but any mind to which the fountains of knowledge have been opened, and which has been taught, in any tolerable degree, to exercise its faculties—finds sources of inexhaustible interest in all that surrounds it; in the objects of nature, the achievements of art, the imaginations of poetry, the incidents of history, the ways of mankind, past and present, and their prospects in the future. It is possible, indeed, to become indifferent to all this, and that too without having exhausted a thousandth part of it; but only when one has had from the beginning no moral or human interest in these things, and has sought in them only the gratification of curiosity.

Now there is absolutely no reason in the nature of things why an amount of mental culture sufficient to give an intelligent interest in these objects of contemplation, should not be the inheritance of every one born in a civilised country. As little is there an inherent necessity that any human being should be a selfish egotist, devoid of every feeling or care but those which centre in his own miserable individuality. Something far superior to this is sufficiently common even now, to give ample earnest of what the human species may be made. Genuine private affections, and a sincere interest in the public good, are possible, though in unequal degrees, to every rightly brought up human being. In a world in which there is so much to interest, so much to enjoy, and so much also to correct and improve, every one who has this moderate amount of moral and intellectual requisites is capable of an existence which may be called enviable; and unless such a person, through bad laws, or subjection to the will of others, is denied the liberty to use the sources of happiness within his reach, he will not fail to find this enviable existence, if he escape the positive evils of life, the great sources of physical and mental suffering—such as indigence, disease, and the unkindness, worthlessness, or premature loss of objects of affection. The main stress of the problem lies, therefore, in the contest with these calamities, from which it is a rare good fortune entirely to escape; which, as things now are, cannot be obviated, and often cannot be in any material degree mitigated. Yet no one whose opinion deserves a moment's consideration can doubt that most of the great positive evils of the world are in themselves removable, and will, if human affairs continue to improve, be in the end reduced within narrow limits. Poverty, in any sense implying suffering, may be completely extinguished by the wisdom of society, combined with the good sense and providence of individuals. Even that most intractable of enemies, disease, may be indefinitely reduced in dimensions by good physical and moral education, and proper control of noxious influences; while the progress of science holds out a promise for the future of still more direct conquests over this detestable foe. And every advance in that direction relieves us from some, not only of the chances which cut short our own lives, but, what concerns us still more, which deprive us of those in whom our happiness is wrapt up. As for vicissitudes of fortune, and other disappointments connected with worldly circumstances, these are principally the effect either of gross imprudence, of ill-regulated desires, or of bad or imperfect social institutions. All the grand sources, in short, of human suffering are in a great degree, many of them almost entirely, conquerable by human care and effort; and though their removal is grievously slow—though a long succession of generations will perish in the breach before the conquest is completed, and this world becomes all that, if will and knowledge were not wanting, it might easily be made—yet every mind sufficiently intelligent and generous to bear a part, however small and unconspicuous, in the endeavour, will draw a noble enjoyment from the contest itself, which he would not for any bribe in the form of selfish indulgence consent to be without.

And this leads to the true estimation of what is said by the objectors concerning the possibility, and the obligation, of learning to do without happiness. Unquestionably it is possible to do without happiness; it is done involuntarily by nineteen-twentieths of mankind, even in those parts of our present world which are least deep in barbarism; and it often has to be done voluntarily by the hero or the martyr, for the sake of something which he prizes more than his individual happiness. But this something, what is it, unless the happiness of others, or some of the requisites of happiness? It is noble to be capable of resigning entirely one's own portion of happiness, or chances of it: but, after all, this self-sacrifice must be for some end; it is not its own end; and if we are told that its end is not happiness, but virtue, which is better than happiness, I ask, would the sacrifice be made if the hero or martyr did not believe that it would earn for others immunity from similar sacrifices? Would it be made if he thought that his renunciation of happiness for himself would produce no fruit for any of his fellow creatures, but to make their lot like his, and place them also in the condition of persons who have renounced happiness? All honour to those who can abnegate for themselves the personal enjoyment of life, when by such renunciation they contribute worthily to increase the amount of happiness in the world; but he who does it, or professes to do it, for any other purpose, is no more deserving of admiration than the ascetic mounted on his pillar. He may be an inspiriting proof of what men *can* do, but assuredly not an example of what they *should*.

Though it is only in a very imperfect state of the world's arrangements that any one can best serve the happiness of others by the absolute sacrifice of his own, yet so long as the world is in that imperfect state, I fully acknowledge that the readiness to make such a sacrifice is the highest virtue which can be found in man. I will add, that in this condition of the world, paradoxical as the assertion may be, the conscious ability to do without happiness gives the best prospect of realising such happiness as is attainable. For nothing except that consciousness can raise a person above the chances of life, by making him feel that, let fate and fortune do their worst, they have not power to subdue him: which, once felt, frees him from excess of anxiety concerning the evils of life, and enables him, like many a Stoic in the worst times of the Roman Empire, to cultivate in tranquillity the sources of satisfaction accessible to him, without concerning himself about the uncertainty of their duration, any more than about their inevitable end.

Meanwhile, let utilitarians never cease to claim the morality of self-devotion as a possession which belongs by as good a right to them, as either to the Stoic or to the Transcendentalist. The utilitarian morality does recognise in human beings the power of sacrificing their own greatest good for the good of others. It only refuses to admit that the sacrifice is itself a good. A sacrifice which does not increase, or tend to increase, the sum total of happiness, it considers as wasted. The only self-renunciation which it applauds, is devotion to the happiness, or to some of the means of happiness, of others; either of mankind collectively, or of individuals within the limits imposed by the collective interests of mankind.

I must again repeat, what the assailants of utilitarianism seldom have the justice to acknowledge, that the happiness which forms the utilitarian standard of what is right in conduct, is not the agent's own happiness, but that of all concerned. As between his own happiness and that of others, utilitarianism requires him to be as strictly impartial as a disinterested and benevolent spectator. In the golden rule of Jesus of Nazareth, we read the complete spirit of the ethics of utility. To do as you would be done by, and to love your neighbour as yourself, constitute the ideal perfection of utilitarian morality. As the means of making the nearest approach to this ideal, utility would enjoin, first, that laws and social arrangements should place the happiness, or (as speaking practically it may be called) the interest, of every individual, as nearly as possible in harmony with the interest of the whole; and secondly, that education and opinion, which have so vast a power over human character, should so use that power as to establish in the mind of every individual an indissoluble association between his own happiness and the good of the whole; especially between his own happiness and the practice of such modes of conduct, negative and positive, as regard for the universal happiness prescribes; so that not only he may be unable to conceive the possibility of happiness to himself, consistently with conduct opposed to the general good, but also that a direct impulse to promote the general good may be in every individual one of the habitual motives of action, and the sentiments connected therewith may fill a large and prominent place in every human being's sentient existence. If the impugners of the utilitarian morality represented it to their own minds in this its true character, I know not what recommendation possessed by any other morality they could possibly affirm to be wanting to it; what more beautiful or more exalted developments of human nature any other ethical system can be supposed to foster, or what springs of action, not accessible to the utilitarian, such systems rely on for giving effect to their mandates.

The objectors to utilitarianism cannot always be charged with representing it in in a discreditable light. On the contrary, those among them who entertain anything like a just idea of its disinterested character, sometimes find fault with its standard as being too high for humanity. They say it is exacting too much to require that people shall always act from the inducement of promoting the general interests of society. But this is to mistake the very meaning of a standard of morals, and confound the rule of action with the motive of it. It is the business of ethics to tell us what are our duties, or by what test we may know them; but no system of ethics requires that the sole motive of all we do shall be a feeling of duty; on the contrary, ninety-nine hundredths of all our actions are done from other motives, and rightly so done, if the rule of duty does not condemn them. It is the more unjust to utilitarianism that this particular misapprehension should be made a ground of objection to it, inasmuch as utilitarian moralists have gone beyond almost all others in affirming that the motive has nothing to do with the morality of the action, though much with the worth of the agent. He who saves a fellow creature from drowning does what is morally right, whether his motive be duty, or the hope of being paid for his trouble; he who betrays the friend that trusts him, is guilty of a crime, even if his object be to serve another friend to whom he is under greater obligations. But to speak only of actions done from the motive of duty, and in direct obedience to principle: it is a misapprehension of the utilitarian mode of thought, to conceive it as implying that people should fix their minds upon so wide a generality as the world, or society at large. The great majority of good actions are intended not for the benefit of the world, but for that of individuals, of which the good of the world is made up; and the thoughts of the most virtuous man need not on these occasions travel beyond the particular persons concerned, except so far as is necessary to assure himself that in benefiting them he is not violating the rights, that is, the legitimate and authorised expectations, of any one else. The multiplication of happiness is, according to the utilitarian ethics, the object of virtue: the occasions on which any person (except one in a thousand) has it in his power to do this on an extended scale, in other words to be a public benefactor, are but exceptional; and on these occasions alone is he called on to consider public utility; in every other case, private utility, the interest or happiness of some few persons, is all he has to attend to. Those alone the influence of whose actions extends to society in general, need concern themselves habitually about so large an object. In the case of abstinences indeed—of things which people forbear to do from moral considerations, though the consequences in the particular case might be beneficial— it would be unworthy of an intelligent agent not to be consciously aware that the action is of a class which, if practised generally, would be generally injurious, and that this is the ground of the obligation to abstain from it. The amount of regard for the public interest implied in this recognition, is no greater than is demanded by every system of morals, for they all enjoin to abstain from whatever is manifestly pernicious to society.

The same considerations dispose of another reproach against the doctrine of utility, founded on a still grosser misconception of the purpose of a standard of morality, and of the very meaning of the words right and wrong. It is often affirmed that utilitarianism renders men cold and unsympathising; that it chills their moral feelings towards individuals; that it makes them regard only the dry and hard consideration of the consequences of actions, not taking into their moral estimate the qualities from which those actions emanate. If the assertion means that they do not allow their judgment respecting the rightness or wrongness of an action to be influenced by their opinion of the qualities of the person who does it, this is a complaint not against utilitarianism, but against having any standard of morality at all; for certainly no known ethical standard decides an action to be good or bad because it is done by a good or a bad man, still less because done by an amiable, a brave, or a benevolent man, or the contrary. These considerations are relevant, not to the estimation of actions, but of persons; and there is nothing in the utilitarian theory inconsistent with the fact that there are other things which interest us in persons besides the rightness and wrongness of their actions. The Stoics, indeed, with the paradoxical misuse of language which was part of their system, and by which they strove to raise themselves above all concern about anything but virtue, were fond of saying, that he who has that has everything; that he, and only he, is rich, is beautiful, is a king. But no claim of this description is made for the virtuous man by the utilitarian doctrine. Utilitarians are quite aware that there are other desirable possessions and qualities besides virtue, and are perfectly willing to allow to all of them their full worth. They are also aware that a right action does not necessarily indicate a virtuous character, and that actions which are blamable, often proceed from qualities entitled to praise. When this is apparent in any particular case, it modifies their estimation, not certainly of the act, but of the agent. I grant that they are, notwithstanding, of opinion, that in the long run the best proof of a good character is good actions; and resolutely refuse to consider any mental disposition as good, of which the predominant tendency is to produce bad conduct. This makes them unpopular with many people; but it is an unpopularity which they must share with every one who regards the distinction between right and wrong in a serious light; and the reproach is not one which a conscientious utilitarian need be anxious to repel.

If no more be meant by the objection than that many utilitarians look on the morality of actions, as measured by the utilitarian standard, with too exclusive a regard, and do not lay sufficient stress upon the other beauties of character which go towards making a human being lovable or admirable, this may be admitted. Utilitarians who have cultivated their moral feelings, but not their sympathies nor their artistic perceptions, do fall into this mistake; and so do all other moralists under the same conditions. What can be said in excuse for other moralists is equally available for them, namely, that, if there is to be any error, it is better that it should be on that side. As a matter of fact, we may affirm that among utilitarians as among adherents of other systems, there is every imaginable degree of rigidity and of laxity in the application of their standard: some are even puritanically rigorous, while others are as indulgent as can possibly be desired by sinner or by sentimentalist. But on the whole, a doctrine which brings prominently forward the interest that mankind have in the repression and prevention of conduct which violates the moral law, is likely to be inferior to no other in turning the sanctions of opinion against such violations. It is true, the question, What does violate the moral law? is one on which those who recognise different standards of morality are likely now and then to differ. But difference of opinion on moral questions was not first introduced into the world by utilitarianism, while that doctrine does supply, if not always an easy, at all events a tangible and intelligible mode of deciding such differences.

It may not be superfluous to notice a few more of the common misapprehensions of utilitarian ethics, even those which are so obvious and gross that it might appear impossible for any person of candour and intelligence to fall into them; since persons, even of considerable mental endowments, often give themselves so little trouble to understand the bearings of any opinion against which they entertain a prejudice, and men are in general so little conscious of this voluntary ignorance as a defect, that the vulgarest misunderstandings of ethical doctrines are continually met with in the deliberate writings of persons of the greatest pretensions both to high principle and to philosophy. We not uncommonly hear the doctrine of utility inveighed against as a *godless* doctrine. If it be necessary to say anything at all against so mere an assumption, we may say that the question depends upon what idea we have formed of the moral character of the Deity. If it be a true belief that God desires, above all things, the happiness of his creatures, and that this was his purpose in their creation, utility is not only not a godless doctrine, but more profoundly religious than any other. If it be meant that utilitarianism does not recognise the revealed will of God as the supreme law of morals, I answer, that a utilitarian who believes in the perfect goodness and wisdom of God, necessarily believes that whatever God has thought fit to reveal on the subject of morals, must fulfil the requirements of utility in a supreme degree. But others besides utilitarians have been of opinion that the Christian revelation was intended, and is fitted, to inform the hearts and minds of mankind with a spirit which should enable them to find for themselves what is right, and incline them to do it when found, rather than to tell them, except in a very general way, what it is; and that we need a doctrine of ethics, carefully followed out, to *interpret* to us the will of God. Whether this opinion is correct or not, it is superfluous here to discuss; since whatever aid religion, either natural or revealed, can afford to ethical investigation, is as open to the utilitarian moralist as to any other. He can use it as the testimony of God to the usefulness or hurtfulness of any given course of action, by as good a right as others can use it for the indication of a transcendental law, having no connexion with usefulness or with happiness.

Again, Utility is often summarily stigmatised as an immoral doctrine by giving it the name of Expediency, and taking advantage of the popular use of that term to contrast it with Principle. But the Expedient, in the sense in which it is opposed to the Right, generally means that which is expedient for the particular interest of the agent himself; as when a minister sacrifices the interests of his country to keep himself in place. When it means anything better than this, it means that which is expedient for some immediate object, some temporary purpose, but which violates a rule whose observance is expedient in a much higher degree. The Expedient, in this sense, instead of being the same thing with the useful, is a branch of the hurtful. Thus, it would often be expedient, for the purpose of getting over some momentary embarrassment, or attaining some object immediately useful to ourselves or others, to tell a lie. But inasmuch as the cultivation in ourselves of a sensitive feeling on the subject of veracity, is one of the most useful, and the enfeeblement of that feeling one of the most hurtful, things to which our conduct can be instrumental; and inasmuch as any, even unintentional, deviation from truth, does that much towards weakening the trustworthiness of human assertion, which is not only the principal support of all present social well-being, but the insufficiency of which does more than any one thing that can be named to keep back civilisation, virtue, everything on which human happiness on the largest scale depends; we feel that the violation, for a present advantage, of a rule of such transcendent expediency, is not expedient, and that he who, for the sake of a convenience to himself or to some other individual, does what depends on him to deprive mankind of the good, and inflict upon them the evil, involved in the greater or less reliance which they can place in each other's word, acts the part of one of their worst enemies. Yet that even this rule, sacred as it is, admits of possible exceptions, is acknowledged by all moralists; the chief of which is when the withholding of some fact (as of information from a male-factor, or of bad news from a person dangerously ill) would save an individual (especially an individual other than oneself) from great and unmerited evil, and when the withholding can only be effected by denial. But in order that the exception may not extend itself beyond the need, and may have the least possible effect in weakening reliance on veracity, it ought to be recognised, and, if possible, its limits defined; and if the principle of utility is good for anything, it must be good for weighing these conflicting utilities against one another, and marking out the region within which one or the other preponderates.

Again, defenders of utility often find themselves called upon to reply to such objections as this—that there is not time, previous to action, for calculating and weighing the effects of any line of conduct on the general happiness. This is exactly as if any one were to say that it is impossible to guide our conduct by Christianity, because there is not time, on every occasion on which anything has to be done, to read through the Old and New Testaments. The answer to the objection is, that there has been ample time, namely, the whole past duration of the human species. During all that time, mankind have been learning by experience the tendencies of actions; on which experience all the prudence, as well as all the morality of life, are dependent. People talk as if the commencement of this course of experience had hitherto been put off, and as if, at the moment when some man feels tempted to meddle with the property or life of another, he had to begin considering for the first time whether murder and theft are injurious to human happiness. Even then I do not think that he would find the question very puzzling; but, at all events, the matter is now done to his hand. It is truly a whimsical supposition that, if mankind were agreed in considering utility to be the test of morality, they would remain without any agreement as to what *is* useful, and

N

would take no measures for having their notions on the subject taught to the young, and enforced by law and opinion. There is no difficulty in proving any ethical standard whatever to work ill, if we suppose universal idiocy to be conjoined with it; but on any hypothesis short of that, mankind must by this time have acquired positive beliefs as to the effects of some actions on their happiness; and the beliefs which have thus come down are the rules of morality for the multitude, and for the philosopher until he has succeeded in finding better. That philosophers might easily do this, even now, on many subjects; that the received code of ethics is by no means of divine right; and that mankind have still much to learn as to the effects of actions on the general happiness, I admit, or rather, earnestly maintain. The corollaries from the principle of utility, like the precepts of every practical art, admit of indefinite improvement, and, in a progressive state of the human mind, their improvement is perpetually going on. But to consider the rules of morality as improvable, is one thing; to pass over the intermediate generalisations entirely, and endeavour to test each individual action directly by the first principle, is another. It is a strange notion that the acknowledgment of a first principle is inconsistent with the admission of secondary ones. To inform a traveller respecting the place of his ultimate destination, is not to forbid the use of landmarks and direction-posts on the way. The proposition that happiness is the end and aim of morality does not mean that no road ought to be laid down to that goal, or that persons going thither should not be advised to take one direction rather than another. Men really ought to leave off talking a kind of nonsense on this subject, which they would neither talk nor listen to on other matters of practical concernment. Nobody argues that the art of navigation is not founded on astronomy, because sailors cannot wait to calculate the Nautical Almanack. Being rational creatures, they go to sea with it ready calculated; and all rational creatures go out upon the sea of life with their minds made up on the common questions of right and wrong, as well as on many of the far more difficult questions of wise and foolish. And this, as long as foresight is a human quality, it is to be presumed they will continue to do. Whatever we adopt as the fundamental principle of morality, we require subordinate principles to apply it by; the impossibility of doing without them, being common to all systems, can afford no argument against any one in particular; but gravely to argue as if no such secondary principles could be had, and as if mankind had remained till now, and always must remain, without drawing any general conclusions from the experience of human life, is as high a pitch, I think, as absurdity has ever reached in philosophical controversy.

The remainder of the stock arguments against utilitarianism mostly consist in laying to its charge the common infirmities of human nature, and the general difficulties which embarrass conscientious persons in shaping their course through life. We are told that a utilitarian will be apt to make his own particular case an exception to moral rules, and, when under temptation, will see a utility in the breach of a rule, greater than he will see in its observance. But is utility the only creed which is able to furnish us with excuses for evil doing, and means of cheating our own conscience? They are afforded in abundance by all doctrines which recognise as a fact in morals the existence of conflicting considerations; which all doctrines do, that have been believed by sane persons. It is not the fault of any creed, but of the complicated nature of human affairs, that rules of conduct cannot be so framed as to require no exceptions, and that hardly any kind of action can safely be laid down as either always obligatory or always condemnable. There is no ethical creed which does not temper the rigidity of its laws, by giving a certain latitude, under the moral responsibility of the agent, for accommodation to peculiarities of circumstances; and under every creed, at the opening thus made, self-deception and dishonest casuistry get in. There exists no moral system under which there do not arise unequivocal cases of conflicting obligations. These are the real difficulties, the knotty points both in the theory of ethics, and in the conscientious guidance of personal conduct. They are overcome practically, with greater or with less success, according to the intellect and virtue of the individual; but it can hardly be pretended that any one will be the less qualified for dealing with them, from possessing an ultimate standard to which conflicting rights and duties can be referred. If utility is the ultimate source of moral obligations, utility may be invoked to decide between them when their demands are incompatible. Though the application of the standard may be difficult, it is better than none at all: while in other systems, the moral laws all claiming independent authority, there is no common umpire entitled to interfere between them; their claims to precedence one over another rest on little better than sophistry, and unless determined, as they generally are, by the unacknowledged influence of considerations of utility, afford a free scope for the action of personal desires and partialities. We must remember that only in these cases of conflict between secondary principles is it requisite that first principles should be appealed to. There is no case of moral obligation in which some secondary principle is not involved; and if only one, there can seldom be any real doubt which one it is, in the mind of any person by whom the principle itself is recognised.

# CHAPTER 3

## OF THE ULTIMATE SANCTION OF THE PRINCIPLE OF UTILITY

THE question is often asked, and properly so, in regard to any supposed moral standard—What is its sanction? what are the motives to obey it? or more specifically, what is the source of its obligation? whence does it derive its binding force? It is a necessary part of moral philosophy to provide the answer to this question; which, though frequently assuming the shape of an objection to the utilitarian morality, as if it had some special applicability to that above others, really arises in regard to all standards. It arises, in fact, whenever a person is called on to *adopt* a standard, or refer morality to any basis on which he has not been accustomed to rest it. For the customary morality, that which education and opinion have consecrated, is the only one which presents itself to the mind with the feeling of being *in itself* obligatory; and when a person is asked to believe that this morality *derives* its obligation from some general principle round which custom has not thrown the same halo, the assertion is to him a paradox; the supposed corollaries seem to have a more binding force than the original theorem; the superstructure seems to stand better without, than with, what is represented as its foundation. He says to himself, I feel that I am bound not to rob or murder, betray or deceive; but why am I bound to promote the general happiness? If my own happiness lies in something else, why may I not give that the preference?

If the view adopted by the utilitarian philosophy of the nature of the moral sense be correct, this difficulty will always present itself, until the influences which form moral character have taken the same hold of the principle which they have taken of some of the consequences—until, by the improvement of education, the feeling of unity with our fellow-creatures shall be (what it cannot be denied that Christ intended it to be) as deeply rooted in our character, and to our own consciousness as completely a part of our nature, as the horror of crime is in an ordinarily well brought up young person. In the meantime, however, the difficulty has no peculiar application to the doctrine of utility, but is inherent in every attempt to analyse morality and reduce it to principles; which, unless the principle is already in men's minds invested with as much sacredness as any of its applications, always seems to divest them of a part of their sanctity.

The principle of utility either has, or there is no reason why it might not have, all the sanctions which belong to any other system or morals. Those sanctions are either external or internal. Of the external sanctions it is not necessary to speak at any length. They are, the hope of favour and the fear of displeasure, from our fellow-creatures or from the Ruler of the Universe, along with whatever we may have of sympathy or affection for them, or of love and awe of Him, inclining us to do His will independently of selfish consequences. There is evidently no reason why all these motives for observance should not attach themselves to the utilitarian morality, as completely and as powerfully as to any other. Indeed, those of them which refer to our fellow-creatures are sure to do so, in proportion to the amount of general intelligence; for whether there be any other ground of moral obligation than the general happiness or not, men do desire happiness; and however imperfect may be their own practice, they desire and commend all conduct in others towards themselves, by which they think their happiness is promoted. With regard to the religious motive, if men believe, as most profess to do, in the goodness of God, those who think that conduciveness to the general happiness is the essence, or even only the criterion of good, must necessarily believe that it is also that which God approves. The whole force therefore of external reward and punishment, whether physical or moral, and whether proceeding from God or from our fellow men, together with all that the capacities of human nature admit of disinterested devotion to either, become available to enforce the utilitarian morality, in proportion as that morality is recognised; and the more powerfully, the more the appliances of education and general cultivation are bent to the purpose.

So far as to external sanctions. The internal sanction of duty, whatever our standard of duty may be, is one and the same—a feeling in our own mind; a pain, more or less intense, attendant on violation of duty, which in properly cultivated moral natures rises, in the more serious cases, into shrinking from it as an impossibility. This feeling, when disinterested, and connecting itself with the pure idea of duty, and not with some particular form of it, or with any of the merely accessory circumstances, is the essence of Conscience; though in that complex phenomenon as it actually exists, the simple fact is in general all encrusted over with collateral associations, derived from sympathy, from love, and still more from fear; from all the forms of religious feeling; from the recollections of childhood and of all our past life; from self-esteem, desire of the esteem of others, and occasionally even self-abasement. This extreme complication is, I apprehend, the origin of the sort of mystical character which, by a tendency of the human mind of which there are many other examples, is apt to be attributed to the idea of moral obligation, and which leads people to believe that the idea cannot possibly attach itself to any other objects than those which, by a supposed mysterious law, are found in our present experience to excite it. Its binding force, however, consists in the existence of a mass of feeling which must be broken through in order to do what violates our standard of right, and which, if we do nevertheless violate that standard, will probably have to be encountered afterwards in the form of remorse. Whatever theory we have of the nature or origin of conscience, this is what essentially constitutes it.

The ultimate sanction, therefore, of all morality (external motives apart) being a subjective feeling in our own minds, I see nothing embarrassing to those whose standard is utility, in the question, what is the sanction of that particular standard? We may answer, the same as of all other moral standards—the conscientious feelings of mankind. Undoubtedly this sanction has no binding efficacy on those who do not possess the feelings it appeals to; but neither will these persons be more obedient to any other moral principle than to the utilitarian one. On them morality of any kind has no hold but through the external sanctions. Meanwhile the feelings exist, a fact in human nature, the reality of which, and the great power with which they are capable of acting on those in whom they have been duly cultivated, are proved by experience. No reason has ever been shown why they may not be cultivated to as great intensity in connexion with the utilitarian, as with any other rule of morals.

There is, I am aware, a disposition to believe that a person who sees in moral obligation a transcendental fact, an objective reality belonging to the province of 'Things in themselves,' is likely to be more obedient to it than one who believes it to be entirely subjective, having its seat in human consciousness only. But whatever a person's opinion may be on this point of Ontology, the force he is really urged by is his own subjective feeling, and is exactly measured by its strength. No one's belief that duty is an objective reality is stronger than the belief that God is so; yet the belief in God, apart from the expectation of actual reward and punishment, only operates on conduct through, and in proportion to, the subjective religious feeling. The sanction, so far as it is disinterested, is always in the mind itself; and the notion therefore of the transcendental moralists must be, that this sanction will not exist *in* the mind unless it is believed to have its root out of the mind; and that if a person is able to say to himself, This which is restraining me, and which is called my conscience, is only a feeling in my own mind, he may possibly draw the conclusion that when the feeling ceases the obligation ceases, and that if he find the feeling inconvenient, he may disregard it, and endeavour to get rid of it. But is this danger confined to the utilitarian morality? Does the belief that moral obligation has its seat outside the mind make the feeling of it too strong to be got rid of? The fact is so far otherwise, that all moralists admit and lament the ease with which, in the generality of minds, conscience can be silenced or stifled. The question, Need I obey my conscience? is quite as often put to themselves by persons who never heard of the principle of utility, as by its adherents. Those whose conscientious feelings are so weak as to allow of their asking this question, if they answer it affirmatively, will not do so because they believe in the transcendental theory, but because of the external sanctions.

It is not necessary, for the present purpose, to decide whether the feeling of duty is innate or implanted. Assuming it to be innate, it is an open question to what objects it naturally attaches itself; for the philosophic supporters of that theory are now agreed that the intuitive perception is of principles of morality and not of the details. If there be anything innate in the matter, I see no reason why the feeling which is innate should not be that of regard to the pleasures and pains of others. If there is any principle of morals which is intuitively obligatory, I should say it must be that. If so, the intuitive ethics would coincide with the utilitarian, and there would be no further quarrel between them. Even as it is, the intuitive moralists, though they believe that there are other intuitive moral obligations, do already believe this to be one; for they unanimously hold that a large *portion* of morality turns upon the consideration due to the interests of our fellow-creatures. Therefore, if the belief in the transcendental origin of moral obligation gives any additional efficacy to the internal sanction, it appears to me that the utilitarian principle has already the benefit of it.

On the other hand, if, as is my own belief, the moral feelings are not innate, but acquired, they are not for that reason the less natural. It is natural to man to speak, to reason, to build cities, to cultivate the ground, though these are acquired faculties. The moral feelings are not indeed a part of our nature, in the sense of being in any perceptible degree present in all of us; but this, unhappily, is a fact admitted by those who believe the most strenuously in their transcendental origin. Like the other acquired capacities above referred to, the moral faculty, if not a part of our nature, is a natural outgrowth from it; capable, like them, in a certain small degree, of springing up spontaneously; and susceptible of being brought by cultivation to a high degree of development. Unhappily it is also susceptible, by a sufficient use of the external sanctions and of the force of early impressions, of being cultivated in almost any direction: so that there is hardly anything so absurd or so mischievous that it may not, by means of these influences, be made to act on the human mind with all the authority of conscience. To doubt that the same potency might be given by the same means to the principle of utility, even if it had no foundation in human nature, would be flying in the face of all experience.

But moral associations which are wholly of artificial creation, when intellectual culture goes on, yield by degrees to the dissolving force of analysis: and if the feeling of duty, when associated with utility, would appear equally arbitrary; if there were no leading department of our nature, no powerful class of sentiments, with which that association would harmonise, which would make us feel it congenial, and incline us not only to foster it in others (for which we have abundant interested motives), but also to cherish it in ourselves; if there were not, in short, a natural basis of sentiment for utilitarian morality, it might well happen that this association also, even after it had been implanted by education, might be analysed away.

But there *is* this basis of powerful natural sentiment; and this it is which, when once the general happiness is recognised as the ethical standard, will constitute the strength of the utilitarian morality. This firm foundation is that of the social feelings of mankind; the desire to be in unity with our fellow creatures, which is already a powerful principle in human nature, and happily one of those which tend to become stronger, even without express inculcation, from the influences of advancing civilisation. The social state is at once so natural, so necessary, and so habitual to man, that, except in some unusual circumstances or by an effort of voluntary abstraction, he never conceives himself otherwise than as a member of a body; and this association is riveted more and more, as mankind are further removed from the state of savage independence. Any condition, therefore, which is essential to a state of society, becomes more and more an inseparable part of every person's conception of the state of things which he is born into, and which is the destiny of a human being. Now, society between human beings, except in the relation of master and slave, is manifestly impossible on any other footing than that the interests of all are to be consulted. Society between equals can only exist on the understanding that the interests of all are to be regarded equally. And since in all states of civilisation, every person, except an absolute monarch, has equals, every one is obliged to live on these terms with somebody; and in every age some advance is made towards a state in which it will be impossible to live permanently on other terms with anybody. In this way people grow up unable to conceive as possible to them a state of total disregard of other people's interests. They are under a necessity of conceiving themselves as at least abstaining from all the grosser injuries, and (if only for their own protection) living in a state of constant protest against them. They are also familiar with the fact of co-operating with others, and proposing to themselves a collective, not an individual interest as the aim (at least for the time being) of their actions. So long as they are co-operating, their ends are identified with those of others; there is at least a temporary feeling that the interests of others are their own interests. Not only does all strengthening of social ties, and all healthy growth of society, give to each individual a stronger personal interest in practically consulting the welfare of others; it also leads him to identify his *feelings* more and more with their good, or at least with an even greater degree of practical consideration for it. He comes, as though instinctively, to be conscious of himself as a being who *of course* pays regard to others. The good of others becomes to him a thing naturally and necessarily to be attended to, like any of the physical conditions of our existence. Now, whatever amount of this feeling a person has, he is urged by the strongest motives both of interest and of sympathy to demonstrate it, and to the utmost of his power encourage it in others; and even if he has none of it himself, he is as greatly interested as any one else that others should have it. Consequently the smallest germs of the feeling are laid hold of and nourished by the contagion of sympathy and the influences of education; and a complete web of corroborative association is woven round it, by the powerful agency of the external sanctions. This mode of conceiving ourselves and human life, as civilisation goes on, is felt to be more and more natural. Every step in political improvement renders it more so, by removing the sources of opposition of interest, and levelling those inequalities of legal privilege between individuals or classes, owing to which there are large portions of mankind whose happiness it is still practicable to disregard. In an improving state of the human mind, the influences are constantly on the increase, which tend to generate in each individual a feeling of unity with all the rest; which, if perfect, would make him never think of, or desire, any beneficial condition for himself, in the benefits of which they are not included. If we now suppose this feeling of unity to be taught as a religion, and the whole force of education, of institutions, and of opinion, directed, as it once was in the case of religion, to make every person grow up from infancy surrounded on all sides both by the profession and the practice of it, I think that no one, who can realise this conception, will feel any misgiving about the sufficiency of the ultimate sanction for the Happiness morality. To any ethical student who finds the realisation difficult, I recommend, as a means of facilitating it, the second of

M. Comte's two principal works, the *Traité de Politique Positive*. I entertain the strongest objections to the system of politics and morals set forth in that treatise; but I think it has superabundantly shown the possibility of giving to the service of humanity, even without the aid of belief in a Providence, both the psychological power and the social efficacy of a religion; making it take hold of human life, and colour all thought, feeling, and action, in a manner of which the greatest ascendancy ever exercised by any religion may be but a type and foretaste; and of which the danger is, not that it should be insufficient, but that it should be so excessive as to interfere unduly with human freedom and individuality.

Neither is it necessary to the feeling which constitutes the binding force of the utilitarian morality on those who recognise it, to wait for those social influences which would make its obligation felt by mankind at large. In the comparatively early state of human advancement in which we now live, a person cannot indeed feel that entireness of sympathy with all others, which would make any real discordance in the general direction of their conduct in life impossible; but already a person in whom the social feeling is at all developed, cannot bring himself to think of the rest of his fellow-creatures as struggling rivals with him for the means of happiness, whom he must desire to see defeated in their object in order that he may succeed in his. The deeply rooted conception which every individual even now has of himself as a social being, tends to make him feel it one of his natural wants that there should be harmony between his feelings and aims and those of his fellow-creatures. If differences of opinion and of mental culture make it impossible for him to share many of their actual feelings— perhaps make him denounce and defy those feelings—he still needs to be conscious that his real aim and theirs do not conflict; that he is not opposing himself to what they really wish for, namely their own good, but is, on the contrary, promoting it. This feeling in most individuals is much inferior in strength to their selfish feelings, and is often wanting altogether. But to those who have it, it possesses all the characters of a natural feeling. It does not present itself to their minds as a superstition of education, or a law despotically imposed by the power of society, but as an attribute which it would not be well for them to be without. This conviction is the ultimate sanction of the greatest happiness morality. This it is which makes any mind, of well-developed feelings, work with, and not against, the outward motives to care for others, afforded by what I have called the external sanctions; and when those sanctions are wanting, or act in an opposite direction, constitutes in itself a powerful internal binding force, in proportion to the sensitiveness and thoughtfulness of the character; since few but those whose mind is a moral blank, could bear to lay out their course of life on the plan of paying no regard to others except so far as their own private interest compels.

# CHAPTER 4

## OF WHAT SORT OF PROOF THE PRINCIPLE OF UTILITY IS SUSCEPTIBLE

IT has already been remarked, that questions of ultimate ends do not admit of proof, in the ordinary acceptation of the term. To be incapable of proof by reasoning is common to all first principles; to the first premises of our knowledge, as well as to those of our conduct. But the former, being matters of fact, may be the subject of a direct appeal to the faculties which judge of fact—namely, our senses, and our internal consciousness. Can an appeal be made to the same faculties on questions of practical ends? Or by what other faculty is cognisance taken of them?

Questions about ends are, in other words, questions what things are desirable. The utilitarian doctrine is, that happiness is desirable, and the only thing desirable, as an end; all other things being only desirable as means to that end. What ought to be required of this doctrine—what conditions is it requisite that the doctrine should fulfil—to make good its claim to be believed?

The only proof capable of being given that an object is visible, is that people actually see it. The only proof that a sound is audible, is that people hear it: and so of the other sources of our experience. In like manner, I apprehend, the sole evidence it is possible to produce that anything is desirable, is that people do actually desire it. If the end which the utilitarian doctrine proposes to itself were not, in theory and in practice, acknowledged to be an end, nothing could ever convince any person that it was so. No reason can be given why the general happiness is desirable, except that each person, so far as he believes it to be attainable, desires his own happiness. This, however, being a fact, we have not only all the proof which the case admits of, but all which it is possible to require, that happiness is a good: that each person's happiness is a good to that person, and the general happiness, therefore, a good to the aggregate of all persons. Happiness has made out its title as *one* of the ends of conduct, and consequently one of the criteria of morality.

But it has not, by this alone, proved itself to be the sole criterion. To do that, it would seem, by the same rule, necessary to show, not only that people desire happiness, but that they never desire anything else. Now it is palpable that they do desire things which, in common language, are decidedly distinguished from happiness. They desire, for example, virtue, and the absence of vice, no less really than pleasure and the absence of pain. The desire of virtue is not as universal, but it is as authentic a fact, as the desire of happiness. And hence the opponents of the utilitarian standard deem that they have a right to infer that there are other ends of human action besides happiness, and that happiness is not the standard of approbation and disapprobation.

But does the utilitarian doctrine deny that people desire virtue, or maintain that virtue is not a thing to be desired? The very reverse. It maintains not only that virtue is to be desired, but that it is to be desired disinterestedly, for itself. Whatever may be the opinion of utilitarian moralists as to the original conditions by which virtue is made virtue; however they may believe (as they do) that actions and dispositions are only virtuous because they promote another end than virtue; yet this being granted, and it having been decided, from considerations of this description, what *is* virtuous, they not only place virtue at the very head of the things which are good as means to the ultimate end, but they also recognise as a psychological fact the possibility of its being, to the individual, a good in itself, without looking to any end beyond it; and hold, that the mind is not in a right state, not in a state conformable to Utility, not in the state most conducive to the general happiness, unless it does love virtue in this manner—as a thing desirable in itself, even although, in the individual instance, it should not produce those other desirable consequences which it tends to produce, and on account of which it is held to be virtue. This opinion is not, in the smallest degree, a departure from the Happiness principle. The ingredients of happiness are very various, and each of them is desirable in itself, and not merely when considered as swelling an aggregate. The principle of utility does not mean that any given pleasure, as music, for instance, or any given exemption from pain, as for example health, is to be looked upon as means to a collective something termed happiness, and to be desired on that account. They are desired and desirable in and for themselves; besides being means, they are a part of the end. Virtue, according to the utilitarian doctrine, is not naturally and originally part of the end, but it is capable of becoming so; and in those who love it disinterestedly it has become so, and is desired and cherished, not as a means to happiness, but as a part of their happiness.

To illustrate this farther, we may remember that virtue is not the only thing, originally a means, and which if it were not a means to anything else, would be and remain indifferent, but which by association with what it is a means to, comes to be desired for itself, and that too with the utmost intensity. What, for example, shall we say of the love of money? There is nothing originally more desirable about money than about any heap of glittering pebbles. Its worth is solely that of the things which it will buy; the desires for other things than itself, which it is a means of gratifying. Yet the love of money is not only one of the strongest moving forces of human life, but money is, in many cases, desired in and for itself; the desire to possess it is often stronger than the desire to use it, and goes on increasing when all the desires which point to ends beyond it, to be compassed by it, are falling off. It may, then, be said truly, that money is desired not for the sake of an end, but as part of the end. From being a means to happiness, it has come to be itself a principal ingredient of the individual's conception of happiness. The same may be said of the majority of the great objects of human life—power, for example, or fame; except that to each of these there is a certain amount of immediate pleasure annexed, which has at least the semblance of being naturally inherent in them; a thing which cannot be said of money. Still, however, the strongest natural attraction, both of power and of fame, is the immense aid they give to the attainment of our other wishes; and it is the strong association thus generated between them and all our objects of desire, which gives to the direct desire of them the intensity it often assumes, so as in some characters to surpass in strength all other desires. In these cases the means have become a part of the end, and a more important part of it than any of the things which they are means to. What was once desired as an instrument for the attainment of happiness, has come to be desired for its own sake. In being desired for its own sake it is, however, desired as *part* of happiness. The person is made, or thinks he would be made, happy by its mere possession; and is made unhappy by failure to obtain it. The desire of it is not a different thing from the desire of happiness, any more than the love of music, or the desire of health. They are included in happiness. They are some of the elements of which the desire of happiness is made up. Happiness is not an abstract idea, but a concrete whole; and these are some of its parts. And the utilitarian standard sanctions and approves their being so. Life would be a poor thing, very ill provided with sources of happiness, if there were not this provision of nature, by which things originally indifferent, but conducive to, or otherwise associated with, the satisfaction of our primitive desires, become in themselves sources of pleasure more valuable than the primitive pleasures, both in permanency, in the space of human existence that they are capable of covering, and even in intensity.

Virtue, according to the utilitarian conception, is a good of this description. There was no original desire of it, or motive to it, save its conduciveness to pleasure, and especially to protection from pain. But through the association thus formed, it may be felt a good in itself, and desired as such with as great intensity as any other good; and with this difference between it and the love of money, of power, or of fame, that all of these may, and often do, render the individual noxious to the other members of the society to which he belongs, whereas there is nothing which makes him so much a blessing to them as the cultivation of the disinterested love of virtue. And consequently, the utilitarian standard, while it tolerates and approves those other acquired desires, up to the point beyond which they would be more injurious to the general happiness than promotive of it, enjoins and requires the cultivation of the love of virtue up to the greatest strength possible, as being above all things important to the general happiness.

It results from the preceding considerations, that there is in reality nothing desired except happiness. Whatever is desired otherwise than as a means to some end beyond itself, and ultimately to happiness, is desired as itself a part of happiness, and is not desired for itself until it has become so. Those who desire virtue for its own sake, desire it either because the consciousness of it is a pleasure, or because the consciousness of being without it is a pain, or for both reasons united; as in truth the pleasure and pain seldom exist separately, but almost always together, the same person feeling pleasure in the degree of virtue attained, and pain in not having attained more. If one of these gave him no pleasure, and the other no pain, he would not love or desire virtue, or would desire it only for the other benefits which it might produce to himself or to persons whom he cared for.

We have now, then, an answer to the question, of what sort of proof the principle of utility is susceptible. If the opinion which I have now stated is psychologically true—if human nature is so constituted as to desire nothing which is not either a part of happiness or a means of happiness, we can have no other proof, and we require no other, that these are the only things desirable. If so, happiness is the sole end of human action, and the promotion of it the test by which to judge of all human conduct; from whence it necessarily follows that it must be the criterion of morality, since a part is included in the whole.

And now to decide whether this is really so; whether mankind do desire nothing for itself but that which is a pleasure to them, or of which the absence is a pain; we have evidently arrived at a question of fact and experience, dependent, like all similar questions, upon evidence. It can only be determined by practised self-consciousness and self-observation, assisted by observation of others. I believe that these sources of evidence, impartially consulted, will declare that desiring a thing and finding it pleasant, aversion to it and thinking of it as painful, are phenomena entirely inseparable, or rather two parts of the same phenomenon; in strictness of language, two different modes of naming the same psychological fact: that to think of an object as desirable (unless for the sake of its consequences), and to think of it as pleasant, are one and the same thing; and that to desire anything, except in proportion as the idea of it is pleasant, is a physical and metaphysical impossibility.

So obvious does this appear to me, that I expect it will hardly be disputed: and the objection made will be, not that desire can possibly be directed to anything ultimately except pleasure and exemption from pain, but that the will is a different thing from desire; that a person of confirmed virtue, or any other person whose purposes are fixed, carries out his purposes without any thought of the pleasure he has in contemplating them, or expects to derive from their fulfilment; and persists in acting on them, even though these pleasures are much diminished, by changes in his character or decay of his passive sensibilities, or are outweighed by the pains which the pursuit of the purposes may bring upon him. All this I fully admit, and have stated it elsewhere, as positively and emphatically as any one. Will, the active phenomenon, is a different thing from desire, the state of passive sensibility, and though originally an offshoot from it, may in time take root and detach itself from the parent stock; so much so, that in the case of an habitual purpose, instead of willing the thing because we desire it, we often desire it only because we will it. This, however, is but an instance of that familiar fact, the power of habit, and is nowise confined to the case of virtuous actions. Many indifferent things, which men originally did from a motive of some sort, they continue to do from habit. Sometimes this is done unconsciously, the consciousness coming only after the action; at other times with conscious volition, but volition which has become habitual, and is put in operation by the force of habit, in opposition perhaps to the deliberate preference, as often happens with those who have contracted habits of vicious or hurtful indulgence. Third and last comes the case in which the habitual act of will in the individual instance is not in contradiction to the general intention prevailing at other times, but in fulfilment of it; as in the case of the person of confirmed virtue, and of all who pursue deliberately and consistently any determinate end. The distinction between will and desire thus understood is an authentic and highly important psychological fact; but the fact consists solely in this—that will, like all other parts of our constitution, is amenable to habit, and that we may will from habit what we no longer desire for itself, or desire only because we will it. It is not the less true that will, in the beginning, is entirely produced by desire; including in that term the repelling influence of pain as well as the attractive one of pleasure. Let us take into consideration, no longer the person who has a confirmed will to do right, but him in whom that virtuous will is still feeble, conquerable by temptation, and not to be fully relied on; by what means can it be strengthened? How can the will to be virtuous, where it does not exist in sufficient force, be implanted or awakened? Only by making the person *desire* virtue—by making him think of it in a pleasurable light, or of its absence in a painful one. It is by associating the doing right with pleasure, or the doing wrong with pain, or by eliciting and impressing and bringing home to the person's experience the pleasure naturally involved in the one or the pain in the other, that it is possible to call forth that will to be virtuous, which, when confirmed, acts without any thought of either pleasure or pain. Will is the child of desire, and passes out of the dominion of its parent only to come under that of habit. That which is the result of habit affords no presumption of being intrinsically good; and there would be no reason for wishing that the purpose of virtue should become independent of pleasure and pain, were it not that the influence of the pleasurable and painful associations which prompt to virtue is not sufficiently to be depended on for unerring constancy of action until it has acquired the support of habit. Both in feeling and in conduct, habit is the only thing which imparts certainty; and it is because of the importance to others of being able to rely absolutely on one's feelings and conduct, and to oneself of being able to rely on one's own, that the will to do right ought to be cultivated into this habitual independence. In other words, this state of the will is a means to good, not intrinsically a good; and does not contradict the doctrine that nothing is a good to human beings but in so far as it is either itself pleasurable, or a means of attaining pleasure or averting pain.

But if this doctrine be true, the principle of utility is proved. Whether it is so or not, must now be left to the consideration of the thoughtful reader.

# CHAPTER 5

# ON THE CONNEXION BETWEEN JUSTICE AND UTILITY

In all ages of speculation, one of the strongest obstacles to the reception of the doctrine that Utility or Happiness is the criterion of right and wrong, has been drawn from the idea of Justice. The powerful sentiment, and apparently clear perception, which that word recalls with a rapidity and certainty resembling an instinct, have seemed to the majority of thinkers to point to an inherent quality in things; to show that the Just must have an existence in Nature as something absolute, generically distinct from every variety of the Expedient, and, in idea, opposed to it, though (as is commonly acknowledged) never, in the long run, disjoined from it in fact.

In the case of this, as of our other moral sentiments, there is no necessary connexion between the question of its origin, and that of its binding force. That a feeling is bestowed on us by Nature, does not necessarily legitimate all its promptings. The feeling of justice might be a peculiar instinct, and might yet require, like our other instincts, to be controlled and enlightened by a higher reason. If we have intellectual instincts, leading us to judge in a particular way, as well as animal instincts that prompt us to act in a particular way, there is no necessity that the former should be more infallible in their sphere than the latter in theirs: it may as well happen that wrong judgments are occasionally suggested by those, as wrong actions by these. But though it is one thing to believe that we have natural feelings of justice, and another to acknowledge them as an ultimate criterion of conduct, these two opinions are very closely connected in point of fact. Mankind are always predisposed to believe that any subjective feeling, not otherwise accounted for, is a revelation of some objective reality. Our present object is to determine whether the reality, to which the feeling of justice corresponds, is one which needs any such special revelation; whether the justice or injustice of an action is a thing intrinsically peculiar, and distinct from all its other qualities, or only a combination of certain of those qualities, presented under a peculiar aspect. For the purpose of this inquiry it is practically important to consider whether the feeling itself, of justice and injustice, is *sui generis* like our sensations of colour and taste, or a derivative feeling, formed by a combination of others. And this it is the more essential to examine, as people are in general willing enough to allow, that objectively the dictates of Justice coincide with a part of the field of General Expediency; but inasmuch as the subjective mental feeling of Justice is different from that which commonly attaches to simple expediency, and, except in the extreme cases of the latter, is far more imperative in its demands, people find it difficult to see, in Justice, only a particular kind or branch of general utility, and think that its superior binding force requires a totally different origin.

To throw light upon this question, it is necessary to attempt to ascertain what is the distinguishing character of justice, or of injustice: what is the quality, or whether there is any quality, attributed in common to all modes of conduct designated as unjust (for justice, like many other moral attributes, is best defined by its opposite), and distinguishing them from such modes of conduct as are disapproved, but without having that particular epithet of disapprobation applied to them. If in everything which men are accustomed to characterise as just or unjust, some one common attribute or collection of attributes is always present, we may judge whether this particular attribute or combination of attributes would be capable of gathering round it a sentiment of that peculiar character and intensity by virtue of the general laws of our emotional constitution, or whether the sentiment is inexplicable, and requires to be regarded as a special provision of Nature. If we find the former to be the case, we shall, in resolving this question, have resolved also the main problem: if the latter, we shall have to seek for some other mode of investigating it.

To find the common attributes of a variety of objects, it is necessary to begin by surveying the objects themselves in the concrete. Let us therefore advert successively to the various modes of action, and arrangements of human affairs, which are classed, by universal or widely spread opinion, as Just or as Unjust.

The things well known to excite the sentiments associated with those names are of a very multifarious character. I shall pass them rapidly in review, without studying any particular arrangement.

In the first place, it is mostly considered unjust to deprive any one of his personal liberty, his property, or any other thing which belongs to him by law. Here, therefore, is one instance of the application of the terms just and unjust in a perfectly definite sense, namely, that it is just to respect, unjust to violate, the *legal rights* of any one. But this judgment admits of several exceptions, arising from the other forms in which the notions of justice and injustice present themselves. For example, the person who suffers the deprivation may (as the phrase is) have *forfeited* the rights which he is so deprived of: a case to which we shall return presently. But also,

Secondly, the legal rights of which he is deprived, may be rights which *ought* not to have belonged to him; in other words, the law which confers on him these rights, may be a bad law. When it is so, or when (which is the same thing for our purpose) it is supposed to be so, opinions will differ as to the justice or injustice of infringing it. Some maintain that no law, however bad, ought to be disobeyed by an individual citizen; that his opposition to it, if shown at all, should only be shown in endeavouring to get it altered by competent authority. This opinion (which condemns many of the most illustrious benefactors of mankind, and would often protect pernicious institutions against the only weapons which, in the state of things existing at the time, have any chance of succeeding against them) is defended, by those who hold it, on grounds of expediency; principally on that of the importance, to the common interest of mankind, of maintaining inviolate the sentiment of submission to law. Other persons, again, hold the directly contrary opinion, that any law, judged to be bad, may blamelessly be disobeyed, even though it be not judged to be unjust, but only inexpedient; while others would confine the licence of disobedience to the case of unjust laws: but again, some say, that all laws which are inexpedient are unjust; since every law imposes some restriction on the natural liberty of mankind, which restriction is an injustice, unless legitimated by tending to their good. Among these diversities of opinion, it seems to be universally admitted that there may be unjust laws, and that law, consequently, is not the ultimate criterion of justice, but may give to one person a benefit, or impose on another an evil, which justice condemns. When, however, a law is thought to be unjust, it seems always to be regarded as being so in the same way in which a breach of law is unjust, namely, by infringing somebody's right; which, as it cannot in this case be a legal right, receives a different appellation, and is called a moral right. We may say, therefore, that a second case of injustice consists in taking or withholding from any person that to which he has a *moral right*.

Thirdly, it is universally considered just that each person should obtain that (whether good or evil) which he *deserves*; and unjust that he should obtain a good, or be made to undergo an evil, which he does not deserve. This is, perhaps, the clearest and most emphatic form in which the idea of justice is conceived by the general mind. As it involves the notion of desert, the question arises, what constitutes desert? Speaking in a general way, a person is understood to deserve good if he does right, evil if he does wrong; and in a more particular sense, to deserve good from those to whom he does or has done good, and evil from those to whom he does or has done evil. The precept of returning good for evil has never been regarded as a case of the fulfilment of justice, but as one in which the claims of justice are waived, in obedience to other considerations.

Fourthly, it is confessedly unjust to *break faith* with any one: to violate an engagement, either express or implied, or disappoint expectations raised by our own conduct, at least if we have raised those expectations knowingly and voluntarily. Like the other obligations of justice already spoken of, this one is not regarded as absolute, but as capable of being overruled by a stronger obligation of justice on the other side; or by such conduct on the part of the person concerned as is deemed to absolve us from our obligation to him, and to constitute a *forfeiture* of the benefit which he has been led to expect.

Fifthly, it is, by universal admission, inconsistent with justice to be *partial*; to show favour or preference to one person over another, in matters to which favour and preference do not properly apply. Impartiality, however, does not seem to be regarded as a duty in itself, but rather as instrumental to some other duty; for it is admitted that favour and preference are not always censurable, and indeed the cases in which they are condemned are rather the exception than the rule. A person would be more likely to be blamed than applauded for giving his family or friends no superiority in good offices over strangers, when he could do so without violating any other duty; and no one thinks it unjust to seek one person in preference to another as a friend, connection, or companion. Impartiality where rights are concerned is of course obligatory, but this is involved in the more general obligation of giving to every one his right. A tribunal, for example, must be impartial, because it is bound to award, without regard to any other consideration, a disputed object to the one of two parties who has the right to it. There are other cases in which impartiality means, being solely influenced by desert; as with those who, in the capacity of judges, preceptors, or parents, administer reward and punishment as such. There are cases, again, in which it means, being solely influenced by consideration for the public interest; as in making a selection among candidates for a government employment. Impartiality, in short, as an obligation of justice, may be said to mean, being exclusively influenced by the considerations which it is supposed ought to influence the particular case in hand; and resisting the solicitation of any motives which prompt to conduct different from what those considerations would dictate.

Nearly allied to the idea of impartiality is that of *equality*; which often enters as a component part both into the conception of justice and into the practice of it, and, in the eyes of many persons, constitutes its essence. But in this, still more than in any other case, the notion of justice varies in different persons, and always conforms in its variations to their notion of utility. Each person maintains that equality is the dictate of justice, except where he thinks that expediency requires inequality. The justice of giving equal protection to the rights of all, is maintained by those who support the most outrageous inequality in the rights themselves. Even in slave countries it is theoretically admitted that the rights of the slave, such as they are, ought to be as sacred as those of the master; and that a tribunal which fails to enforce them with equal strictness is wanting in justice; while, at the same time, institutions which leave to the slave scarcely any rights to enforce, are not deemed unjust, because they are not deemed inexpedient. Those who think that utility requires distinctions of rank, do not consider it unjust that riches and social privileges should be unequally dispensed; but those who think this inequality inexpedient, think it unjust also. Whoever thinks that government is necessary, sees no injustice in as much inequality as is constituted by giving to the magistrate powers not granted to other people. Even among those who hold levelling doctrines, there are as many questions of justice as there are differences of opinion about expediency. Some Communists consider it unjust that the produce of the labour of the community should be shared on any other principle than that of exact equality; others think it just that those should receive most whose wants are greatest; while others hold that those who work harder, or who produce more, or whose services are more valuable to the community, may justly claim a larger quota in the division of the produce. And the sense of natural justice may be plausibly appealed to in behalf of every one of these opinions.

Among so many diverse applications of the term Justice, which yet is not regarded as ambiguous, it is a matter of some difficulty to seize the mental link which holds them together, and on which the moral sentiment adhering to the term essentially depends. Perhaps, in this embarrassment, some help may be derived from the history of the word, as indicated by its etymology.

In most, if not in all, languages, the etymology of the word which corresponds to Just, points distinctly to an origin connected with the ordinances of law. *Justum* is a form of *jussum*, that which has been ordered. Δίκαιον comes directly from δίκη, a suit at law. *Recht*, from which came *right* and *righteous*, is synonymous with law. The courts of justice, the administration of justice, are the courts and the administration of law. *La justice*, in French, is the established term for judicature. I am not committing the fallacy imputed with some show of truth to Horne Tooke, of assuming that a word must still continue to mean what it originally meant. Etymology is slight evidence of what the idea now signified is, but the very best evidence of how it sprang up. There can, I think, be no doubt that the *idée mère*, the primitive element, in the formation of the notion of justice, was conformity to law. It constituted the entire idea among the Hebrews, up to the birth of Christianity; as might be expected in the case of a people whose laws attempted to embrace all subjects on which precepts were required, and who believed those laws to be a direct emanation from the Supreme Being. But other nations, and in particular the Greeks and Romans, who knew that their laws had been made originally, and still continued to be made, by men, were not afraid to admit that those men might make bad laws; might do, by law, the same things, and from the same motives, which if done by individuals without the sanction of law, would be called unjust. And hence the sentiment of injustice came to be attached, not to all violations of law, but only to violations of such laws as *ought* to exist, including such as ought to exist, but do not; and to laws themselves, if supposed to be contrary to what ought to be law. In this manner the idea of law and of its injunctions was still predominant in the notion of justice, even when the laws actually in force ceased to be accepted as the standard of it.

It is true that mankind consider the idea of justice and its obligations as applicable to many things which neither are, nor is it desired that they should be, regulated by law. Nobody desires that laws should interfere with the whole detail of private life; yet every one allows that in all daily conduct a person may and does show himself to be either just or unjust. But even here, the idea of the breach of what ought to be law, still lingers in a modified shape. It would always give us pleasure, and chime in with our feelings of fitness, that acts which we deem unjust should be punished, though we do not always think it expedient that this should be done by the tribunals. We forego that gratification on account of incidental inconveniences. We should be glad to see just conduct enforced and injustice repressed, even in the minutest details, if we were not, with reason, afraid of trusting the magistrate with so unlimited an amount of power over individuals. When we think that a person is bound in justice to do a thing, it is an ordinary form of language to say, that he ought to be compelled to do it. We should be gratified to see the obligation enforced by anybody who had the power. If we see that its enforcement by law would be inexpedient, we lament the impossibility, we consider the impunity given to injustice as an evil, and strive to make amends for it by bringing a strong expression of our own and the public disapprobation to bear upon the offender. Thus the idea of legal constraint is still the generating idea of the notion of justice, though undergoing several transformations before that notion, as it exists in an advanced state of society, becomes complete.

The above is, I think, a true account, as far as it goes, of the origin and progressive growth of the idea of justice. But we must observe, that it contains, as yet, nothing to distinguish that obligation from moral obligation in general. For the truth is, that the idea of penal sanction, which is the essence of law, enters not only into the conception of injustice, but into that of any kind of wrong. We do not call anything wrong, unless we mean to imply that a person ought to be punished in some way or other for doing it; if not by law, by the opinion of his fellow-creatures; if not by opinion, by the reproaches of his own conscience. This seems the real turning point of the distinction between morality and simple expediency. It is a part of the notion of Duty in every one of its forms, that a person may rightfully be compelled to fulfil it. Duty is a thing which may be *exacted* from a person, as one exacts a debt. Unless we think that it may be exacted from him, we do not call it his duty. Reasons of prudence, or the interest of other people, may militate against actually exacting it; but the person himself, it is clearly understood, would not be entitled to complain. There are other things, on the contrary, which we wish that people should do, which we like or admire them for doing, perhaps dislike or despise them for not doing, but yet admit that they are not bound to do; it is not a case of moral obligation; we do not blame them, that is, we do not think that they are proper objects of punishment. How we come by these ideas of deserving and not deserving punishment, will appear, perhaps, in the sequel; but I think there is no doubt that this distinction lies at the bottom of the notions of right and wrong; that we call any conduct wrong, or employ, instead, some other term of dislike or disparagement, according as we think that the person ought, or ought not, to be punished for it; and we say, it would be right to do so and so, or merely that it would be desirable or laudable, according as we would wish to see the person whom it concerns, compelled, or only persuaded and exhorted, to act in that manner.[1]

This, therefore, being the characteristic difference which marks off, not justice, but morality in general, from the remaining provinces of Expediency and Worthiness; the character is still

[1] See this point enforced and illustrated by Professor Bain, in an admirable chapter (entitled 'The Ethical Emotions, or the Moral Sense'), of the second of the two treatises composing his elaborate and profound work on the Mind.

to be sought which distinguishes justice from other branches of morality. Now it is known that ethical writers divide moral duties into two classes, denoted by the ill-chosen expressions, duties of perfect and of imperfect obligation; the latter being those in which, though the act is obligatory, the particular occasions of performing it are left to our choice; as in the case of charity or beneficence, which we are indeed bound to practise, but not towards any definite person, nor at any prescribed time. In the more precise language of philosophic jurists, duties of perfect obligation are those duties in virtue of which a correlative *right* resides in some person or persons; duties of imperfect obligation are those moral obligations which do not give birth to any right. I think it will be found that this distinction exactly coincides with that which exists between justice and the other obligations of morality. In our survey of the various popular acceptations of justice, the term appeared generally to involve the idea of a personal right—a claim on the part of one or more individuals, like that which the law gives when it confers a proprietary or other legal right. Whether the injustice consists in depriving a person of a possession, or in breaking faith with him, or in treating him worse than he deserves, or worse than other people who have no greater claims, in each case the supposition implies two things—a wrong done, and some assignable person who is wronged. Injustice may also be done by treating a person better than others; but the wrong in this case is to his competitors, who are also assignable persons. It seems to me that this feature in the case—a right in some person, correlative to the moral obligation—constitutes the specific difference between justice, and generosity or beneficence. Justice implies something which it is not only right to do, and wrong not to do, but which some individual person can claim from us as his moral right. No one has a moral right to our generosity or beneficence, because we are not morally bound to practise those virtues towards any given individual. And it will be found with respect to this as to every correct definition, that the instances which seem to conflict with it are those which most confirm it. For if a moralist attempts, as some have done, to make out that mankind generally, though not any given individual, have a right to all the good we can do them, he at once, by that thesis, includes generosity and beneficence within the category of justice. He is obliged to say, that our utmost

exertions are *due* to our fellow-creatures, thus assimilating them to
a debt; or that nothing less can be a sufficient *return* for what society
does for us, thus classing the case as one of gratitude; both of which
are acknowledged cases of justice. Wherever there is a right, the
case is one of justice, and not of the virtue of beneficence: and
whoever does not place the distinction between justice and morality
in general, where we have now placed it, will be found to make no
distinction between them at all, but to merge all morality in
justice.

Having thus endeavoured to determine the distinctive elements
which enter into the composition of the idea of justice, we are ready
to enter on the inquiry, whether the feeling, which accompanies
the idea, is attached to it by a special dispensation of nature, or
whether it could have grown up, by any known laws, out of the
idea itself; and in particular, whether it can have originated in
considerations of general expediency.

I conceive that the sentiment itself does not arise from anything
which would commonly, or correctly, be termed an idea of
expediency; but that though the sentiment does not, whatever
is moral in it does.

We have seen that the two essential ingredients in the sentiment
of justice are, the desire to punish a person who has done harm,
and the knowledge or belief that there is some definite individual
or individuals to whom harm has been done.

Now it appears to me, that the desire to punish a person who
has done harm to some individual is a spontaneous outgrowth
from two sentiments, both in the highest degree natural, and which
either are or resemble instincts; the impulse of self-defence, and the
feeling of sympathy.

It is natural to resent, and to repel or retaliate, any harm done
or attempted against ourselves, or against those with whom we
sympathise. The origin of this sentiment it is not necessary here
to discuss. Whether it be an instinct or a result of intelligence, it is,
we know, common to all animal nature; for every animal tries to
hurt those who have hurt, or who it thinks are about to hurt,
itself or its young. Human beings, on this point, only differ from
other animals in two particulars. First, in being capable of sympathising, not solely with their offspring, or, like some of the more

noble animals, with some superior animal who is kind to them, but with all human, and even with all sentient, beings. Secondly, in having a more developed intelligence, which gives a wider range to the whole of their sentiments, whether self-regarding or sympathetic. By virtue of his superior intelligence, even apart from his superior range of sympathy, a human being is capable of apprehending a community of interest between himself and the human society of which he forms a part, such that any conduct which threatens the security of the society generally, is threatening to his own, and calls forth his instinct (if instinct it be) of self-defence. The same superiority of intelligence, joined to the power of sympathising with human beings generally, enables him to attach himself to the collective idea of his tribe, his country, or mankind, in such a manner that any act hurtful to them, raises his instinct of sympathy, and urges him to resistance.

The sentiment of justice, in that one of its elements which consists of the desire to punish, is thus, I conceive, the natural feeling of retaliation or vengeance, rendered by intellect and sympathy applicable to those injuries, that is, to those hurts, which wound us through, or in common with, society at large. This sentiment, in itself, has nothing moral in it; what is moral is, the exclusive subordination of it to the social sympathies; so as to wait on and obey their call. For the natural feeling would make us resent indiscriminately whatever any one does that is disagreeable to us; but when moralised by the social feeling, it only acts in the directions conformable to the general good: just persons resenting a hurt to society, though not otherwise a hurt to themselves, and not resenting a hurt to themselves, however painful, unless it be of the kind which society has a common interest with them in the repression of.

It is no objection against this doctrine to say, that when we feel our sentiment of justice outraged, we are not thinking of society at large, or of any collective interest, but only of the individual case. It is common enough certainly, though the reverse of commendable, to feel resentment merely because we have suffered pain; but a person whose resentment is really a moral feeling, that is, who considers whether an act is blameable before he allows himself to resent it—such a person, though he may not say expressly to himself that he is standing up for the interest of society, certainly does feel that he is asserting a rule which is for the benefit of others as well as for his own. If he is not feeling this—if he is regarding the act solely as it affects him individually—he is not consciously just; he is not concerning himself about the justice of his actions. This is admitted even by anti-utilitarian moralists. When Kant (as before remarked) propounds as the fundamental principle of morals, 'So act, that thy rule of conduct might be adopted as a law by all rational beings,' he virtually acknowledges that the interest of mankind collectively, or at least of mankind indiscriminately, must be in the mind of the agent when conscientiously deciding on the morality of the act. Otherwise he uses words without a meaning: for, that a rule even of utter selfishness could not *possibly* be adopted by all rational beings—that there is any insuperable obstacle in the nature of things to its adoption— cannot be even plausibly maintained. To give any meaning to Kant's principle, the sense put upon it must be, that we ought to shape our conduct by a rule which all rational beings might adopt *with benefit to their collective interest.*

To recapitulate: the idea of justice supposes two things; a rule of conduct, and a sentiment which sanctions the rule. The first must be supposed common to all mankind, and intended for their good. The other (the sentiment) is a desire that punishment may be suffered by those who infringe the rule. There is involved, in addition, the conception of some definite person who suffers by the infringement; whose rights (to use the expression appropriated to the case) are violated by it. And the sentiment of justice appears to me to be, the animal desire to repel or retaliate a hurt or damage to oneself, or to those with whom one sympathises, widened so as to include all persons, by the human capacity of enlarged sympathy, and the human conception of intelligent self-interest. From the latter elements, the feeling derives its morality; from the former, its peculiar impressiveness, and energy of self-assertion.

I have, throughout, treated the idea of a *right* residing in the injured person, and violated by the injury, not as a separate element in the composition of the idea and sentiment, but as one of the forms in which the other two elements clothe themselves. These elements are, a hurt to some assignable person or persons on the one hand, and a demand for punishment on the other. An examination of our own minds, I think, will show, that these two things include all that we mean when we speak of violation of a right. When we call anything a person's right, we mean that he has a valid claim on society to protect him in the possession of it, either by the force of law, or by that of education and opinion. If he has what we consider a sufficient claim, on whatever account, to have something guaranteed to him by society, we say that he has a right to it. If we desire to prove that anything does not belong to him by right, we think this done as soon as it is admitted that society ought not to take measures for securing it to him, but should leave him to chance, or to his own exertions. Thus, a person is said to have a right to what he can earn in fair professional competition; because society ought not to allow any other person to hinder him from endeavouring to earn in that manner as much as he can. But he has not a right to three hundred a-year, though he may happen to be earning it; because society is not called on to provide that he shall earn that sum. On the contrary, if he owns ten thousand pounds three per cent. stock, he *has* a right to three hundred a-year; because society has come under an obligation to provide him with an income of that amount.

To have a right, then, is, I conceive, to have something which society ought to defend me in the possession of. If the objector goes on to ask, why it ought? I can give him no other reason than general utility. If that expression does not seem to convey a sufficient feeling of the strength of the obligation, nor to account for the peculiar energy of the feeling, it is because there goes to the composition of the sentiment, not a rational only, but also an animal element, the thirst for retaliation; and this thirst derives its intensity, as well as its moral justification, from the extraordinarily important and impressive kind of utility which is concerned. The interest involved is that of security, to every one's feelings the most vital of all interests. All other earthly benefits are needed by one person, not needed by another; and many of them can, if necessary, be cheerfully foregone, or replaced by something else; but security no human being can possibly do without; on it we depend for all our immunity from evil, and for the whole value of all and every good, beyond the passing moment; since nothing but the gratification of the instant could be of any worth to us, if we could be deprived of anything the next instant by whoever was

P

momentarily stronger than ourselves. Now this most indispensable of all necessaries, after physical nutriment, cannot be had, unless the machinery for providing it is kept unintermittedly in active play. Our notion, therefore, of the claim we have on our fellow-creatures to join in making safe for us the very groundwork of our existence, gathers feelings around it so much more intense than those concerned in any of the more common cases of utility, that the difference in degree (as is often the case in psychology) becomes a real difference in kind. The claim assumes that character of absoluteness, that apparent infinity, and incommensurability with all other considerations, which constitute the distinction between the feeling of right and wrong and that of ordinary expediency and inexpediency. The feelings concerned are so powerful, and we count so positively on finding a responsive feeling in others (all being alike interested), that *ought* and *should* grow into *must*, and recognised indispensability becomes a moral necessity, analogous to physical, and often not inferior to it in binding force.

If the preceding analysis, or something resembling it, be not the correct account of the notion of justice; if justice be totally independent of utility, and be a standard *per se*, which the mind can recognise by simple introspection of itself; it is hard to understand why that internal oracle is so ambiguous, and why so many things appear either just or unjust, according to the light in which they are regarded.

We are continually informed that Utility is an uncertain standard, which every different person interprets differently, and that there is no safety but in the immutable, ineffaceable, and unmistakable dictates of Justice, which carry their evidence in themselves, and are independent of the fluctuations of opinion. One would suppose from this that on questions of justice there could be no controversy; that if we take that for our rule, its application to any given case could leave us in as little doubt as a mathematical demonstration. So far is this from being the fact, that there is as much difference of opinion, and as much discussion, about what is just, as about what is useful to society. Not only have different nations and individuals different notions of justice, but in the mind of one and the same individual, **justice** is not some one rule, principle or maxim, but many, which do not always coincide in their dictates, and in choosing between which, he is guided either by some extraneous standard, or by his own personal predilections.

For instance, there are some who say, that it is unjust to punish any one for the sake of example to others; that punishment is just, only when intended for the good of the sufferer himself. Others maintain the extreme reverse, contending that to punish persons who have attained years of discretion, for their own benefit, is despotism and injustice, since if the matter at issue is solely their own good, no one has a right to control their own judgment of it; but that they may justly be punished to prevent evil to others, this being the exercise of the legitimate right of self-defence. Mr. Owen, again, affirms that it is unjust to punish at all; for the criminal did not make his own character; his education, and the circumstances which surrounded him, have made him a criminal, and for these he is not responsible. All these opinions are extremely plausible; and so long as the question is argued as one of justice simply, without going down to the principles which lie under justice and are the source of its authority, I am unable to see how any of these reasoners can be refuted. For in truth every one of the three builds upon rules of justice confessedly true. The first appeals to the acknowledged injustice of singling out an individual, and making him a sacrifice, without his consent, for other people's benefit. The second relies on the acknowledged justice of self-defence, and the admitted injustice of forcing one person to conform to another's notions of what constitutes his good. The Owenite invokes the admitted principle, that it is unjust to punish any one for what he cannot help. Each is triumphant so long as he is not compelled to take into consideration any other maxims of justice than the one he has selected; but as soon as their several maxims are brought face to face, each disputant seems to have exactly as much to say for himself as the others. No one of them can carry out his own notion of justice without trampling upon another equally binding. These are difficulties; they have always been felt to be such; and many devices have been invented to turn rather than to overcome them. As a refuge from the last of the three, men imagined what they called the freedom of the will; fancying that they could not justify punishing a man whose will is in a thoroughly hateful state, unless it be supposed to have come into that state through no influence of anterior circumstances. To escape from the other difficulties, a favourite contrivance has been the fiction of a contract, whereby at some unknown period all the members of society engaged to obey the laws, and consented to be punished for any disobedience to them; thereby giving to their legislators the right, which it is assumed they would not otherwise have had, of punishing them, either for their own good or for that of society. This happy thought was considered to get rid of the whole difficulty, and to legitimate the infliction of punishment, in virtue of another received maxim of justice, *Volenti non fit injuria*; that is not unjust which is done with the consent of the person who is supposed to be hurt by it. I need hardly remark, that even if the consent were not a mere fiction, this maxim is not superior in authority to the others which it is brought in to supersede. It is, on the contrary, an instructive specimen of the loose and irregular manner in which supposed principles of justice grow up. This particular one evidently came into use as a help to the coarse exigencies of courts of law, which are sometimes obliged to be content with very uncertain presumptions, on account of the greater evils which would often arise from any attempt on their part to cut finer. But even courts of law are not able to adhere consistently to the maxim, for they allow voluntary engagements to be set aside on the ground of fraud, and sometimes on that of mere mistake or misinformation.

Again, when the legitimacy of inflicting punishment is admitted, how many conflicting conceptions of justice come to light in discussing the proper apportionment of punishments to offences. No rule on the subject recommends itself so strongly to the primitive and spontaneous sentiment of justice, as the *lex talionis*, an eye for an eye and a tooth for a tooth. Though this principle of the Jewish and of the Mahomedan law has been generally abandoned in Europe as a practical maxim, there is, I suspect, in most minds, a secret hankering after it; and when retribution accidentally falls on an offender in that precise shape, the general feeling of satisfaction evinced bears witness how natural is the sentiment to which this repayment in kind is acceptable. With many, the test of justice in penal infliction is that the punishment should be proportioned to the offence; meaning that it should be exactly measured by the moral guilt of the culprit (whatever be their standard for measuring moral guilt): the consideration, what amount of punishment is necessary to deter from the offence, having nothing to do with the question of justice, in their estimation: while there are others to whom that consideration is all in all; who maintain that it is not just, at least for man, to inflict on a fellow-creature, whatever may be his offences, any amount of suffering beyond the least that will suffice to prevent him from repeating, and others from imitating, his misconduct.

To take another example from a subject already once referred to. In a co-operative industrial association, is it just or not that talent or skill should give a title to superior remuneration? On the negative side of the question it is argued, that whoever does the best he can, deserves equally well, and ought not in justice to be put in a position of inferiority for no fault of his own; that superior abilities have already advantages more than enough, in the admiration they excite, the personal influence they command, and the internal sources of satisfaction attending them, without adding to these a superior share of the world's goods; and that society is bound in justice rather to make compensation to the less favoured, for this unmerited inequality of advantages, than to aggravate it. On the contrary side it is contended, that society receives more from the more efficient labourer; that his services being more useful, society owes him a larger return for them; that a greater share of the joint result is actually his work, and not to allow his claim to it is a kind of robbery; that if he is only to receive as much as others, he can only be justly required to produce as much, and to give a smaller amount of time and exertion, proportioned to his superior efficiency. Who shall decide between these appeals to conflicting principles of justice? Justice has in this case two sides to it, which it is impossible to bring into harmony, and the two disputants have chosen opposite sides; the one looks to what it is just that the individual should receive, the other to what it is just that the community should give. Each, from his own point of view, is unanswerable; and any choice between them, on grounds of justice, must be perfectly arbitrary. Social utility alone can decide the preference.

How many, again, and how irreconcilable, are the standards of justice to which reference is made in discussing the repartition of taxation. One opinion is, that payment to the State should be in numerical proportion to pecuniary means. Others think that justice dictates what they term graduated taxation; taking a higher percentage from those who have more to spare. In point of natural justice a strong case might be made for disregarding means altogether, and taking the same absolute sum (whenever it could be got) from every one: as the subscribers to a mess, or to a club, all pay the same sum for the same privileges, whether they can all equally afford it or not. Since the protection (it might be said) of law and government is afforded to, and is equally required by all, there is no injustice in making all buy it at the same price. It is reckoned justice, not injustice, that a dealer should charge to all customers the same price for the same article, not a price varying according to their means of payment. This doctrine, as applied to taxation, finds no advocates, because it conflicts so strongly with man's feelings of humanity and of social expediency; but the principle of justice which it invokes is as true and as binding as those which can be appealed to against it. Accordingly it exerts a tacit influence on the line of defence employed for other modes of assessing taxation. People feel obliged to argue that the State does more for the rich than for the poor, as a justification for its taking more from them: though this is in reality not true, for the rich would be far better able to protect themselves, in the absence of law or government, than the poor, and indeed would probably be successful in converting the poor into their slaves. Others, again, so far defer to the same conception of justice, as to maintain that all should pay an equal capitation tax for the protection of their persons (these being of equal value to all), and an unequal tax for the protection of their property, which is unequal. To this others reply, that the all of one man is as valuable to him as the all of another. From these confusions there is no other mode of extrication than the utilitarian.

Is, then, the difference between the Just and the Expedient a merely imaginary distinction? Have mankind been under a delusion in thinking that justice is a more sacred thing than policy, and that the latter ought only to be listened to after the former has been satisfied? By no means. The exposition we have given of the nature and origin of the sentiment, recognises a real distinction; and no one of those who profess the most sublime contempt for the consequences of actions as an element in their morality, attaches more importance to the distinction than I do. While I dispute the pretensions of any theory which sets up an imaginary standard of justice not grounded on utility, I account the justice which is grounded on utility to be the chief part, and incomparably the most sacred and binding part, of all morality. Justice is a name for certain classes of moral rules, which concern the essentials of human well-being more nearly, and are therefore of more absolute obligation, than any other rules for the guidance of life; and the notion which we have found to be of the essence of the idea of justice, that of a right residing in an individual, implies and testifies to this more binding obligation.

The moral rules which forbid mankind to hurt one another (in which we must never forget to include wrongful interference with each other's freedom) are more vital to human well-being than any maxims, however important, which only point out the best mode of managing some department of human affairs. They have also the peculiarity, that they are the main element in determining the whole of the social feelings of mankind. It is their observance which alone preserves peace among human beings: if obedience to them were not the rule, and disobedience the exception, every one would see in every one else an enemy, against whom he must be perpetually guarding himself. What is hardly less important, these are the precepts which mankind have the strongest and the most direct inducements for impressing upon one another. By merely giving to each other prudential instruction or exhortation, they may gain, or think they gain, nothing: in inculcating on each other the duty of positive beneficence they have an unmistakable interest, but far less in degree: a person may possibly not need the benefits of others; but he always needs that they should not do him hurt. Thus the moralities which protect every individual from being harmed by others, either directly or by being hindered in his freedom of pursuing his own good, are at once those which he himself has most at heart, and those which he has the strongest interest in publishing and enforcing by word and deed. It is by a person's observance of these that his fitness to exist as one of the fellowship of human beings is tested and decided; for on that depends his being a nuisance or not to those with whom he is in contact. Now it is these moralities primarily which compose the obligations of justice. The most marked cases of injustice, and those which give the tone to the feeling of repugnance which characterises the sentiment, are acts of wrongful aggression, or wrongful exercise of power over some one; the next are those which consist in wrongfully withholding from him something which is his due; in both cases, inflicting on him a positive hurt, either in the form of direct suffering, or of the privation of some good which he had reasonable ground, either of a physical or of a social kind, for counting upon.

The same powerful motives which command the observance of these primary moralities, enjoin the punishment of those who violate them; and as the impulses of self-defence, of defence of others, and of vengeance, are all called forth against such persons, retribution, or evil for evil, becomes closely connected with the sentiment of justice, and is universally included in the idea. Good for good is also one of the dictates of justice; and this, though its social utility is evident, and though it carries with it a natural human feeling, has not at first sight that obvious connexion with hurt or injury, which, existing in the most elementary cases of just and unjust, is the source of the characteristic intensity of the sentiment. But the connection, though less obvious, is not less real. He who accepts benefits, and denies a return of them when needed, inflicts a real hurt, by disappointing one of the most natural and reasonable of expectations, and one which he must at least tacitly have encouraged, otherwise the benefits would seldom have been conferred. The important rank, among human evils and wrongs, of the disappointment of expectation, is shown in the fact that it constitutes the principal criminality of two such highly immoral acts as a breach of friendship and a breach of promise. Few hurts which human beings can sustain are greater, and none wound more, than when that on which they habitually and with full assurance relied, fails them in the hour of need; and few wrongs are greater than this mere withholding of good; none excite more resentment, either in the person suffering, or in a sympathising spectator. The principle, therefore, of giving to each what they deserve, that is, good for good as well as evil for evil, is not only included within the idea of Justice as we have defined it, but is a proper object of that intensity of sentiment, which places the Just, in human estimation, above the simply Expedient.

Most of the maxims of justice current in the world, and commonly appealed to in its transactions, are simply instrumental to carrying into effect the principles of justice which we have now spoken of. That a person is only responsible for what he has done voluntarily, or could voluntarily have avoided; that it is unjust to condemn any person unheard; that the punishment ought to be proportioned to the offence, and the like, are maxims intended to prevent the just principle of evil for evil from being perverted to the infliction of evil without that justification. The greater part of these common maxims have come into use from the practice of courts of justice, which have been naturally led to a more complete recognition and elaboration than was likely to suggest itself to others, of the rules necessary to enable them to fulfil their double function, of inflicting punishment when due, and of awarding to each person his right.

That first of judicial virtues, impartiality, is an obligation of justice, partly for the reason last mentioned; as being a necessary condition of the fulfilment of the other obligations of justice. But this is not the only source of the exalted rank, among human obligations, of those maxims of equality and impartiality, which, both in popular estimation and in that of the most enlightened, are included among the precepts of justice. In one point of view, they may be considered as corollaries from the principles already laid down. If it is a duty to do to each according to his deserts, returning good for good as well as repressing evil by evil, it necessarily follows that we should treat all equally well (when no higher duty forbids) who have deserved equally well of *us*, and that society should treat all equally well who have deserved equally well of *it*, that is, who have deserved equally well absolutely. This is the highest abstract standard of social and distributive justice; towards which all institutions, and the efforts of all virtuous citizens, should be made in the utmost possible degree to converge. But this great moral duty rests upon a still deeper foundation, being a direct emanation from the first principle of morals, and not a mere logical corollary from secondary or derivative doctrines. It is involved in the very meaning of Utility, or the Greatest Happiness Principle. That principle is a mere form of words without rational signification, unless one person's happiness, supposed equal in degree (with the proper allowance made for kind), is counted for exactly as much as another's. Those conditions being supplied, Bentham's dictum, 'everybody to count for one, nobody for more than one,' might be written under the principle of utility as an explanatory commentary.[1] The equal claim of everybody to happiness in the estimation of the moralist and of the legislator, involves an equal claim to all the means of happiness, except in so far as the inevitable conditions of human life, and the general interest, in which that of every individual is included, set limits to the maxim; and those limits ought to be strictly construed. As every other maxim of justice, so this is by no means applied or held applicable universally; on the contrary, as I have already remarked, it bends to every person's ideas of social expediency. But in whatever case it is deemed applicable at all, it is held to be the dictate of justice. All persons are deemed to have a *right* to equality of treatment, except when some recognised social expediency requires the reverse. And hence all social inequalities which have ceased to be considered expedient, assume the character not of simple inexpediency, but of injustice, and appear so tyrannical, that people are apt to wonder how they ever could have been

[1] This implication, in the first principle of the utilitarian scheme, of perfect impartiality between persons, is regarded by Mr. Herbert Spencer (in his *Social Statics*) as a disproof of the pretensions of utility to be a sufficient guide to right; since (he says) the principle of utility presupposes the anterior principle, that everybody has an equal right to happiness. It may be more correctly described as supposing that equal amounts of happiness are equally desirable, whether felt by the same or by different persons. This, however, is not a *pre*-supposition; not a premise needful to support the principle of utility, but the very principle itself; for what is the principle of utility, if it be not that 'happiness' and 'desirable' are synonymous terms? If there is any anterior principle implied, it can be no other than this, that the truths of arithmetic are applicable to the valuation of happiness, as of all other measurable quantities.

[Mr. Herbert Spencer, in a private communication on the subject of the preceding Note, objects to being considered an opponent of utilitarianism, and states that he regards happiness as the ultimate end of morality; but deems that end only partially attainable by empirical generalisations from the observed results of conduct, and completely attainable only by deducing, from the laws of life and the conditions of existence, what kinds of action necessarily tend to produce happiness, and what kinds to produce unhappiness. With the exception of the word 'necessarily', I have no dissent to express from this doctrine; and (omitting that word) I am not aware that any modern advocate of utilitarianism is of a different opinion. Bentham, certainly, to whom in the *Social Statics* Mr. Spencer particularly referred, is, least of all writers, chargeable with unwillingness to deduce the effect of actions on happiness from the laws of human nature and the universal conditions of human life. The common charge against him is of relying too exclusively upon such deductions, and declining altogether to be bound by the generalisations from specific experience which Mr. Spencer thinks that utilitarians generally confine themselves to. My own opinion (and, as I collect, Mr. Spencer's) is, that in ethics, as in all other branches of scientific study, the consilience of the results of both these processes, each corroborating and verifying the other, is requisite to give to any general proposition the kind and degree of evidence which constitutes scientific proof.]

tolerated; forgetful that they themselves perhaps tolerate other inequalities under an equally mistaken notion of expediency, the correction of which would make that which they approve seem quite as monstrous as what they have at last learnt to condemn. The entire history of social improvement has been a series of transitions, by which one custom or institution after another, from being a supposed primary necessity of social existence, has passed into the rank of a universally stigmatised injustice and tyranny. So it has been with the distinctions of slaves and freemen, nobles and serfs, patricians and plebeians; and so it will be, and in part already is, with the aristocracies of colour, race, and sex.

It appears from what has been said, that justice is a name for certain moral requirements, which, regarded collectively, stand higher in the scale of social utility, and are therefore of more paramount obligation, than any others; though particular cases may occur in which some other social duty is so important, as to overrule any one of the general maxims of justice. Thus, to save a life, it may not only be allowable, but a duty, to steal, or take by force, the necessary food or medicine, or to kidnap, and compel to officiate, the only qualified medical practitioner. In such cases, as we do not call anything justice which is not a virtue, we usually say, not that justice must give way to some other moral principle, but that what is just in ordinary cases is, by reason of that other principle, not just in the particular case. By this useful accommodation of language, the character of indefeasibility attributed to justice is kept up, and we are saved from the necessity of maintaining that there can be laudable injustice.

The considerations which have now been adduced resolve, I conceive, the only real difficulty in the utilitarian theory of morals. It has always been evident that all cases of justice are also cases of expediency: the difference is in the peculiar sentiment which attaches to the former, as contradistinguished from the latter. If this characteristic sentiment has been sufficiently accounted for; if there is no necessity to assume for it any peculiarity of origin; if it is simply the natural feeling of resentment, moralised by being made coextensive with the demands of social good; and if this feeling not only does but ought to exist in all the classes of cases to which the idea of justice corresponds; that idea no longer presents itself as a stumbling-block to the utilitarian ethics. Justice remains the appropriate name for certain social utilities which are vastly more important, and therefore more absolute and imperative, than any others are as a class (though not more so than others may be in particular cases); and which, therefore, ought to be, as well as naturally are, guarded by a sentiment not only different in degree, but also in kind; distinguished from the milder feeling which attaches to the mere idea of promoting human pleasure or convenience, at once by the more definite nature of its commands, and by the sterner character of its sanctions.